Praise for *Volleyball with the Cuna Indians*

"There is nobody in the world quite like Mr. Ebensten, and there has never been a book quite like this. Even if, like me, you skip the bits about gay sex, you will find it marvelously loaded with wit, astonishment, elegant writing, entertaining prejudice, and plain human affection."
—Jan Morris

"Delightful . . . full of surprises . . . Ebensten is a good writer, a tart and keen-eyed observer, and, best of all, a comfortably gay man who loves to travel. He tells many a good story and leaves in the names, the places, and the sex."
—*Genre*

"I knew *Volleyball with the Cuna Indians* would be informative, but it is also funny—outrageously funny. Woven with the useful facts about little-known places are hilarious experiences with Lady Diana Cooper on the one hand and ninety-eight Italian motorcycle cops on the other. It is a book not to be missed."
—Quentin Crisp

"This memoir of six decades of travel from Monte Carlo to the Galapagos offers an engaging and entertaining combination of sex and old-world charm. Hanns Ebensten is a scintillating travel guide."
—Neil Miller, author of *Out in the World*

"Stylish, cultivated, witty, and frankly gay, Ebensten draws often hilarious portraits of travelers whom readers would not otherwise meet, and places rarely visited."
—*Publishers Weekly*

"Yikes. This is the kind of travel anecdote that gives new meaning to the term 'wanderlust.' . . . Ebensten exudes a reverence for other worlds that borders on the transcendental and proves he has achieved something rare. In the end . . . he looks like the best kind of traveler."

PENGUIN BOOKS

VOLLEYBALL WITH THE CUNA INDIANS

Hanns Ebensten has arranged and conducted tours, cruises, and expeditions to remote, unusually interesting, and adventurous places for forty years. His agency, Hanns Ebensten Travel, Inc., in Key West, Florida, celebrated its twentieth anniversary in 1992. He is a regular contributor to *Christopher Street*, *Archaeology Magazine*, *The Advocate*, and the *Society for Hellenic Travel Review*, among other publications.

VOLLEYBALL WITH THE CUNA INDIANS

AND OTHER GAY TRAVEL ADVENTURES

Hanns Ebensten

PENGUIN BOOKS

PENGUIN BOOKS
Published by the Penguin Group
Penguin Books USA Inc., 375 Hudson Street, New York, New York 10014, U.S.A.
Penguin Books Ltd, 27 Wrights Lane, London W8 5TZ, England
Penguin Books Australia Ltd, Ringwood, Victoria, Australia
Penguin Books Canada Ltd, 10 Alcorn Avenue, Toronto, Ontario, Canada M4V 3B2
Penguin Books (N.Z.) Ltd, 182–190 Wairau Road, Auckland 10, New Zealand

Penguin Books Ltd, Registered Offices: Harmondsworth, Middlesex, England

First published in the United States of America by Viking Penguin,
a division of Penguin Books USA Inc., 1993
Published in Penguin Books 1994

1   3   5   7   9   10   8   6   4   2

"A Night in Gay Paree," "The Ninety-eight Motorcycle Cops of Florence," "A Pastry in
Monte Carlo," "First Night in the Promised Land," "How the Grand Canyon Went Gay,"
"Easter Island Revisited" (under the title "The Navel of the World"), portions of "Fellow
Travelers" (under the title "Encounters with Superstuds"), and "Clothes Make the Man"
first appeared in *Christopher Street*. Portions of "Modern Wanderers in a Biblical Wilderness"
(under the title "Blasphemy in Blue") first appeared in *Archaeology Magazine*.

Grateful acknowledgment is made for permission to reprint an excerpt from "Give Me the
Man" by Leo Robin and Karl Hajos. Copyright © 1930 by Famous Music Corporation.
Copyright renewed 1957 by Famous Music Corporation.

THE LIBRARY OF CONGRESS HAS CATALOGUED THE HARDCOVER AS FOLLOWS:
Ebensten, Hanns.
Volleyball with the Cuna Indians and other gay travel adventures/
by Hanns Ebensten.
p.   cm.
ISBN 0-670-84993-6 (hc.)
ISBN 0 14 01.7879 1 (pbk.)
1. Ebensten, Hanns—Journeys.   2. Voyages and travels.   3. Gays—Travel.
I. Title.
G465.E24 1993   93–18684   910.4—dc20

Printed in the United States of America
Set in Garamond No. 3
Designed by Brian Mulligan

CONTENTS

1	Meeting a Black King	1
2	A Night in Gay Paree	18
3	The Ninety-eight Motorcycle Cops of Florence	26
4	A Pastry in Monte Carlo	35
5	With Scholarship, Wit, Beauty, and Zest to Trebizond	49
6	First Night in the Promised Land	82
7	The Mystique of Mustique	90
8	How the Grand Canyon Went Gay	101
9	Volleyball with the Cuna Indians	111
10	Gays in the Galápagos	130
11	Who Was Nick?	145
12	Staying with the Monks	158
13	Easter Island Revisited	177
14	The Mountain of the Gods	184

15   Modern Wanderers in a Biblical Wilderness   198

16   A Journey to Vilcabamba   215

17   With Fatso in Turkey   244

18   The Nile by Felucca   268

19   Fellow Travelers   287

20   Clothes Make the Man   312

21   Tea on the Terrace   324

For Brian

VOLLEYBALL WITH THE CUNA INDIANS

1

MEETING

A BLACK

KING

IN DECEMBER OF 1934, at the age of eleven, I left Germany with my parents to settle in Swaziland, a country of which I had never heard and that was so small and insignificant it did not appear on many maps of Africa. Situated between what were then the Union of South Africa and Portuguese East Africa, often named the Switzerland of Africa, it is an independent kingdom that was at the time under the protection of Great Britain. When my father announced that we were to emigrate to it, he immediately arranged for me to have private English lessons three times each week; but my stepmother said that with a few exceptions that only proved the rule—Shakespeare, Lord Byron, and Oscar Wilde—English was a language of commerce, and she would pick up what was absolutely necessary of it when we were there.

Adolf Hitler had taken control of Germany the previous year. Like most industrialists, my father had at first approved of his aims—he would destroy communism; he would put the idlers to work building roads; he would make Germany strong and proud again. Like many Jews, my father chose to believe that Hitler's anti-Semitism was not directed at the "good Jews," whose families had lived in Germany for centuries, but against the despised *Ostjuden,* who had arrived from the ghettos of Russia and Poland in alarming numbers in the past thirty years and who ostentatiously flaunted their new wealth. My stepmother was a great beauty, and one day, when she was waiting for a train at a railroad station in Berlin, Hitler had come striding along the platform with his entourage, stopped short, saluted, and bowed low, and had told her that she was a very beautiful woman. Could this charming, gallant man be all bad?

But as soon as Hitler had come to power and showed his fangs, my father realized that we must make haste to leave Germany. For him, this decision was an act of desperation in order to survive; my young Christian stepmother, an admiral's daughter and the sister of an officer in the Wehrmacht, was appalled but considered it her duty to go with him—had she not married him for better or for worse?—but I was thrilled by the prospect of going to live in "darkest Africa," the "Black Continent," in the land of Rider Haggard's *King Solomon's Mines,* which I had read in translation, as well as the tales of African adventure by Karl May. When I told my school fellows about it, even those admired ones who were members of the Hitler Youth, which I had so desperately wanted to join but from which I was excluded, were envious of *me* for a change.

We crossed the frontier at Basel into Switzerland and safety. It was forbidden to transfer or take money out of Germany, so my stepmother wore three thick, very wide bracelets over her dress sleeve, like cheap, massive costume junk—they were pure platinum, had been specially made by a friendly jeweler, and constituted all my father's savings; and he took them to a bank in Basel the morning after we arrived there.

To provide us with privacy on this painful railroad journey from our homeland into the unknown, my parents made good use of my presence. My stepmother wept most of the time. "Oh, Paulchen, be good to me!" she sobbed. "I will, I will," he promised. Whenever anyone attempted to enter our compartment, I was told to throw a tantrum and stamp and scream; I was happy to oblige, and no one came to sit with us.

We were to take a ship from Genoa early in January, but my stepmother had persuaded my father (who was twice her age and doted on her) to let us spend Christmas and New Year's in Florence. "Grant me just two last weeks to soak up European culture before you take me to that dreadful Africa," she said. We did not stay at the luxurious Grand Hotel, where my father had taken her on their honeymoon, but a world away (although also on the Lung'arno) at the simple Pensione Balestri. "We are emigrants now," he told her, "and must begin to live modestly."

I was insufferably precocious and had studied travel literature on all the places through which we would pass on our way to South Africa, so that when the train from Florence stopped earlier than expected and my parents saw signs reading GENOVA on the station platform and hurriedly gathered up our baggage and prepared to get off, I sat smugly and said, "We are not yet in Genoa; first the train must go through a tunnel." My father slapped me, twice, hard across the face, and ordered me to stop my nonsense and help carry our cases off the train. When we stood on the platform and the train had left, I was proved right—it was Genova Brignole, a suburb, and we had not reached Genoa's main railroad station, where our hotel was located.

Next day we boarded the SS *Giulio Cesare* and settled in our cabin. There were then still six hours before sailing time, so my stepmother made my father take her ashore to visit the famous Campo Santo cemetery in the hills above Genoa, filled with Italy's most ornate and elaborate funerary monuments. They did not consider this a suitable place for an impressionable child. When the ship sailed, my parents had not returned, and when the passengers heard of this, they made a great fuss of me and many ladies comforted me and many gentlemen told me I must be brave—but I was not in the least worried, relished my sudden importance, and was delighted to be rid of my stern old father and my silly, pretty stepmother, whose mental age was far below mine. For many years I had prayed that the Gypsies would come in the night and steal me away from home; and this was almost as good.

Much to my disappointment, my parents reboarded the ship next day at Marseilles, frantic with remorse and worry, to receive a raucous reception from the passengers—but not from me. "It was entirely your father's fault," my stepmother told me. "He was too mean to pay for a taxi from the Campo Santo back to the ship, and the tramcar was so slow and took us to the wrong place. And then we had to sit up all night to Marseilles in a horrible train."

After Gibraltar, the weather became warm and the passengers put on light tropical clothes and lay in deck chairs. A handsome Italian boxer took a liking to me and made me share his deck chair and cuddled me. My parents approved of this. I was a spoiled sissy, and my father said, "Mario is a good example for him and will teach him to become more manly."

I adored Mario, who had thick black hair and a bushy mustache and wore white gym clothes. I fantasized that I was really his son and that when he took me to live with him, he would make me go out and steal for him.

At Dakar, my parents took a sight-seeing drive in a horse-drawn carriage, but this time they did not leave me behind on the ship. My stepmother was shocked by the filth and stench, and alarmed by the people in the streets. "Oh, they are all so *black*," she cried. "I never realized they would be as black as that."

Suddenly loud voices called out from many towers, and all the men in the streets unrolled bits of carpet or sacking and threw themselves onto the ground and prayed. Our driver stopped the carriage and joined them. My stepmother was frightened, but my father had lived twenty years in Muslim countries and was quite familiar with the five daily calls to prayer.

In Cape Town, when the colored porters swarmed on board, my stepmother was somewhat reassured. "Oh, Paulchen, here they are only *half-black*," she said.

We traveled by overnight train—not the grand Blue Train, because we were emigrants, not tourists—to Johannesburg, which was disappointingly like a city in Europe and not at all what I had expected of Africa, and then drove to Swaziland to inspect the tin mine my father was planning to buy.

My father fussed with our papers when he expected the Swaziland frontier post to appear, but there was none. Instead, we knew that we had crossed from the Union of South Africa into the kingdom of Swaziland when the dirt road abruptly ended and became a well-maintained tarmac highway. "We are under the protection of Great Britain now," said my father.

The long drive across the flat Transvaal veld had been dull and quite unlike the descriptions in the stories of African adventure; but soon after Mbabane, the little capital of Swaziland that took us only a minute or two to drive through, the road descended several thousands of feet in a series of sharp bends and then we were suddenly, unmistakably, in the hot, humid tropical lowlands. It was at last the Africa of which I had read, the Africa I had imagined, the exotic Africa of the storybooks, the land Rider Haggard called "little less than an earthly paradise." Here, now, were the bare-breasted women in heavy skirts of cowhide and goatskin, carrying grotesquely large bundles on their heads, the men naked except for small pieces of animal skin over their private parts, the children wearing nothing except narrow waistbands of beads or plaited grass around their hideously extended bellies. Here was all the lush, strange tropical vegetation I had expected to see. Here giraffes stood quite still, their heads taller than some weirdly twisted trees that had no leaves but masses of scarlet flowers. We caught glimpses of zebras galloping in herds through the tall grass. Crocodiles were said to lurk in the rivers. We saw steep cliffs from which, my father said with relish, adulterous women had been cast down to their death until recent times to the sounds of drums.

For a boy not yet in his teens who had never before been out of Europe except for a barely remembered cruise up the Nile at the age of six, all this was high adventure indeed.

We stayed at a rough inn in the Ezulwini Valley that catered to commercial travelers, for this was long before tourists ventured to Swaziland. The guest accommodations consisted of straw-covered rondavels standing under huge trees some distance from the main house, which was also a general store. We had to use flashlights to walk to dinner; and the innkeeper, trying to scare us—and succeeding in alarming my stepmother—warned us never to walk under the trees and always to keep our eyes open for snakes: the dreaded black mamba, which dropped silently from its hiding place among the leaves to strike and instantly kill passersby, and the huge boa constrictor, which lay coiled around the branches and was almost indistinguishable from them until it pounced with incredible speed to entangle its victims and crush them slowly to death. It could devour a whole sheep, or a boy like me—it had a marked preference for white children—and then slept for weeks, replete and obscenely swollen, while it digested its prey.

I knew that this was wildly exaggerated, if not totally untrue, but how thrilling nevertheless to be in darkest Africa, where such horrors were possible!

We drove to inspect the tin mine, not far from the inn, and were conducted around by the foreman. It was a great brown scar on the green mountainside. My father was disgusted by the obvious deception that had been contrived in an infantile effort to impress us: as we walked along above the pits in which the barefooted miners were working, wearing loincloths or khaki shorts and merrily chanting, they passed up to us impressively large lumps of tin-bearing ore as gifts for my stepmother, as if they had that moment hacked them out of the earth.

We were shown the house that was to be our home, built by a former manager, set among banana trees and overlooking a river. It was quite large, with high ceilings to keep its rooms cool in summer, and fireplaces, because winter nights were often cold; a porch ran around three of its sides. Even my stepmother had to agree that with the essential additions of a modern tiled kitchen and bathroom, it might be made habitable.

My father was enthusiastic. "This will be our *Esszimmer;* and here I will have the wall knocked down to make one big *Wohnzimmer* with our Biedermeier furniture and the porcelain Buddha and the Indian curtains, and our large Böcklin landscape on this wall. This will be the boy's bedroom, next to ours, and I will have a nice bathroom put in here between them. The two small bedrooms will be for guests. And I promise you a kitchen just as modern and good as in Berlin, or even better!"

He strode along the porch, measuring it with his footsteps. "This part I will have extended and enclosed with screens, like in Java, so you can sit here nice and cool above the river and have your afternoon *Kaffee und Kuchen* brought to you and listen to the gramophone and read your *Grüner Heinrich* until your old man comes home from the mine to give you a kiss. And servants cost nothing here; you shall have a dozen of them, trained at the German mission, and the best cook in Swaziland."

Encouraged by this rosy picture, my stepmother became reconciled to the prospect of being exiled in this strange, savage country. It was so conveniently located, halfway between Johannesburg—where the stores had German sausages and marzipan and the Elvas plums she liked so much, and where I was to attend one of the boarding schools of the good Jesuits or the Marist brothers—and Lourenço Marques on the coast. Every weekend, my stepmother decided, she and my father would drive either to Johannesburg to be with me or to lively Lourenço Marques, where the sidewalks were paved in swirling patterns like in Rio de Janeiro and all the rich white people of South Africa stayed at the Polana Hotel on the beach.

✧

A German businessman in Mbabane was assisting my father with his application for our residence permits at the British high commissioner's office and his negotiations for the purchase of the tin mine, and he and his wife also offered to introduce my parents to the respectable members of the small European community. "There are dances and garden parties almost every week, and we even have amateur theatricals occasionally down in Bremersdorp," he told my father. "Your beautiful lady wife will create a sensation in our circle." He took us to pay our obligatory courtesy visit to the queen mother at Lobamba, the royal kraal.

This was a large complex of circular straw huts, some of very great size, with sleeping accommodations for many hundreds of women and children, and enclosures for cattle, and long reed windbreakers all around them. The Great Hut, under the charge of Lomawa, the queen mother, was decorated with skulls that I hoped to be of humans, enemies killed in battles, but that were merely those of cows and antlered deer. Hundreds of the king's children by his numerous wives lived here with their grandmother. The king was Lomawa's only child, and he maintained wives in kraals throughout his country where several wives shared one hut, as in a harem, from which one would be summoned to the king's personal hut when he visited it during his tours of the country. "He is not interested in any of them except as breeders," I overheard the German businessman tell my father.

"Yes, it is the same in the East," said my father.

We had been instructed to bring a gift of chewing tobacco for the queen mother, who was said to be extremely fond of it; and my parents thought it would be a nice touch if I presented it to her. Lomawa had ruled Swaziland for twenty-one years after the death of her husband until her son came of age and she allowed him—reluctantly, it was said—to ascend the throne. She was still powerful and feared, and her word was law. Any foreigner of whom she did not approve was soon expelled from the country on some pretext. My father was not unfamiliar with such matriarchs; he had learned during his years in India's princely states and in Java that the success of a commercial enterprise often depended on the goodwill of the local potentate's wife or mother. "You must make an effort to endear yourself to the queen mother," he told my stepmother. "She is more important here than the king; make her become your friend."

But how could she possibly become a friend of the fat, dour, ugly, illiterate old woman to whom we were presented, who wore the skin of a whole leopard over her bare shoulders? Lomawa sat on the ground, surrounded by her women and a great number of children, and scowled at us. We were led to mats placed on the earth floor, six feet from her and facing her, and when I was prompted to step up to her with the gift of the chewing tobacco, tied with a ribbon and accompanied by a posy of flowers, she uttered no word of thanks and passed the present carelessly to one of her attendants.

My father then made her the formal, respectful speech he had learned by heart, and it was translated into siSwati by one of the attendants. The queen mother was clearly not pleased with it and not impressed favorably by this fat, sweating old man who said that the young overdressed woman was his wife, and that the pale, willowy child was his son; but through her interpreter she began to question my father rather shrewdly.

If this, as he claimed, was his only child, surely he had made other children by other women long ago? She, too, she said, had only one child, the king, but her husband, the king before him, had had many hundreds of children by many other women. That was the way of men. That was how it should be. A man who made only one child was not a man. "Your woman and the child are too thin and look sickly. Be sure to feed them better and attend to their health," she said, and when this ominous pronouncement had been duly translated, she dismissed us from her presence.

The visit had clearly not been a success.

But the businessman from Mbabane, who knew old Lomawa's ways, was not discouraged. "She showed some interest in you," he told my father. "That is good. Two American Methodists came last month with ridiculously lavish presents, and she screamed abuse at them and turned them away. You will find the king much more agreeable."

He had planned to arrange for my father to meet the king in Mbabane, where the king lived with his chief wife and their family in a well-furnished European stone house and where he wore suits and a bowler hat and carried a cane; but Sobhuza II was visiting the royal kraal in a few days' time to inaugurate a new regiment of young warriors, and this would be a good opportunity for us to see the ceremonies, and for the king and my father to have a talk in private, away from the watchful eyes of the British high commissioner and his overzealous minions. He made the arrangements for us to be received at the royal kraal, said he would meet us there to effect introductions, and on the appointed day we drove back to Lobamba.

This time the royal kraal presented a completely different appearance. Instead of being a place of women and children with only a few old men in evidence, there were now no females in sight, and few children. It was a military camp, filled with hundreds of near-naked youths and men, and older men in long cloaks carrying staffs and with feathers in their hair. Scores of the young men squatted together in groups on the ground, sounding drums, making a deafening, alarming din, smoking something that sent up a foul stink. Their shields and bows and clubs lay about in untidy piles. Others strutted aimlessly to and fro. The German businessman was there to greet us and introduce us to some of the old men, who were officials of some kind; he explained that the youths we saw had recently been taken from their homes to form a new regiment in which they would serve several years, during which time they were not allowed to marry or have women.

"How good and wise that is," said my stepmother, "to make them lead pure lives."

The German, who had lived many years in Swaziland and knew its ways, smiled. "Not so," he said. "Their law only forbids them to spill their manhood *to make children.*" And as he emphasized the last words he smirked, and my father showed that he understood his implication.

"Yes," my father sighed. "It is the same among the troops in the East."

Waiting for the king to arrive and inaugurate this new Locust Regiment, the youths began to march up and down and around the reed windbreakers in what appeared to us as a pitifully haphazard, disorganized manner. "They need a few Prussian officers here, to teach them discipline," said my father. Then hundreds of these happy, untrained young warriors formed themselves into untidy rows and raced toward one another, screaming and howling and brandishing their bows and sticks and shields, and at the last moment before colliding stopped short in their tracks and stamped their bare feet so that clouds of dust arose. Like all such tribal cere-

monies, these were far too long and repetitive to be appreciated by
spectators who were uninitiated into their meanings and complexi-
ties, and we became bored. With so many naked men around us,
there was also an increasingly pungent, sickly, male smell, mixed
with that of the weed the older men were smoking, and my stepmother wanted to press her cologne-scented handkerchief to her
nose, but my father forbade her to do so.

It was a relief to us when frenzied shouting arose: the king's car
had been sighted. The men broke ranks and ran toward it and then
beside it as it drove slowly up the hill. Some of the old officials who
had welcomed us on arrival now cleared a path for us to a vantage
point from which we could watch the highly polished large black
chauffeur-driven car come toward us.

It came to a stop near us. Professor Hilda Kuper, the official
biographer of King Sobhuza II and who lived in Swaziland at that
time, has informed me that it was a Buick, but I saw it as a splendid
Rolls-Royce that day in 1935, and in my mind I see it as such today.
The monarch of a country under the protection of Great Britain
should have traveled in nothing less than that.

The king wore tribal garb, so that when he stepped out of his
black car his appearance was both incongruous and highly dramatic. Except for a short skirt of spotted animal fur, he was naked,
barefooted, and bareheaded. He had some amulets around his arms
and ankles, and wore a necklace of large white shells. There was a
small piece of red cloth in his hair. Sobhuza II, the king of Swaziland, the *Ngwenyama,* or Lion, of his country, was thirty-six years of
age, a magnificent, heavily bearded, muscular man in his prime. He
was not black, not inky-black like the people of Dakar at whose
sight my stepmother had been so repelled; his skin was that even,
smooth, burnt-cinnamon color that was at the time termed "nigger
brown" and highly fashionable in the couture world, a pleasant
brown like that of the smiling Moor who rolled his eyes in the

animated electric sign advertising Sarotti chocolates high above the Kurfürstendamm in Berlin.

My stepmother, who had anxiously inquired whether she should curtsy to the king, had been told by the Mbabane business-man that this was neither customary nor expected; a handshake would suffice. She was disappointed. She had been brought up to honor and respect royalty; and a king was a king, even if he was as black as ink—or nigger brown. She decided to formalize the occa-sion by making a bob as she shook his hand.

The king was most gracious. Unlike his dour mother, it was obvious that he appreciated my stepmother's elegant dress with the matching wide-brimmed hat, gloves, and shoes; he addressed us in English, which he had learned at a mission school in the Union of South Africa, asked our names, tousled my hair, inquired about our ship journey, wanted to know why his country was called the Switz-erland of Africa, and talked about his visit to London in 1922.

Having been advised that we were German, but not that my father spoke English fluently, he had brought along one of his ad-visers, a German missionary, who translated his siSwati when he realized that my stepmother had not yet learned any English. He hoped, he told her, that she would enjoy the new life in his peaceful country and be happy there.

My stepmother was delighted with him, but displayed incred-ible lack of tact when, intending to say something nice to him, she asked how he, being so well educated and after having been to England, could bear to live in a straw hut and sleep on the bare ground. My father was deeply shocked and dismayed by her gaffe, and even I realized how stupid she had shown herself to be, how much the king would be affronted. But he smiled indulgently and said a few words in siSwati for the missionary to translate. *"Gnädige Frau, Heimat bleibt Heimat,"* he told her.

My stepmother was very much touched by this sentiment and

burst into tears, thinking of her *Heimat,* which she had forsaken in order to accompany my father and me into exile.

The king then led my father and the Mbabane consultant away to have their talk, and the German missionary escorted my stepmother to visit the women, who were preparing a meal to feed the thousands of men assembled at the royal kraal that day. She was glad to hear that the formidable queen mother would not be in evidence.

"The boy is quite safe here," said the missionary. "Let him make friends with the children." But I was never at ease with children of my own age and thought their hopping and skipping games and their casting of pebbles quite ridiculous; I was always drawn toward older youths or adult men, and did not feel shy or embarrassed when I walked toward the young men of the new Locust Regiment, who were standing and sitting against a long, curving reed fence, eating corn and laughing and smoking their little wooden pipes. They were as curious about me as I was interested in them, and touched my soft, pale-blond hair—my stepmother washed it once a week with the yolks of three eggs—and my metal belt buckle with the Florentine lily on it, and were most intrigued by my wristwatch, which had no numerals on it, only big dots where the 12, 3, 6, and 9 should have been. The youths of this new regiment were only a few years older than I—I was as tall as many of them—and I longed to be one of them, to live, like them, away from home. What a triumph it would be, to be the only white, blond warrior among this band of jovial Negroes, parading with them and eating mealies with them, wearing only a bit of animal fur to cover my private parts, with gaudy feathers and a red cloth fetish in my hair, amulets and strange charms around my arms and legs, shell necklaces to indicate my rank, sleeping in their communal thatched hut, huddled together for warmth, smoking that forbidden hemp they carried in the pipes hanging from the thong around their waists. They were like the brave Spartans of whom I had read, and like them they loved only one another. O happy band, from whose ranks, the German businessman had told us, the king selected the most trusted to be his messengers and personal attendants.

Playfully, they urged me to smoke one of their pipes, and I knew that it was forbidden for me, but with great daring I took a few puffs of the horrid, rank smoke and could not help gasping and looking disgusted by it. How they laughed at me; what good fellows they all were! Then they squatted on the ground, many of them, as if commanded to do so, and as I stood by and wondered what they were doing, whether it was perhaps a prayer like in Dakar, I realized with a shock of fascination that they were shamelessly urinating, copiously and loudly, and that warm, foaming rivulets coursed from under their haunches and sent up a great smell, and the dry soil became wet and glistened.

When my stepmother and the German missionary, returning from their visit to the women's huts, came upon this mass display of micturating warriors, she was horrified and called me to her and hurried me away and remonstrated with the missionary for being quite unperturbed.

"But it is *disgusting*!" she cried. "I don't care if you say it *is* their custom. You should have it stopped. I have never seen anything so filthy in my life—and in full view of the boy! What terrible ideas it will put in his head!"

She was so deeply shocked that she could barely be polite to the king when his conference with my father ended and we all said good-bye to him. On the advice of the businessman from Mbabane, we did not remain and intrude on the inauguration ceremony of the Locust Regiment and the king's address, nor for the uninhibited feasting and drinking that were to follow and would last long into the night and were likely to shock my stepmother.

✧

The meeting with the king had greatly depressed my stepmother.
Poor, silly young woman: she had married an old man for the security he could offer her; now he was no longer rich and had brought
her to this godforsaken uncivilized land without any of the basic
comforts that would make life possible, where she was to make
friends with an illiterate so-called queen. Her sense of duty had
made her come along with a man she did not love and a spoiled little
boy who was not hers. "Oh, Paulchen," she implored my father
when we drove from the royal kraal back to the inn at Ezulwini, "I
think we have made a terrible mistake. Maybe that Hitler is not so
bad after all—remember how nice he was to me that day at the
Bahnhof am Zoo? We should have stayed there where we were so
happy, in our lovely house, with all our nice friends, where everyone
knew us, you with your weekly *Herrenabend* and your *Skat* and my
Schiller-verein and the theater and everything. Here we will always
be strangers, and there is nothing except the heat and that dreadful
mambo-wambo snake and wild beasts howling in the night and
men making pee-pee. The naked king is quite right—*Heimat bleibt
Heimat!*" Tears rolled down her beautiful face. "Please, Paulchen,
let us go home, where we belong."

My father sympathized with her and tried to comfort her but
told her that there was no turning back. He was grim and knew he
had failed her. I lay on the backseat of the car and began to relish a
new and delicious fantasy. No longer did I want the Gypsies to
come in the night and steal me from my parents; instead,
Ngwenyama, the Lion of Swaziland, had chosen me from among all
the youths of his Locust Regiment to be his trusted personal attendant. He taught me to hunt wild beasts with bow and arrow, and
made me sleep at his feet in his straw hut, and, when it became cold

just before dawn, took me under his rough blanket to lie snug and warm against his strong, lean, chocolate-colored body.

But I was never to see King Sobhuza II again. The Swaziland adventure was short-lived. My father became disenchanted with the prospects of the tin mine and did not buy it, much to the relief of my stepmother. We returned to Johannesburg and a prosaic, financially precarious existence there; but we had foiled death in the gas chambers, which would have been our fate in Germany.

2

A

NIGHT

IN GAY

PAREE

SOON AFTER THE END of World War II, when it was again possible to visit the continent of Europe, and when I lived in England, I went with two friends for a week to Paris. It was to be a dream come true. We were in our early twenties, quite innocent, and on a very tight budget.

We took the day train from London and arrived in the evening at the Gare Saint-Lazare, which conveniently and dramatically brings the traveler right into the center and bustle of Paris. As we stood in the square outside the station and breathed the heady air and ambience of Paris, we felt that it was a major achievement merely to have arrived there. We walked with our luggage to the Rue du Colisée, where, we had heard, there were small hotels that offered cheap rooms for "men who liked the color green" or who were "musical"—the word "gay," in those days, was used only to mean lively, merry, lighthearted, given to pleasure.

At the Hôtel du Colisée they showed us a three-bedded room; but each of us hoped, although we had never discussed this among us, to meet a rich beau who, in return for certain favors granted,

would pay for our dinners and theater tickets and other amuse-
ments—so we took three single rooms. There was a rudimentary
bathroom along the corridor.

My friends were as graceful as a pair of swans, and within
twenty-four hours of our arrival had established amiable relationships—John's friend was a tall black American, the leading dancer
in the revue at the Lido nightclub; Neville's amour was an Egyptian
playboy whose mother was a very well connected grande dame, so
that he could take the three of us to a showing of the highly publi-
cized New Look collection at Christian Dior, for which it was impossible to obtain tickets. He had enormous hands. "We all know
what *that* implies," gloated Neville.

I was the ugly duckling of this trio; and after the day's dutiful
cultural sight-seeing, when darkness fell and the lights lit up and
Paris became truly *la ville lumière* and as romantic as we had expected, and when my friends went off to dinner with their protec-
tors, I was left to my own devices. I had barely enough money for
food; the cost of theater and even cinema tickets was prohibitive;
and the cheapest way to spend the evening was to go to the *bain
vapeur* in the nearby Rue de Penthièvre, a bathhouse in a working-
class district chiefly patronized by men who lived in that area and
had no bathrooms in their homes. But there was an army barracks
close by; and some of the young soldiers had no more money for
entertainments than I had, so they went there to while away many
hours, and there was some furtive sexual activity in dark corners and
where the steam was most dense.

But toward the end of our week's stay I felt that I had to see
more of Paris by night than the interior of that sordid, unclean
bathhouse; I would splurge just once and go to the famous Boeuf sur
le Toit bar, the meeting place of all the richest, most famous, most
talented, most beautiful homosexuals, where, it was said, one could
see Mr. Jean Cocteau with his gorgeous lover, Mr. Jean Marais,

almost every night. Young men—painters, playwrights, poets, actors, musicians—had been discovered there, careers had been born. It was a must for an impecunious, ambitious young man.

I rested in bed all afternoon and early evening in order to look my best. I brushed my best suit, made sure I had kept a clean shirt for the occasion, selected my most handsome tie. A drop of eau de cologne went behind each ear; more was sprinkled onto the pristine white hand-hemmed Irish linen handkerchief that was arranged to peep just a little more flamboyantly than usual from the jacket's breast pocket. With hair brushed vigorously *en brosse* and considerable trepidation, I entered the door of this elegant, dimly lit bar.

Drinks were exorbitant in price, I had been warned, but less so at the bar than at tables. I went to the bar, where not many places were taken, and sat down three stools away from a little woman in a rather mannish gray tailor-made costume of skirt and jacket with matching hat. I ordered *"un gin-fizz"* because a tall drink can be made to last a long, long time.

The mirror behind the bar reflected the whole room, and in it I began to notice that the men seated at the tables behind me were glancing at me—no, openly looking at me. I was very surprised, but there was no doubt of it—they were looking at me, watching me, studying me—and I was tremendously flattered and elated by this attention. Was it because I was a new face there? Was it my crew cut, not yet fashionable at that time in Paris? Whatever it was, I glowed in all those admiring looks; I preened; pretending not to have noticed them, I turned left, I turned right, I gave the room the benefit of first one profile, then the other; I toyed with my glass; I dipped a finger into the gin and made it fizz and extracted my finger and ever so slowly, sensuously, licked it. I was a vamp of the silent screen; I looked dreamily into the far distance; and then in a bold move I swiveled slowly, seductively around on my stool, leaned back on one elbow against the bar, posed with my legs thrust apart, and looked directly at the men who were looking at me.

But they were not looking at me; they had never looked at me, had not seen all my ridiculous posing and preening and the sexy way I had licked my finger. No, not one of them had paid me any attention; their eyes were all directed to my right, on the drab little woman three stools away—and no wonder, for now that I had become used to the dim lighting I saw that this woman was Miss Marlene Dietrich.

Oh, the shock of it! The realization stunned me so much and I was so mortified that I gulped down the remainder of my gin-fizz and dared not spend money on another when the efficient barman immediately came to serve me. The entire, pretentious bar, all the men and that famous actress in it, the whole of Paris, had become hateful. I wanted to run away, but sat on as though glued to the seat of my humiliation, pretending to the barman that I was waiting for someone: a rich admirer, a handsome lover, the editor of the *Spectator,* who had asked me to allow him to publish my story about meeting the king of Swaziland, a theatrical producer who had begged me to design the décor and costumes for his next opera at La Scala, at Covent Garden, at Bayreuth. But, as in the best-remembered line of my favorite book, "It was all play . . . a striving and a striving, and an ending in nothing." I was a miserable failure.

And then, as in a dream or a film with a happy ending, a tall and well-dressed man rose from one of the tables and on his way out of the bar made a little detour and came right up to me and without stopping said, "Do you plan to waste more time here or will you go home with me now?"

I was rescued; and I followed him out of that dark bar and to a taxi that drove us around the Place de l'Étoile into the tree-lined Avenue d'Iéna to a late-nineteenth-century mansion that had been

converted into apartments, and in an incredible fin de siècle elevator that was all glass and bronze we rode up to his flat.

He switched on a table lamp, and I found myself in a small, very
neat studio room, sparsely furnished in what seemed to be a military
style, with framed photographs of quaint groups of soldiers of long
ago all over the walls. "This is not my home, you know; I live mostly
in England. It's just my little Paris pied-à-terre, a foot on the
ground, you know. I have others in Cairo and Lahore."

I was impressed. My rescuer was clearly a rich and cultivated
man. As Oscar Wilde had pointed out, the possession of several
addresses inspires confidence—and not only in tradesmen. His
charmingly Olde Worlde upper-class English accent was most reassuring, too. I knew he was a real gentleman and that I would come
to no harm with him.

While I looked at the photographs, he had taken the fur rug off
the narrow bed and folded it neatly. "Go to bed," he told me. "I'll
join you." And he went to the bathroom, from which he reappeared
when I was between the sheets. I caught a glimpse of him, naked
and very thin and tall, a silhouette against the doorway, before he
turned out the light behind him and came to bed. He smelled clean
and good, and we were both tired, and I went to sleep in his arms.

✧

When I awoke next morning, pale daylight was coming into the
room through the window blinds. My host appeared from the bathroom in a magnificent floor-length Eastern robe and went into the
kitchen. "I'll make us a pot of hot chocolate before you leave," he
called out. It was a strong hint that he did not want me to linger,
and I was disappointed.

I dressed and walked around the room to look more closely at
the framed sepia photographs that filled the walls, all of which
depicted groups of late-nineteenth-century soldiers of the British

army—"officers and gentlemen"—sitting with spiked and plumed shikar helmets held on their laps, their ceremonial swords or sabers beside them, wearing highly polished spurred boots almost to their knees, very tight trousers, and uniform jackets crisscrossed over and over with masses of heavy braid and tassels, fancy facings on the sleeves and on the high-necked collars, and ornamented epaulets. Their legs were always thrust far apart in manly poses; most of them sported fierce mustaches. Behind them, or demurely posed at the sides of the pictures, were their native servants in turbans and white robes with wide sashes across their chests, some holding regimental mascots—mostly dogs but the occasional goat. In the background there were tents, trestle tables laid for elaborate meals featuring many bottles of wine, bungalows set among palm trees, or the veranda of a gymkhana club.

Some of the pictures were not of large groups but showed only four, five, or six officers, bachelors all, at their ease in front of the stuccoed white chummery in which they lived, one reposing gracefully on the ground and the others sitting on campstools behind him, with their household servants, their grooms, their polo ponies, and their pets arranged artistically around them.

All these military group portraits were handsomely framed behind glass, and on their cardboard mats they bore in black or in embossed gold letters the name of the regiment, the date and location where its members had thus been perpetuated, and, in small type, the name of each man pictured there. It was a delightful, unusual collection of photographs, and when my host returned with the hot chocolate I complimented him on them. "They're so amusing, so quaint, such fun," I said. "Wherever did you find them all?"

"*Find* them? What *can* you mean?" he said, quite sternly. "They're mine, of course. They're my regiment; I'm in every one of them."

It was impossible to extricate myself from my faux pas. "But they're all so old," I said, feebly.

"Of course they're old. So am I. I fought at Majuba Hill, you know."

This was inconceivable. I had gone to school in Johannesburg and knew South African history. *"Majuba Hill!"* I cried. "But the Battle of Majuba Hill was in 1881!"

"So it was, and a bloody mess it was, too. I was a nineteen-year-old subaltern."

He walked to the two windows and snapped down the little acorns at the bottom of the blinds so that they rolled up and let in the sunlight. It shone upon him like a spotlight. He was not Frankenstein's monster, not quite; but the gentleman with whom I had shared a bed was all too obviously eighty-six years old.

It was a shock, and I felt extremely foolish, but the lighting in the bar, in the street outside it, in the taxi, in the lobby and elevator of the apartment building, had all been very dim. The flat had been lit only by the small table lamp. I had never clearly seen his face the previous evening; all that had mattered to me was that a kindly and well-spoken gentleman had rescued me from that hateful bar and taken me to his cozy bed.

"But who are you? Are you a general?" I asked this ancient warrior who had played an active part in the rise of the British Empire and then witnessed its fall.

"What does that matter?" he said. "No questions, no pack drill."

We drank the hot chocolate, which was delicious.

He had been up the Nile with Wolseley in 1885 and in the Afghan Frontier Campaign of 1897 and then back in Egypt and the Sudan in 1898 and at the Battle of Omdurman.

"Omdurman! The cavalry charge—Winston Churchill was in

that," I said in awe. I was an ardent admirer of Britain's great war-time prime minister.

"Yes, and what a nuisance he was, too."

After that he had returned to South Africa and fought in the Boer War. "And in the First World War?" I asked.

"That was not a war for gentlemen," he said curtly.

He wanted me to leave. I finished my hot chocolate; we shook hands; he took me to the glass-and-bronze elevator and watched me descend in it.

I did not know whether to feel ashamed or proud of my exploit as I walked down the Avenue des Champs-Élysées to the Rue du Colisée to have breakfast with John and Neville and exchange accounts of our night's adventures. Unlike wines and violins, bed companions are not prized for their age. I felt that I had made myself ridiculous—but, on the other hand, I had inadvertently become an interesting link with the past.

3

THE

NINETY-EIGHT

MOTORCYCLE

COPS OF

FLORENCE

WE LAUGHED with derision in England in the early 1950s when Arthur Frommer's *Europe on 5 Dollars a Day* guides appeared; we were doing it on less than half that, and in considerable style.

With the equivalent of $280 I paid for my round-trip rail ticket to Italy and spent an entire summer in the village of Forio on the island of Ischia in the Bay of Naples, staying in the comfortable guest room of a fisherman and his family, with my own basic bathroom and a terrace shaded by a grapevine. The room cost less than a dollar a night, and another dollar paid for three daily meals at the village trattorias. I lived like a prince. (A real one, Prince Heinrich von Hesse, clandestinely crossed the bay in a speedboat each evening from Capri to spend the night with a German beauty who was my daytime companion and photographed me as a damp beachcomber with playing cards scattered around me for *Die Elegante Welt,* a fashion magazine.)

I walked all around the island and made detailed drawings for a record of the deterioration of the old churches since they had been documented in the late nineteenth century. With a statuesque black district attorney from Chicago and half a dozen local friends I climbed Mount Epomeo and spent a night singing in a hermit's cave near the summit, to see the sunrise next morning. The family with whom the German beauty was staying owned a vineyard; when the grapes were ripe, we helped to pick them, and she hitched up her skirt and I rolled up my trousers and we assisted in the stamping of the grapes. Most of the summer visitors were single men of all ages and nationalities, drawn there because the Ischian men had the well-deserved reputation for being most accommodating. All the fishermen in Forio vied with one another to be hired at wonderfully affordable rates for an hour's "fishing trip" out at sea— the traditional and discreet way of making romantic assignations. The helpful owner of Filippo's waterfront *locanda* provided expert firsthand advice: "The young brother is the best-looking but still a bit shy; the older brother is better; the father is one of the best on the island, very good value; the grandfather is a real satyr and loves it so much he often gives another hour without extra charge."

In nearby Lacco Ameno we lay for hours in ancient stone troughs, covered from head to foot with the hot, therapeutic mud that had attracted Romans there twenty centuries before. The poet W. H. Auden and his friend Chester Kallman lived squalidly in a run-down house in the village. One evening, sitting on the harbor wall, I exchanged sweaters with the ex-king of Spain. Altogether, a perfect summer on two dollars a day.

Early in October it became chilly and rainy; it was time to leave, but I still had enough money left for a week in Florence and a few days in Zurich before returning to England to teach art and geography to the three pretty little granddaughters of Bertrand Russell.

In Florence, I stayed at the youth hostel on the Piazza Beccaria, a vast fortresslike building that had been an army barracks until World War II. There were enormous dormitories, each occupying a whole floor, with hundreds of double-tiered bunks. At 11:00 P.M.

the inmates were locked in for the night. I believe that somewhere in the building there was a separate entrance for women and a dormitory for them. I never saw it: the sexes were completely segregated in those happy times.

The tourist season was over, so that only about thirty young men were lodged in one section of a dormitory, where they talked loud and long about their travel experiences, never mentioning any visits to churches, art galleries, palaces, castles, museums, or scenic sights, but boasting of the free meals they had obtained from gullible drivers who had picked them up at the roadside, of innkeepers they had bilked by departing before dawn, of trains in which they had traveled long distances without paying the fare, locked inside the toilet.

It was forbidden to bring food into the dormitory, but almost all the hostelers did so, although the trattorias in the nearby Borgo la Croce provided substantial three-course meals for around fifty cents. Two blond German youths lay in the bunk above me—amazingly daring and courageous of them, in those days—and took alternate bites from a pungent sausage. An athletic Californian had hitchhiked all over Europe for six months in threadbare sneakers, swim trunks, and a tracksuit, without a change of clothes. Unless he was offered a free bed for the night and until it became too cold, he had slept in fields and parks. He ate a small carton of yogurt each day for breakfast, lunch, and dinner.

Early one afternoon there was a great deal of commotion. Due to the fear of a Communist demonstration planned for next day, ninety-eight motorcycle cops had been rushed to Florence to supplement the local police force; and they were being billeted at the youth hostel.

The arrival of these Cocteau-like angels of death turned the dormitory into a homosexual's dream come true. Helmeted like ancient gods, these sturdy, gorgeous men began to fill the huge hall: they wore black leather jackets, black turtleneck sweaters, jodhpurs, and boots up to their knees; they had holsters strapped around their waists and menacing billy clubs and handcuffs hanging from their heavy belts. Many of them had fierce mustaches and eyes hidden behind sinister dark glasses. Their officers—who were lodged in less Spartan quarters elsewhere in the city—had apparently briefed them not to intimidate the hostelers by their greater number and air of authority but to give the tourists preference at the washbasins and showers. They selected their bunks, spread their blankets, unburdened themselves of their weapons, lit cigarettes, and held themselves aloof.

An English friend of mine had asked me to contact a Swedish writer who lived in Florence, and I had telephoned this Mr. Nils Bjorn on my arrival. He was one of the numerous financially secure northern European "confirmed bachelors" who have for many centuries made the delectable city of Florence their preferred home, finding there all they most desire on earth: the art and architecture of the Renaissance with its Hellenistic sources, splendidly ornate church ceremonies, the society of grand ladies with titles going back two thousand years, and the occasional peasant lad to be led secretly up the service stairs to share their bed. Each winter, Mr. Bjorn wisely returned to his family mansion in Stockholm, which was well heated. The people of Florence pretend that they have no winter, and consequently freeze from November to April.

I sensed his consternation when I told him over the telephone that I was staying at the youth hostel. The Piazza Beccaria was not in a respectable part of the city. Had I stayed at one of the many simple *pensioni* that catered to thrifty art lovers, he might not have been unduly worried; but someone who was at that lowly hostel had to be viewed with great apprehension. In the usual European method of first assessing a stranger's credentials on neutral ground before inviting him into one's home, he suggested that we meet for morning coffee at the Piazza della Signoria. Only tourists frequented it: his Florentine friends would be most unlikely to see him there with me.

I had been shown photographs of him in England and recognized him sitting at a table when I arrived; and as soon as he saw that I was dressed in clean and well-pressed gray flannel trousers, a somber tie, and a decent tweed jacket, he led me away to one of the fashionable *caffès* on the Via Tornabuoni. "They know one there, dear boy, and serve one well."

He was very kind and most helpful. He gave me precise advice on which paintings to concentrate on in the Uffizi Gallery, what to look for especially in the Pitti Palace; which churches could be omitted without detriment. He told me at what time of day the Duomo was least crowded and at what hour of sunlight the reliefs on the Baptistry doors appeared to their best advantage. He recommended books to read on the Medici popes. He had made a study of Savonarola and talked brilliantly on that strange and horrible period of Florentine history. It was an education to listen to him.

When he felt adequately assured that my presence in his home would bring no disgrace upon it, he formally invited me later that week to his apartment—"to see a few of one's treasured possessions, dear boy, and take afternoon tea with some charming ladies of one's acquaintance."

Mr. Bjorn's apartment occupied the main floor of a palace on the Lungarno Torigiani, the tall, slender windows of its reception rooms overlooking the river Arno and toward the Duomo and the Palazzo Vecchio. It was very large and very fine, with wonderful painted ceilings, and crowded to suffocation with beautiful pieces of old furniture, paintings, hangings, vases filled with flowers and scarlet ostrich feathers, statues, and endless small objets d'art and silver-framed photographs of men and women in court dress displayed on spindly tables. The cushions that sat in rows on the armchairs and sofas were of medieval cloths and edged with golden cords. Two elderly maidservants fussily brought in an elaborate tea—pretty, tiny cakes, minuscule sandwiches, and water ices. There was a plethora of lace cloths, napkins, little forks and spoons, sugar tongs, utensils to squeeze the lemon slices into the thin Capo di Monte cups.

The other guests were three noble Florentine ladies, all beautifully dressed with the utmost simplicity. They did not remove their elaborate hats and white gloves. The most important—as was obvious by the way in which our host and the younger ladies deferred to her—was a frail old princess: she did not speak or understand English, and my Italian was far too limited to enable me to address more than a trite sentence or two to her.

Mr. Bjorn was naturally adept at all the social graces and adroitly kept polite conversation going to and fro across his dainty tea table, partly in English and partly in Italian, until one of the younger ladies turned to me and inquired where I was staying in Florence. I replied that I was at the youth hostel on the Piazza Beccaria. There was a moment of silence, as though I had voiced a profanity in that sacred chamber. Ashamed for me, feeling acutely responsible to the ladies for my presence, and desperately embarrassed, Mr. Bjorn attempted to salvage the situation with a torrent of English and Italian. "Not at all what you think—a perfectly charming place—such nicely appointed bedrooms for the thrifty young people—quite the ideal place to stay—just like a hotel, indeed better than some of them one knows—so clever of Mr. Ebensten to have selected it for his sojourn in our city. . . ."

I could not bear to listen to this pretense and subterfuge, and when he halted in his fairy tale I said that on the contrary, the hostel was of the utmost simplicity but clean, that there were no bedrooms but that I would sleep that night in a huge dormitory with ninety-eight policemen.

Mr. Bjorn blanched, and the ladies who understood English looked thoroughly alarmed; but the old princess asked them to translate what I had said, and when they had done so with hesitation, lifted her hands with delight and announced, "Oh, what bliss! How I wish *I* would sleep tonight with ninety-eight policemen."

The others took their lead from her; apprehension turned into hilarity, and I remained persona grata for the remainder of the tea party, although I fear that I had not endeared myself to the exceedingly decorous Mr. Nils Bjorn.

✧

The shrewd old princess proved to be right: that night *was* bliss.

Even before lights-out at 11:00 P.M., there was no mistaking the aura of sexuality that almost a hundred armed motorcycle cops had brought with them into the dismal dormitories. They loitered in the dimly lit washrooms, in corridors, and on the iron circular stairs between the floors, posed in the open doors of toilets and shower cubicles, stripped to the waist, cigarette between lips, smirking sensuously, groping their genitalia under their uniform pants, occasionally hissing invitingly: *"Cazzo grande, cazzo duro."*

The bold, blond German sausage-eaters were the first to take advantage of the rare treats that were being offered. In dark corners of the washrooms I saw them fill their mouths eagerly with the policemen's *cazzos,* which were as large and hard as they had promised. *"Mensch, das ist ja ganz toll!"* they cried as they drew breath to attend to the next cop, and the next.

After lights-out, their and other hostelers' trysts with the cops at first took place with some attempts at privacy; but when it became apparent that there was no one of authority to stop the action, that no one interfered, it became no longer furtive but open and general. It was the older policemen who set the tone for that night's pleasures—men in their thirties and forties, married and with children, whose complete masculinity could not be in doubt and who, by forcing slim young tourists to their knees in phallic worship and holding them there while being serviced, demonstrated added proof of their male dominance.

As the night progressed, and with far too few compliant hostelers to meet the demands of so many aroused policemen, the cops began without shame to fellate one another and to proceed to anal intercourse. It was, as the indefatigable German youths called out to each other again and again, totally crazy; and I witnessed erotic scenes that far exceeded the imaginative couplings with which the celebrated Tom of Finland was then beginning to delight and excite us, depicting sexual encounters involving cops, bikers, sailors, and cowboys. "This sure beats even the Embarcadero Y," confided the young Californian hiker, who demonstrated remarkable powers of endurance that long night, during much of which he permitted himself to be playfully handcuffed to an iron pipe, naked, facing a tiled wall.

By no means did all the policemen join in the unabated escapades that night. Many of them, and some hostelers, slept oblivious of the silent though frantic activities around them or pretended to sleep and lay in silent disapproval of the orgy; but the antics of the others lasted so long and became so energy-consuming that I wondered whether these tough motorcycle cops would have enough stamina left next morning to be able to quell the anticipated Communist riot.

✧

As it turned out, there was no political demonstration next day, and during the afternoon all the policemen roared back to Bologna,

Milan, and Pisa on their motorbikes. The cavernous dormitory seemed sad and neglected that night, with only its handful of impecunious hostelers. On the following morning I took the train through the Saint Gotthard tunnel to the cold north.

4

A

PASTRY IN

MONTE

CARLO

I DISLIKE being someone's guest in a restaurant. Sometimes it cannot be avoided, as recently when a friend from Ohio was in Key West (where I now live) and invited me to dinner at Louie's Backyard, our most expensive restaurant. I told him that it was quite unnecessary for him to be so extravagant, and suggested other pleasant eating places, but he had set his heart on Louie's. As always on such occasions, I felt awkward and selected the least costly dish, while the other guests started with shrimps and clams and went on to elaborate exotic tropical salads and the artistically arranged *grands plats* in which Louie's specializes. Instead of wine or the practically obligatory chic Perrier with its slice of lemon, I drank tap water.

And despite my sweet tooth, when the desserts were offered, I declined. The others chose from the many rich confections with fancy names for which Louie's is best known, and when my host persisted in urging me to order one, I succumbed, but when it was brought to me, I knew that I could not accept it and with great embarrassment sent it back to the kitchen, because the sight of it had suddenly lifted me out of Louie's Backyard—it was not the Atlantic outside the glass doors but the Mediterranean, it was August the fifth, 1955, and I was in the Restaurant Le Snack—"just off the cheese," as Madame de Carné had said—in Monte Carlo.

✧

London in the 1950s had no gay bars or clubs—homosexual men met furtively in the parks at night or spent long evenings creeping from one smelly public urinal to the next—an activity known as "cottaging," which was generally frustrating and occasionally resulted in a fine or imprisonment. The alternative was to respond to the ambiguously worded, numbered cards that daring owners of obscurely located tobacconist shops permitted to be displayed in their windows: "PROFESSOR PAYNE has vacancies for students: beginners welcome"; "ACTIVE EX-GUARDSMAN welcomes old friends and new in his Mayfair flat"; or "GREEK TEACHER gives lessons in your home: satisfaction guaranteed." Replies in sealed envelopes were passed on by the shop to the advertiser, whose anonymity was thus assured.

I had responded to some of these advertising cards, always with dismal results, but was tempted early in 1955 to try once more by seeing a neatly lettered card:

> ART CONNOISSEUR
> *seeks well-equipped young man*
> *to fill position of personal*
> *secretary*

I knew, of course, what this advertisement implied—but what had I to lose by answering it? At thirty-two, I felt justified in still considering myself to be young, and I was unquestionably well equipped to be a secretary, although I had no doubt that it was not typing abilities the Art Connoisseur was looking for.

Two days after I had handed in my reply at the shop, the Connoisseur telephoned me and, after a brief conversation, suggested that we meet for dinner. He would pick me up in his car outside the Royal Court Theatre in Sloane Square. "Describe yourself," he said.

"Five foot ten, crew cut, and I'll be wearing gray pants and a tweed jacket," I told him. How experienced in making such dubious assignations this Connoisseur was, I thought—if he did not like what he saw standing on the sidewalk, he could just drive on.

But he did stop the car and beckoned to me to sit beside him and we drove to a restaurant in Chelsea. He was not much older than I and good-looking, and I realized immediately that he was one of those fortunate men whom Noël Coward had called "scions of a noble breed," the infinitely privileged product of a great public (which in England means private) school and Oxford University. He was a keen sportsman—he mentioned cricket, polo, skiing, and bob sleighing—and positively exuded wealth but did his best to put me at ease; and although he quickly made it clear that I was not the bed companion for whom he had advertised, my table talk and my table manners seemed to pass muster, so that as we parted after the meal he told me he would contact me soon and invite me to dinner at his house. It could have been a polite way of terminating the brief acquaintance, but he did telephone me and then told me his name—Anthony Beauchamp—and spelled the surname for me: "It's pronounced the same as Beecham pills and the conductor, but my people came over with William the Conqueror."

A week later a butler admitted me to a large house on Eaton Square, where Anthony Beauchamp introduced me to his older American friend, Mr. Austin Riddle, and a dozen splendid people who were assembled in a room with a huge seventeenth-century tapestry depicting the four continents then known; two servants handed round trays of sherry. It was as if I had entered a film set; but although I was not a little awed by the company and the Corot over the fireplace, I was reassured to see that my black corduroy suit was suitable for the occasion and by hearing Anthony tell the other guests that I was an author. A little careful research on his part since our first meeting had established that I was poor but honest and had no embarrassing relatives or friends or any criminal associations. I was a young man who could be nurtured. *Pierced Hearts and True Love,* my history of the art of tattooing, had been published in 1953 and been an astonishing success, with a second large printing a few months later; it had received highly enthusiastic press reviews, been discussed on the BBC, and its fame was assured when the Communist *Daily Worker* condemned it. Next year my first novel, *All Play,* appeared—"a witty and penetrating account of life among artistic and theatrical circles in London today," said one reviewer. ("Artistic," in those distant days of decorum, was understood to mean "homosexual," a word then never mentioned in polite society.)

The conversation at dinner was mainly about people I did not know and could not even identify because most of them were referred to by pet names—Buffy, Tigger, Mooncalf. When I left, I did not know whether I had made a good impression or been a failure, and was considerably surprised a few weeks later to receive a letter from Mr. Riddle in which he invited me to spend two weeks in August with him and Tony Beauchamp at their villa in the South of France. I wrote and accepted with pleasure but was somewhat perplexed. Would I be painfully out of my depth? What would I wear? What tips were expected of a guest at a villa at Saint-Jean-Cap-Ferrat? Why, indeed, had I been invited?

When I spoke with Tony Beauchamp later on the telephone to confirm my arrival by train, I hinted at my trepidation. "If one has a writer staying as one's houseguest, one expects either to be entertained by his witty conversation all day or, if he is the quiet, morose type, he must read his journal cozily in the evenings," he said.

I did not know to what type I belonged, but I promised to keep a journal.

I could manage the cost of a third-class round-trip rail ticket to the South of France, but I possessed no clothes remotely suitable for that playground of the rich and famous. Tony had told me that he and Austin avoided the smart Riviera set and that formal clothes were not required; but my serviceable gray flannel trousers, my blue jeans and leather jacket, and my black corduroy suit would be useless and out of place. The English working classes did not in those days go to the Mediterranean for summer vacations—*plage* clothes were made for the rich and were correspondingly expensive. Most fortuitously, I lived opposite a catering-outfitter store, where I bought two pairs each of white and of blue-and-white-checkered chef's trousers, and rope-soled kitchen shoes; in London's dockland I found thin blue-and-white cotton sailor's jerseys; and from a vacation spent on a North Sea trawler I had a hand-knitted white traditional seaman's sweater for cool evenings. None of this was stylish, it all looked cheap, but I hoped that it would be redeemed by my cherished Royal Navy officer's belt with its impressive brass buckle, a gift from a friend who had worn it at the Japanese surrender in Tokyo Bay.

To arrive at one's destination slowly, by train, sharpens the anticipation. Twenty-four hours after having left London, when dawn broke as the train ran along the Riviera coast, all was enchantment. Those legendary names on the station platforms—Saint-Raphaël, Cannes, Antibes, Nice—the glimpses of beautiful, well-tended hotels and villas and sand beaches where colored umbrellas were being set up in rows—the masses of flowers and the green, green trees—there were even *palm trees*! "After Nice there's a tunnel, so be ready to get off at Beaulieu-sur-Mer," Tony had said; and there he was, despite the early hour, on the platform, and drove me to the Villa Eugénie.

I had read about the Villa Eugénie at Saint-Jean-Cap-Ferrat in an architectural magazine, where it was described as being "shaded by pine trees, a paradise built above the white rocks"; but neither this nor the grandeur of Tony and Austin's London house had prepared me for the opulent, sequestered estate we entered. The villa was still shuttered at that hour, and Tony took me up to my room. Because I had sat up all night on the train, he suggested that I rest until luncheon to meet Austin and the other houseguests—a most congenial old lady, Miss Smith, a Quaker heiress from Philadelphia, and Alexander Pomfret, an Englishman, the young but already exceedingly successful editor of a highly respected art magazine. He was witty and handsome, so that great ladies of European high society doted on him and vied with one another to have him at their dinner parties. He was a great snob and insufferably rude to those he considered his inferiors—which was most of the world's population. He was what was then referred to as "a pain in the neck"—a pain that is today said to be felt in a lower part of the human anatomy.

The bad witch of this fairy-tale enclave was Tony and Austin's social secretary, Miss Valentine, a most forbidding lady of advanced years who thoroughly understood and briskly dealt with the members of the Riviera's beau monde and their parasites. She was an Englishwoman and believed that it was not wealth, importance, or power that was of supreme importance, but ancient lineage, which she called "good blood." When arranging the placement for a luncheon or dinner party at the Villa Eugénie, she thus ranked a British earl over a French marquise but below a maharani.

Early next morning I went through the villa's garden down to the sea-bathing place for which the Villa Eugénie was most renowned. Austin Riddle's mother, who had entertained on a lavish scale, had had an artificial cove blasted out of the rocks so that the duke and duchess of Windsor could swim there in complete privacy, unobserved from any passing boat. My solitary swim was one of the most luxuriously memorable experiences of my life, and when I stepped out of the water there was a houseman who wrapped me in a huge soft towel with the villa emblem—he must have watched me from the house. Having dried me, he inquired whether Monsieur would like to go up and change and then have his *petit déjeuner* served to him on the terrace. Monsieur was happy to do so; and presently the butler, assisted by a servant, set a table for me and brought coffee, fresh orange juice, hot croissants and wonderful apricot confiture, and several morning papers in English and French.

I had never been so incredibly cosseted in such glamorous, gracious surroundings. It was an astonishing, exhilarating experience; but the insidious danger for someone not accustomed or born to such a life-style is that it acts on the novice like a powerful, habit-forming drug that, unless it is courageously given up, corrupts and ultimately destroys the addict.

I did not know or understand the ways of the rich and felt that my obnoxious fellow guest Alexander Pomfret was taking advantage of our hosts' hospitality. He spent every afternoon at the nearby and even grander Villa La Fiorentina of the notorious Lady Kenmare (who was reputed to have murdered her four fabulously rich husbands), where he frolicked around the pool with her son, Rory Cameron, and other lovely young men in abbreviated bathing slips. Immediately after dinner he took himself off to Nice, where he was having an *affaire* with a skater in the ice show. The large villa car was driven only by the chauffeur and used to take the cook to market and the maids to the dentist; Tony and Austin's car was never available when they needed it—Alex had commandeered it; and when he returned from La Fiorentina, he went on and on about the famous people he met there: "Count and Countess Stroganoff—she's simply *covered* with those amazing jewels they managed to bring out of Russia in 1917—the Prince and Princess Hildesheim—she was a Hohenzollern, you know—Pussy Vagobert, who used to be Lord Bismuth's lover until he dropped him for that Peruvian gold digger." It was all very amusing, but I considered it tactless of him when he boasted that "everyone on the Riviera, even the Rainiers and the Aquavivas," would be at Lady Kenmare's White Ball, since Tony and Austin had not been invited. I thought it bad of him to attend it, but he did look stunning in my white seaman's sweater, which he borrowed for the event. He enthused that everything was to be white: white lanterns in the trees, white flowers, everyone wearing white, nothing but white food—even the drinks would be all white.

"Milk?" Austin said.

In their desire to leave nothing undone to assure their houseguests' happiness, Tony and Austin had arranged for us to swim at the heated outdoor *piscine* of the Grand Hôtel du Cap-Ferrat, where the beau monde could be seen acquiring expensive suntans and eating freshly caught *moules* served in ice-filled silver buckets, accompanied by *kir* in slender glasses.

Alexander Pomfret took me there one morning and imperiously called out "Villa Eugénie" as we swept in through the gate; but it seemed ludicrous to me to swim in a pool, no matter how large it was or how rich the bathers, when we had our own glorious sea-bathing place at the villa. The admirable Miss Smith agreed. "It costs Tony and Austin four hundred francs every time one of us goes there," she said. "And who wants to be among all those obscenely fat Indochinese crooks and their expensive Parisian prostitutes anyway?" I never accompanied Alex there again.

One day Mr. Cecil Roberts came to luncheon. He was the enormously prolific author of novels that appealed chiefly to female readers. Humbly born—it was said that his mother had been a servant in a country house in Norfolk or Suffolk—he had worked hard to endear himself to many rich titled ladies, in whose châteaux, palazzi, and villas he spent most of his time. "Here," he cried, handing Miss Valentine a book, "is my thirty-second baby!" (He pronounced it "bebby.") It was a novel set in Alassio. "They've made me an honorary citizen of Alassio and are presenting me with a key. Charming of them, isn't it?"

Throughout the meal he spoke of archduchesses, mediatized princesses, and countesses, to all of whom he referred by their pet names. Any men he mentioned were generals, air marshals, or heads of state. He had just been in Vienna again. "Oh, the red plush, the boys' choir, the Prater, the *Gemütlichkeit*—there's a book in it."

Did we know—surely we did—well, it bore repeating—that the empress Elizabeth of Austria, the one who had walked thirty feet after having been fatally stabbed in the back in Geneva—had held him on her lap? Yes, when he was a child—a little *bebby*—in a country house in Norfolk—or was it Suffolk?

And then he talked of his earnings, all those royalties simply pouring in, after all those years, almost all his thirty-one books still in print, in all sorts of curious languages—one did not know how to cope with it all—should one sell foreign rights outright to assist with the horrendous British income tax? Writing came so easy, by now, but the financial problems never stopped.

Miss Valentine, playing hostess, graciously turned to me. "I hear you are also a writer, but I take it you have no such problems?"

"No, not as yet," I said.

The other luncheon guests were the maharaja of Nagpur (seated on Mr. Riddle's right) and his pretty Persian catamite with hideously varnished, pointed fingernails (next to me). They were motoring to Italy and calling on friends en route. Immediately after coffee the maharaja looked at his sumptuous wristwatch. "*Quelle horreur!* I must be in Portofino in time for dinner with the Aquavivas! I must pass on," he announced. "Dear Miss Valentine, please be so good as to have my motor brought round."

"We say *press* on, Your Highness," Miss Valentine corrected him, rang the bell to summon a servant, and instructed the man to summon the maharaja's prewar Daimler, whose color exactly matched that of the turbaned chauffeur's *eau-de-Nil* uniform.

"Did you hear Tubby Nagpur say he had to pass on when he meant *press* on?" said Tony when he and Austin returned, having seen off their guests. "Delicious!"

Another day, Tony and Austin took us to Monte Carlo for luncheon with Austin's sister, a *principessa,* her two well-behaved teenage sons in sailor suits, and Madame de Carné, an old friend of Austin's late mother's, who had been decorated for her heroic work with the French Resistance during World War II and was living in reduced circumstances with the Dubonnets, about whom she complained that they were making her walk their dog. "Poor Paul has a cash register instead of a heart," she told us. She suggested that we eat at "an amusing little snack place just off the cheese"—fashionable people referred to Monte Carlo's main square in that flippant way.

This little snack place was the Restaurant Le Snack and extremely expensive, what is today known as a tourist trap. Madame de Carné talked, talked, talked, and very entertaining it was—how Austin at the age of twelve had absolutely refused to dance with a fat, ugly little girl who was Barbara Hutton; how, when he was a teenager, she had driven with him in his mother's car to Carcassonne and how the people in the hotel there had assumed that it was the classic first *affaire* of a young man with an older, experienced woman. I wondered whether Austin enjoyed all these reminiscences, and later, when I asked him, he said, "Dear Madame de Carné—a great *raconteuse* but given to embroidering."

Tony added to the general merriment when he described how the maharaja of Nagpur had said he had to pass on when he meant to say *press* on. "They never get it quite right, do they?" said Alexander Pomfret.

At the end of the meal, a basket of fruit was placed on the table and an immense silver platter of tempting pastries was proffered. For someone with a passion for sweets, like me, it was a vision of heaven. There were caramelized *palmiers;* astonishing *babas au rhum; mille-feuilles; tuiles aux amandes; tartes aux fraises, aux abricots,* and *aux pêches; éclairs* so fresh and light that they would truly melt in the mouth as quick as a flash of lightning, which their name means; and the tongue-shaped *couques,* which had been created in the 1920s at the Café de Paris.

After considerable and difficult deliberation I selected a *mille-feuille,* and it was very good.

Madame de Carné peeled and sliced a pear; I have never seen it done more elegantly and efficiently.

We parted from Madame de Carné and the *principessa* and her sons outside the restaurant and drove toward the hills above Nice, where Tony and Austin were paying a visit to an old, ailing friend. On the outskirts of Monte Carlo, Tony called out, *"Arrêtez! Arrêtez un moment!"* to the chauffeur, dashed into a *pâtisserie,* and came out eating a pastry. Miss Smith reprimanded him for such gluttony. "Well, I think it's better to pay twenty-five francs than to make one's host pay two hundred francs for the same thing in a snob restaurant," said Tony.

I felt dreadful, so humiliated. And it was so unfair—I had eaten only a small first course, not a main dish, taken no wine or coffee; and the apples and pears and grapes the others had selected had no doubt also cost eight times market price. And Tony did not stop— no, during that afternoon drive he reverted again and again to my extravagance, to that wretched pastry I had so unthinkingly ordered. When he and Austin went to see their friend and Alexander flirted with a youth in a village antique shop, Miss Smith and I went for a walk. I asked her what I should do—should I make some excuse and say I must leave the Villa Eugénie immediately? Should I depart secretly during the night? Should I leave an envelope with two hundred francs in it for Tony? She was very understanding and sympathetic. "Do no such silly thing," she said. "The *gratin bien lavé* are often extremely generous, but also capricious, and occasionally callous. Tony has these idiotic little economies. Don't let it upset you and go out of all proportion; get it out of your system and talk to him about it tonight."

After dinner at the Villa Eugénie that evening, Alexander Pomfret drove to Villefranche with Rory Cameron to pick up sailors— an American warship was in port. Miss Smith went to bed early. I sat on miserably with Tony and Austin and did not read from my journal.

Tony said, "Goodness, Hanns, tonight you really *are* quiet and morose."

"He is in a brown study," said Austin.

I took that for my cue and burst out with my hurt feelings; despite my gratitude to them for having invited me to the villa, I desperately wanted Tony to apologize to me.

Instead he said, icily, "It was wrong of you to make Austin and me waste two hundred francs on you for a pastry that one can get in a shop for twenty-five francs."

I burst into tears and ran up to my room and cried and cried, and packed my things to be ready to leave early next morning.

But next morning Austin came to me and asked me to have breakfast with him on his balcony, something he had not done before—we all breakfasted separately at the Villa Eugénie—and he was kind and charming, and it was clear that the incident of the pastry was to be forgotten. So I went to my room and put my clothes back into the cupboard and the chest of drawers.

For the remainder of my stay I felt distinctly uncomfortable. Would Tony notice if I sprinkled too much Parmesan on my spaghetti? If I dropped more lumps of sugar into my tea than anyone else? When the day of my departure came, I would not let him drive me to the station or send me with the chauffeur, in case he might say I made him and Austin waste gasoline on me. Although Austin thought it very odd of me, I carried my luggage along the road into Saint-Jean and took the bus from there to Beaulieu-sur-Mer. I was not meant to be a bird in a gilded cage.

✧

Anthony Beauchamp died a few years later, when he was thrown by his polo pony. Alexander Pomfret and Rory Cameron also died before they became old. They were all greatly missed by many friends in Europe and in America, but I remember them not as Noël Coward's "scions of a noble breed" but as examples of the English upper-class men of whom he said that they are "uncertain, coy, and hard to please." Tony's untimely death was a tragic loss for the older Austin Riddle, but made it easier for me to continue my friendship with this real gentleman, whose goodness and wisdom I admired and treasured. I was honored when he was one of my two sponsors for U.S. citizenship. I dined at his family house on Gramercy Square in Manhattan; I spent weekends at his farm in Pennsylvania; I sailed in his yacht along the coast of Turkey—but never in the role of a *jeune homme bien placé,* for which I was not suited and which did not suit me. I had become wary of being hurt. The incident of the pastry in Monte Carlo has molded my behavior. I have trod very, very carefully ever since, and paid for my own pastries, and never been humiliated in that way again. I do not regret what happened on August the fifth, 1955. It was part of my learning experience, a short, sharp pain, as of a vaccination or inoculation, which has provided me with immunity for the rest of my life.

5

WITH SCHOLARSHIP, WIT, BEAUTY, AND ZEST TO TREBIZOND

IN AUGUST OF 1958 readers of *The Queen,* that British monthly chronicle of all that was chic, stylish, and desirable, could read in Lord Kinross's social diary of people, places, and events that a party of celebrities was departing for a cruise to the Black Sea ports of Russia and Turkey, following the path of the Argonauts.

Hoping to clamber among the peaks of the Caucasus and to bathe off the beaches of the Crimea, he reported, were Lady Juliet Duff, who was especially anxious to visit the palace of her aristocratic Russian ancestors, the Voronzov family, near Yalta, Lady Diana Cooper, and Dame Rose Macaulay. Accompanying them would be Prince Dimitri Obolensky "and a writer named Mr Hanns Ebensten who is an expert on tattooing, a subject on which he wrote an entertaining and authoritative book. But whether, in Russia, he will be able to pursue his researches into this peculiar habit remains to be seen. I daresay he will have to confine himself, in this regard, to the observation, as they sunbathe, of the passengers and, as they toil, of the crew."

My old friend Patrick Kinross was an acknowledged expert on

Turkey. He had stayed at the British consulate on the hill above Trebizond in 1951, and his book *Within the Taurus* the following year had started a fashion for "Turkey books" by British writers, of whom Rose Macaulay—then not yet a dame of the British Empire—had been the most eminent; as a result of her visit, *The Towers of Trebizond,* part novel, part travel book, had appeared to enormous acclaim in 1956. She was in her seventies, as thin as a scarecrow and alarmingly frail-looking, but as full of fun and mischief as a girl. She took a lively interest in things around her, and everything amused her. Like all hardworking, competent writers, she kept her eyes and ears open for anything that might come in handy for a future book or article. When she had afternoon tea with me in my flat one Sunday, she wandered into the bedroom and looked at the photographs of bikers pinned to a wall.

"Oh, so you are one of those young men who like leather jackets," she said; and when I confessed that I was and owned one, she made me put it on. I felt distinctly awkward in it, pouring Earl Grey tea and handing her cucumber sandwiches. It was definitely not an occasion for which a black leather jacket was de rigueur.

I had also met the other two of this trio of revered old ladies. Lady Juliet Duff, whose mother had brought the Ballets Russes to England before World War I, had known Diaghilev and Nijinsky; she was the patroness of my friend Simon Fleet, who shared my interest in bikers, and borrowed his black leather pants for gardening in the country—"So useful for doing the roses." Having recently broken a hip, she walked with the aid of a cane, which enhanced her stately bearing.

Lady Diana Cooper was a legendary personage—the most famous, remarkable, and celebrated woman of her time, and the most beautiful woman in the world. Groomed by her ducal family to become queen of England, she had instead married for love; she had starred alternately as the Nun and the Madonna in England and in the United States in Max Reinhardt's spectacular production of *The Miracle;* her outrageous, uninhibited behavior was legendary, and she was featured only slightly disguised—if at all—in the novels of Evelyn Waugh and Nancy Mitford. She was a grandmother in her sixties, and no little artifice was doubtless required to retain her beauty: that flawless glowing skin, the absence of even the tiniest wrinkle, the firm throat, the pale-golden hair, those haunting eyes of a piercing, innocent, babylike blue. It is occasionally said of a woman that she lights up any room she enters, but with Lady Diana this was literal truth. Lord Kinross's small, dark basement dining room, where I first met her, was transformed into a candle-lit *galerie des glaces* when I followed her down into it.

And how thoughtful she was. I was poor and very shy in grand society. She expertly and kindly put me at my ease. "Patrick tells me we are to be shipmates—and Juliet and dear Simon, and Dame Rose. What fun we'll all have!"

✧

Unlike the other cruise passengers, whom I had escorted on the train from London to Venice, where we boarded the SS *Hermes,* Lady Juliet Duff and Lady Diana Cooper and Dame Rose, squired by Simon Fleet, joined us there, swirling up the Canale della Giudecca in the spic-and-span motor launch of the British consulate, all brass and mahogany and with the Union Jack making a splendid show in the breeze. As an efficient cruise director, I ran down the gangway of the SS *Hermes* to lead them to their cabins. There was a bunch of flowers, in cellophane, in Dame Rose's; she drew back and cried that this could not be her cabin—it did not occur to her, one of the brightest stars in the galaxy of contemporary English writers, a national treasure, recently honored by Queen Elizabeth, that anyone had sent her flowers. I assured her there was no mistake.

The good ship SS *Hermes* was fully booked. All the 198 passengers were, of course, equal; but some, as in George Orwell's *Animal Farm,* were more equal than others. Within an hour of embarking, the ladies Cooper and Duff had gathered a charmed circle of grandees around them. They had discovered Sir Colin and Lady Anderson in the passenger list—he was the owner of the Peninsula & Oriental Shipping Line, and the possessor of a fine collection of Pre-Raphaelite paintings; Miss Smith, the daughter of the great Lord Birkenhead; and a friend of Dame Rose's, Mr. Stewart Perowne, the eminent scholar, author, traveler, and éminence grise at British embassies in the Levant.

These members of *le gratin* claimed as their right the best table in the ship's dining room and set eight deck chairs together on the most choice part of the sheltered deck, on which they left books, maps, and personal items bearing their names as proof of ownership.

Soon after we left Venice, as we sailed out of the lagoon into the Adriatic, two little men came to me. They wore identical outfits quite unsuitable for this cruise: white tennis shirts, open at the neck and with short sleeves, little white shorts, and white shoes with ankle socks—as if they were about to burst into a song-and-dance routine. They seemed unaware that their bizarre costumes were exposing them to ridicule on this Society for Hellenic Travel cruise whose male members wore somber suits or cavalry-twill trousers and blazers, regimental or school ties, and serviceable stout shoes. This was not, after all, a pleasure jaunt for the hoi polloi but a quest for knowledge, a learning experience. Who *were* these angry little men?

"I am Professor Jack Warren Lavender," said the prematurely bald one with the round red face.

"And I am Professor Jack Lacey," said the one with the spectacles, "and we have a serious complaint about our cabin—which should be described as a broom closet!"

I consulted the list of cabins. "You reserved and paid for a double inside cabin at the minimum rate," I said, "and the cabin which you occupy is precisely that. It has an upper and a lower berth, individual bedside reading lights, an electric fan in a safety cage, and plenty of hooks for hanging clothes. It measures six feet six inches by six feet, and is seven feet nine inches high, giving it a capacity of three hundred and two cubic feet. It conforms exactly with the description of it in the cruise brochure. You have no valid cause for complaint."

"But what about the *bathroom*!" they whined. "There is only one for twenty cabins, at the end of the corridor—and it is locked!" I told them to find the bathroom steward and tell him on what day and at what time they wanted him to draw their bath and open the door for them.

"On what *day*? But we want a bath *every day*!" they cried.

I could not believe my ears. I had never heard of such a thing. What men were they, that they had to wash away their guilt every day? Every cabin in the SS *Hermes* provided the luxury of running water; each evening—and, if absolutely necessary, also in the morning—one ran one's wet washcloth around one's private parts and under each armpit. A tub bath was a special treat in which one indulged once a week—maybe once a fortnight.

"But we are *Americans*," cried the professors. "Don't you understand? Americans take a bath every day."

I showed them the passenger list. "We have other Americans with us," I said. "Here you see Mr. and Mrs. Arnold Whitridge. They are, I believe, what is in your country called VSPs—very socially prominent. I have received no complaint from them."

I really could not put up with their nonsense. Indeed, the few bathrooms were used less for bathing than as places of assignation. The bathroom stewards were the ship whores and pimps, and cheerfully offered themselves or any crew member whom a passenger fancied for a half hour's pleasure at a negotiable fee in the bathrooms of which they held the keys.

✧

After dinner on the first night of the cruise, Simon Fleet invited me to join the charmed circle on deck: Lady Diana was to read some recent letters from her son John Julius, who was *en poste* at the British embassy in Beirut.

No entertainment was provided on this Hellenic cruise—no vulgar deck games during the day, no music and dancing in the evenings. No one would have dreamed of doing anything as frivolous as to play cards. Most passengers were in their seventies or older, and retired immediately after dinner and rose very early, hungry for breakfast.

The letters of John Julius Norwich were vastly indiscreet about the goings-on in the embassy in Beirut, and made highly entertaining reading; they had clearly been written for a wide audience and for later publication. They were a tough act to follow, and I was flattered but uncertain of success when Simon asked me to tell the company the story of Elizabeth Slattery and her baby, which he had heard me tell before—indeed, I often told it and had perfected it over the years. Elizabeth Slattery was one of my pupils when I taught at Stonelands, a school run on the controversial system of education founded by A. S. Neill. Elizabeth was fourteen, mentally somewhat retarded, but cheerful and chubby and caused no trouble. She became strangely fat about the middle, then grotesquely so. "Elizabeth Slattery is having a *baby,* a *baby,* a fat little *baby*!" sang the other children, and her condition did look remarkably like it. The principal questioned her. "What nonsense, Lucy: it's only baby fat," said Elizabeth. But by July she was enormous. There could be no doubt. A doctor was called to come and examine her. She was seven months pregnant.

"It was the ice-cream man!" announced the other children. The ice-cream man came to the school gate three times a week in his van, and although Elizabeth rarely had any pocket money, it was noticed that she always lingered after the others had bought their ices, and later appeared back at school greedily licking an Eskimo Pie or a strawberry cone.

Mrs. Lucy Francis was horrified by the prospect of the impending scandal, until she realized that the ice-cream man came only from April to September, while Elizabeth must have been impregnated late in December. She was greatly relieved: the school had been closed from December 15 to January 5 for the Christmas–New Year holiday. The girl had been seduced during her stay at home, and Mrs. Francis questioned her again. "You must not be shy, Elizabeth, you must tell me who it was."

"No one," said Elizabeth smugly. "It's the same as it was with the dear Virgin Mary. An Immaculate Conception, they call it. I am carrying a little Jesus in my belly."

"Please don't be ridiculous, Elizabeth," said Mrs. Francis. "And don't talk nonsense, or sacrilege. Who was it?"

"Well, Lucy, it must have been on Christmas Eve," explained Elizabeth. "You see, Mum and Dad and I went to the pub, and Dad had ever so many port-and-lemons; and when we went to bed—you see, Mum and Dad and I sleep in one big bed, it's ever so cozy—Dad wanted to do Mum, but she said he was stinking drunk and turned her back on him, so he did me instead. So that's when the mischief must have been done."

The conclusion of this moral tale was received with raptures. It had just the earthy bawdiness that appealed to Lady Diana. She laughed and laughed and clapped her hands with delight, and the others took their cue from her and all applauded me. I was thrilled by their reception of my story and grateful to Simon Fleet for having given me the opportunity to tell it, as a result of which I was adopted as a member of the charmed circle for the remainder of the cruise.

✧

At Itéa, Simon Fleet and Stewart Perowne astonished the passengers by plunging from the ship's ladder into the wine-red sea—for men in their late fifties, they had admirably slim, trim bodies—and Simon bought tall wooden shepherd's crooks for himself, Lady Diana, and Lady Juliet, which they carried ashore on all excursions with great aplomb. We drove up to Delphi and dined on a terrace under a huge orange moon.

✧

In Athens, Mr. Mark Ogilvy Grant gave a dinner party for the ladies Diana and Juliet; they were to bring their favorite shipmates.

Mr. Cecil Beaton and Mr. Patrick Leigh Fermor met the members of the charmed circle in the bar of the Hotel Grande Bretagne, from where Mr. Ogilvy Grant had asked them to arrange for us all to be driven to his house. Three large black chauffeur-driven cars conveyed us like a funeral procession, but when we arrived, Mr. Beaton refused to pay the drivers the amounts on which they insisted. "Quite ridiculous! Do they take us for tourists?"

Mr. Ogilvy Grant, who was at the door to greet his guests, also indignantly rejected the demands for payment. "I told you to get taxis, Cecil," he cried. "I'm not paying for these opulent hired cars of yours!"

The Andersons, Miss Smith, and Mr. Perowne, and the ladies Diana and Juliet, with Simon Fleet between them, quickly entered the house to avoid any unpleasantness. The drivers screamed abuse, and Mr. Ogilvy Grant and Mr. Leigh Fermor screamed back in their fluent demotic Greek, acquired when they fought with the Greek partisans during World War II. To appease the drivers, I offered to pay. "You keep out of this!" shouted my host, who threw the drivers some drachma notes, far less than they had demanded, pulled us inside his house, and closed the door behind us. Strange indeed are the ways of the rich and famous. For some time the drivers gave loud expression of their anger by sounding their car horns.

Dinner was a buffet on the roof terrace of the house, lit by oil lamps, the Acropolis on the left, the Lycabettus Hill on the right, Mount Hymettus pale in the distance.

Mr. Cecil Beaton told Lady Diana and Lady Juliet that Truman Capote had heard that he was to see them in Athens during the cruise and had asked him to beg the ladies to be nice to two friends of his who were also aboard the SS *Hermes.*

"Who are they?" they asked.

"Two professors—Jack Warren Lavender and Jack Lacey."

"Do you know them?" they asked me. "Do tell."

I explained that they were the two men in white shorts. Surely they had noticed them?

"Oh, the Dolly Sisters! That's what we call them," said Lady Diana. "Dearest Cecil, not even for you, or for that dread Mr. Capote, can we possibly be nice to the Dolly Sisters! Oh, you should see them—little white slippers, and sweet little white socks—"

"No, Diana," Lady Juliet corrected her, "not plain white: don't forget the colored stripes, matching so exactly those of their sweet little Boy Scout belts with those adorable little brass clasps."

"Quite right, I forgot the stripes. And they wear shorts—even into the dining room for luncheon—well, I ask you, they're at least forty. Hanns, you must know, you've seen all our passports with our guilty secrets—do tell—oh, why do middle-aged American men dress like schoolboys? No, Cecil, we cannot be nice to the Dolly Sisters—well, I daresay we'll have to ask them to dine at our table, just once."

"But we'll never be able to avoid them for the rest of the cruise if we do," said Lady Juliet.

"Oh, dear; Mr. Capote has a lot to answer for."

Mr. Ogilvy Grant made no effort to make me feel welcome on his roof. My friend Tony had been his lover, and he knew quite well who I was but preferred to pretend that I was someone whom Simon Fleet or Stewart Perowne had picked up that evening in the Grande Bretagne bar. The notion that homosexuals help one another socially is a fallacy: all too often they sense competition and are antagonistic to fellow deviates. It was Lady Diana who passed me a plate and a napkin for the buffet and who contrived a diversion to give me a useful occupation when I was left out of the others' conversation about Evelyn Waugh: ". . . used to be such fun, but that snobbishness is eating away at his talent like a cancer . . . still writes like an angel . . . so difficult not to forgive him his vileness . . . but what an odious little man he has become . . ." She tipped the contents of her shopping basket, which she carried with her everywhere instead of a handbag, onto the floor next to me, and asked me to sort out its contents.

A basket does not lend itself to tidy arrangements and is by no means ideal for filing travel documents; but I did my best. There was her passport, with the photograph of herself taken by Cecil Beaton for the famous Bestegui Ball in Venice some years before, dressed and coiffed as the Tiepolo Cleopatra—how astonished the Soviet officials who granted her visa must have been to see this jewel-bedecked seventeenth-century lady in her extremely low-cut bodice with her ample bosom exposed. There were many traveler's checks, some in neat folders, others loose; there were pound and lira and drachma notes in all sorts of denominations, all madly mixed up, and coins of many kinds, including pretty octagonal ones and others with holes in them; there were keys galore, some lonely, others clipped together with a tag reading CHÂTEAU SAINT-FIRMIN, CHANTILLY; letters from her son; photographs; postcards;

makeup and pills; two apples and bits of half-chewed chocolate; needles and thread; three handkerchiefs—none too clean; and an ashtray filched from the bar of the Grande Bretagne—everything, in fact, that an English gentlewoman requires on her travels.

While the others gossiped, I repacked the basket. Mr. Ogilvy Grant managed, after some prompting by Lady Diana, to provide me with rubber bands and paper clips, and I made up bundles of each currency and clipped them together with slips of paper noting their conversion rates. I could not resist reading some of the postcards, which she had written and addressed (in pencil) but not yet mailed, and was gratified to see that she was enjoying the cruise, though the card addressed to Mr. Stavros Niarchos compared our dear shabby SS *Hermes* most unfavorably with his yacht, in which she had sailed the previous summer.

I was proud of my efforts when I handed the basket with its neatly ordered contents back to her. She thanked me effusively. "Oh, do look how clever Hanns has organized me! How can I ever live up to it?"

"Such Teutonic precision," said Mr. Ogilvy Grant. He loathed everything German.

We returned to the SS *Hermes* after midnight—this time, thriftily, in taxis—and sailed at 2:00 A.M. for Skyros, where a short afternoon stop had been contrived to break the monotony of a full day's sailing between Athens and the Bosphorus. There was no shore excursion; we merely went ashore in the ship's boats to swim or walk along a beach, and some of us ordered coffee at a small taverna whose owner gave us scissors to cut grapes from the vine above our heads. It was a very simple, idyllic interlude.

Someone expressed regret that we were not to visit the grave of Rupert Brooke, the World War I poet.

"Better not," said Lady Diana. "There's a hideous modern statue, a male nude with a big—well, you know what I mean."

"Maybe the Dolly Sisters would appreciate it," said Mr. Stewart Perowne.

When we were all back and accounted for aboard the SS *Hermes*, she started her engines; and then Simon Fleet came running in great agitation—Lady Diana was prostrate with shame and despair: she had left her basket on the beach. We hurried to the bridge to inform the captain, who immediately ordered the engines to stop; but a boat was already seen coming toward us from the beach, rowed frantically by two men while a third triumphantly held up the basket. A rope was let down the side of the ship as the boat came alongside, and the basket was tied to it and hauled up. The passengers lined the railings and cheered. Lady Diana briskly checked that nothing was missing, and Simon asked her for a hundred-drachma note to send down to reward the honest men. She searched among the neatly banded money and gave a note to him.

"Fifty drachmae is quite enough, Simon," she said.

He tied the note through a knot in the rope and sent it down. Everyone applauded again, the boatmen waved, and we sailed on.

✧

And then a really dreadful thing happened: Stewart Henry Perowne believed that he had fallen in love with me. It was, as he took great pains to explain to me, a completely asexual love, the utterly pure love of an older man for a younger, the same love Hadrian had felt for Antinoüs. (He was working on a biography of the emperor.) "No honorable man would have a carnal relationship with a lad whom he adored as Hadrian did his beloved Bithynian," he told me. This was reassuring, because the thought of physical contact with this tremendously distinguished gentleman was not pleasant: he was as bald as an egg (and at that time baldness was not yet fashionable and considered to be sexy) and had the halitosis and unwashed-body odor that denote a member of the English upper classes, who, aware of these failings, are so confident in their superiority that they do not take any measures to make themselves less repulsive to those who must come into close contact with them. I was thirty-five, no longer young, and had never been handsome, so that it was flattering to have made a conquest, in so short a time, and without the least effort or intention to achieve it, of this great scholar—recipient of the Order of the British Empire; knight of the Order of Saint John of Jerusalem; son of a bishop of Worcester; graduate of Hailesbury School and Corpus Christi College, Cambridge, and Harvard; discoverer of the ancient city of Aziris; author of many learned books, including the lauded biography of Herod the Great; adviser on Arab affairs to the Palestine Government Service, the British government, and the United Nations; governor of Barbados; husband of the equally distinguished Freya Stark, with whom he had plotted in Aden and Baghdad and who had written of him that he was "gay"—which, at that time, meant merely joyous, merry, and happy—"slim, well-dressed, enthusiastic, with a sparkle that matched the sunlight." A fine man to have captivated—but oh! the embarrassment of being watched from early morning to late evening by the 197 passengers as my besotted swain followed me with dogged devotion wherever I went, hung about outside the cruise office when I pretended that I had work to do there, and joined me whenever I talked to anyone on deck or in the lounge and took over the conversation. There was no escape—it was like being an unwillingly enrolled actor on a moving, multiple-level stage, feeling the audience's derision and distaste for this ludicrous performance that was being acted out before them.

When the SS *Hermes* approached Istanbul, the passengers lined the railings. "Like coming into Liverpool," said Lady Diana, playing the enfant terrible. I did not appreciate her drollery and wanted desperately to savor the sea approach to this most romantic of port cities in silence and solitude. I made my way past the anchor winch to the prow of the ship and waited for the minarets to take shape.

In a moment Stewart Perowne was beside me, close to me. I knew that all the cameras and binoculars that had been trained on the dim silhouette of the distant city were now directed at us. The *Queen* photographer with his ruthlessly obtrusive camera was certain not to miss this opportunity. I wanted the ship to sink, bow first, to save me from this intolerably mortifying situation.

"That is the faint gray skyline of Constantinople," said Stewart Perowne, "for I cannot bear to call this Byzantine city by its modern name. Look closely, dear Hanns, and you will see the remains of the walls constructed by Theodosius the Second in the fifth century to repel the advance of your ancestor Attila the Hun with his Golden Horde. Imagine that terrible day in May of 1453, when the sultan Mehmed the Second, wearing pale-blue boots, made his entry into it, riding a mule to show his humility, with the sword of the Prophet Muhammad in his hand, shouting to his Muslim soldiers, 'God be praised! You are the conquerors of Constantinople!'—and then the dreadful pillage began."

I did see the dim line of decaying walls; but it was not May, 1453, of which I thought, but of the spectacle he and I made, pressed close together in the prow of the SS *Hermes*.

"And here are the glorious minarets and domes, rising as on tiers from the shore to the seven hills—that is the Sultan Ahmed Mosque—always be sure to refer to it thus—only vulgar people call it the Blue Mosque. Late, of course, early seventeenth century, and not a patch architecturally on Santa Sophia, which, as you well know, precedes it by almost nine hundred years—but very fine and generally the most admired of the great mosques, though not quite to my taste. Note the six pencil-slim minarets—a unique feature.

The small domes below are those of the Church of Saints Sergius and Bacchus—imagine, Justinian and the lovely and much maligned Empress Theodora had it built because they believed that these two saints had saved their lives. Such piety, dear Hanns. And there is Santa Sophia, of which Procopius, who is surely always by your bedside, wrote that 'this church presents a most glorious spectacle, excelling both by its size and the harmony of its measures.' What can one add to that? Imagine the great Justinian entering it at sunrise on December the twenty-sixth in 537, Saint Stephen's Day. 'At last the holy morn had come, and the great door of the newly built temple groaned on its opening hinges, and when the interior was seen, sorrow fled from the heart of all as the sun lit the glories of the temple.' Isn't that lovely, dear Hanns? When we return to the city, I will take you up into the galleries to look down into the immense space and show you the graffiti of pilgrims and visitors covering a thousand years—even the runes of your other ancestors, the marauding Vikings. And now see the walls of the Topkapi, the great palace of the Ottoman sultans, with its former kitchens crammed with quite unbelievable and still largely uncataloged treasures: Chinese porcelains and armor and jeweled garments and thrones, as well as the absurd rich kitsch which those tasteless sultans so adored. Oh, how I shall enjoy leading you through its courts: that of the wicked Janissaries, who were said to be addicted to certain unnatural practices which I cannot mention, the lovely Second Court, with its cypress trees, and through the Gate of Felicity into the private part of the palace to the Circumcision Room—oh, dearest Hanns, were you submitted to this barbaric custom which I so despise, despite my love for all things Arabic? And we shall wander through the Tulip Garden and the pretty Baghdad Kiosk, hand in hand, because that is quite proper and customary for two men to do in the Muslim world—and that last pavilion of the palace, that white monstrosity, was built in 1840, quite Western and grotesque—as I said, those nineteenth-century sultans had absolutely no taste."

We had reached what I knew to be the mouth of the Golden Horn. How long, O Lord, how long would this erudite scholar's travelogue continue?

"This is the Golden Horn, and here the Bosphorus begins. That is Seraglio Point, where the nasty Ottoman sultans conveniently dumped any unwanted or faithless concubines into the sea, neatly sewn in sacks. And that is the Galata Bridge—oh, Hanns, do promise never, never to stroll on it after dark: that is when depraved men stalk there in search of their innocent prey. The mosque beside it is called the New Mosque—new, meaning 1597—or the Valide Mosque, begun by the *valide,* or queen mother, of the sultan Mehmed the Third, and, after the great fire of 1660, of which you have of course read, rebuilt as an act of piety by the mother of Mehmed the Fourth. Grelot wrote of it that 'it is a jewel of Ottoman architecture to serve as an eternal monument to her generous enterprises.' How neglected it is, how grimy with soot; it has none of the perfection of the great Sinan's earlier mosques, but oh! Hanns, it epitomizes Constantinople for me—and see how gratifying, all the good men of the city crowding to enter and pray in it. Oh, I much prefer it to that flashy though magnificent Süleymaniye Mosque, which dominates the skyline behind it. And now we are sailing along the shore of Pera, and that is the Galata Tower, which the Genoese crusaders built in 1304; but close your eyes, dear Hanns, to all those horrid modern towers of hotels and offices and banks— if they were not there, you could see the gracious former embassies of the Western powers, now merely consulates, alas, since that naughty Atatürk moved his capital to dismal Ankara."

The ship sailed past the Dolmabahce Palace, in deep water close to the European shore.

"That is the Dolmabahce Palace," Stewart told me, "all nine hundred hideous feet of it; and I shall most certainly not take you *there*—oh, Hanns, how it would distress you—the world's largest and ugliest chandeliers and carpets and hundreds of clocks and sets of tableware in the very worst possible taste. And now we are well and truly sailing on the Bosphorus, where Io, the beloved of Zeus, hid from his jealous spouse, Hera, in the guise of a heifer—for that, as you know, is what Bosphorus means: 'the ford of the cow.' Now we truly follow the path of Jason and his merry lads in the *Argo* on their search for the Golden Fleece. Here Darius crossed from Asia to Europe in 512 B.C. Here Belisarius fought the whale, and here Gyllus saw the largest shark he had ever encountered. And now look at the Asian shore, there, where I am pointing—do look, Hanns—at the Beylerbeyi Palace, where the dear Empress Eugénie of France stayed en route to open the Suez Canal, and the sad old Emperor Franz Josef of Austria, and our own King Edward the Eighth with that Mrs. Simpson—and quickly turn back to the European shore, that is Roberts College on the hill, a wonderful example of what American enthusiasm and philanthropy can achieve—never, never despise the great American dollar, dear Hanns."

I had no intention ever to do so. What curious ideas this admirer of mine had about me.

"And now we have reached the narrowest point, just two hundred and twenty feet across, where Darius and his army crossed by means of a bridge of boats, and that is the Rumeli Hisar, to protect the narrows, built by the Sultan Mehmed a year before he conquered Constantinople. Oh, and there—look again at the Asian shore— the Sweet Waters of Asia, the favorite resort of the Ottoman grandees and their ladies, where Lady Mary Wortley Montagu, the wife of our eighteenth-century ambassador, spent so many happy afternoons. There, opposite on the European shore, we now pass Tarabya, the Greek Therapia, named for its healing spring—those are the former summer embassies of the great Western powers with their gardens and parks—that is the British embassy, where that most gentle of men, Harold Nicolson, was made to help his governess build a useless hut in the park and where he was later *en poste* and gave such delicious luncheon parties. Turn again to the Asian shore—do look, Hanns—that is Anadulu Kavagi, the Giant's Grave: ' 'Tis a grand sight from off the Giant's Grave / To watch the progress of these rolling seas / Between the Bosphorus as they lash and lave / Europe and Asia, you being quite at ease'—but of course you know all the best of Byron by heart, as I do. And that is Fil Burnu, the Elephant Point, named thus for no reason that I understand."

Oh, would he never stop? Would this damn Bosphorus never end? We passed Garipçe, the Town of Vultures, where King Phineus lived and was plagued by the Harpies, who seized his food until Jason and his kindly lads chased them away, and Anadolu Feneri Burnu, named after the lighthouse—*fener*—and the rock of Rumeli Feneri, the so-called Pillar of Pompey, the ancient Symplegades, the Clashing Rocks, which blissfully at long last marked the end of the Bosphorus on its European shore. Opposite, on the Asian shore, there remained only Kabakoz Limani, the Harbor of the Wild Walnuts, and then the SS *Hermes* passed Yum Burnu, where Jason took aboard a stone anchor for the good ship *Argo*, the Cape of Good Omen—". . . and is it not indeed a good omen, dearest Hanns, that you should see it first with me? Like Jason, you and I will surely find the Golden Fleece together."

It was over; the European and the Asian shores receded; after an eternity of two hours the Bosphorus was behind us; we were in the open waters of the Black Sea.

It was the moment to escape. I hurried below and hid in the fetid four-berth inside cabin that I shared with the *Queen* photographer, who was seldom in it, preferring to spend every night with a passenger who occupied a cabin with a porthole. Presently an envelope containing a card was pushed under the door: "You remind me of the tribute paid to a former prelate in an epitaph in Killarney Cathedral: 'He charmed every ear, and vanquished every heart.' "

✧

We knew that a civic reception had been planned for our arrival in Odessa, the first cruise of stinking-rich Western capitalists since before World War II. We were up by six in the morning and breakfast was at seven, so that we would be ready to go ashore promptly at 8:00 A.M.—but Soviet bureaucracy and inefficiency intervened. The SS *Hermes* was ordered to drop her anchor three miles offshore, and there we lay in a sweltering heat haze while a hundred officials in a variety of musical-comedy uniforms boarded the ship and set up trestle tables and demanded food and drink and began with maddening slowness to inspect the passenger manifest, passports, and visa lists. Health forms and currency-declaration forms were asked for: we had none, as none had been requested previously. Although all lists and visas were in perfect order, it seemed at some moments that we would be denied entry into Soviet waters. The Intourist guides, who had boarded with the officials and were to be with us from Odessa until we left Sukhumi, our last Soviet port, went down to their cabins. Two of them, great big hulking fellows, had been assigned to fill the bunks in my and the *Queen* photographer's four-berth cabin; they changed into striped flannel pajamas and wool nightcaps and went to sleep.

After four hours of frustration, alternating between hope and despair, we were permitted to proceed. We ordered luncheon to be served in order to have as much of the afternoon remaining for sight-seeing in Odessa, and docked while we were eating. The lady mayor, a brass band, and thousands of schoolchildren were on the dock, waiting for us behind guarded barriers. The band struck up its version of "God Save the Queen," the sounds of which aroused considerable merriment when heard in the dining room. The Intourist people were most upset and told me to order the passengers to interrupt their meal and go ashore so that they could be greeted by the mayor and receive their welcome bouquets. "The children have been assembled there since daybreak, on their feet without food or water; many have fainted in the heat. How can you disappoint them so?"

How indeed. I made an announcement in the dining room and gently requested the passengers to go ashore, for only a few moments, to make an appearance to the waiting crowd; but it was not well received until Lady Diana rose and proceeded down the gangway, which had the result of making many others follow her splendid example. She wore a pleated white skirt, cut very full, a naval blazer, and an admiral's cap, and created a sensation on the dock. "It is Marlene Dietrich!" said some of the people of Odessa who were worldly-wise and had seen Western films. In her wake we others shook hands with the jolly fat lady mayor, accepted the wilted flowers the children held out to us, had hammer-and-sickle pins fixed to our jackets. All was friendship and goodwill. Then we followed Lady Diana back up the gangway and resumed our meal.

The sight-seeing tour of Odessa—"You have forced us to curtail it, due to your late arrival," the Intourist people complained to me—took us to a champagne factory (no samples, alas) and the railroad station. Professor Jack Warren Lavender enjoyed a special treat instead: he suffered from toothache, and Intourist was quite delighted to rush him to Odessa's dental hospital, of which they were extremely proud and where dozens of dentists and nurses vied with one another to share in treating this rara avis, a real live American professor, which good fortune had swept into their hands.

What we all wanted to see, had expected to be shown, and asked for was the famous long flight of stone steps so excitingly featured in the Eisenstein film *Potemkin;* but the Intourist guides denied any knowledge of them, and then, when we insisted on being taken to them, said they dared not alter the program and that the steps were not a "cultural attraction" fit for tourists. But we were not to be trifled with; we had maps of Odessa, and we pointed out that the steps were on our direct route back to the ship. "The steps are nothing," said the guides.

The guides were right. The great Eisenstein was a cheat. The steps of Odessa are neither long nor impressive. The scene of the perambulator bouncing down and down that seemingly endless staircase was cleverly created by a trick, by moving the camera up, and up, and up yet again. The steps are quite short and were a huge disappointment to us all. "I want my money back," said Lady Diana.

In the evening there was *Rigoletto* sung in Ukrainian. By saying that I could not join the members of the charmed circle because I had to go over the program for Yalta with the Intourist people, and changing into a seaman's sweater after the passengers had left the ship for the opera house, I managed to explore the seamy dock area, where many drunks lay ignored in the streets and alleys, and sailors consumed prodigious quantities of potent kvass, became belligerent, fought, vomited, and taunted some old, hideously painted queens. It was all refreshingly noncultural, a glimpse behind the façade of Soviet cleanliness and prudishness. The Intourist people would have died of shame if they had known what I was seeing; and Simon Fleet was madly envious when I told him about it.

In Yalta we were taken to Chekhov's house and to the Voronzov Palace, the summer home of Lady Juliet's Russian ancestors, where the portrait of one of their ladies did indeed strongly resemble her. She posed for photographs under it.

"This palace was builded by twenty thousand serfs in the English Tudor style," announced the guide.

"Nonsense," said Lady Juliet, very loud, and stamped her shepherd's crook on the marble floor. "It was builded by Mr. Blore, an Englishman, and my ancestors' architect."

We were then set down on what was called a beach, an expanse of jagged black stones lapped by a chilly sea, densely crowded with pajama-clad Soviet workers enjoying their doubtlessly well deserved but, by our standards, dismal recuperative holiday. A row of ice-cream vending machines was the big attraction here, and Russian ice cream is very good indeed; but the machines were all out of order.

None of the members of the charmed circle had signed up for the expedition to Bakhchisarai, which was limited to thirty participants and involved many hours of travel through the dark in an ancient bus with wooden seats, a night at an inn where, it was rumored, four persons were to be accommodated in each bed, and an hour for seeing the insignificant remains of a minor Tatar palace. The promised hardships of this trip had made it so popular that Dame Rose had been unable to secure a reservation for it; but another old lady backed out when she saw the bus and gave her prized place to Dame Rose. We saw her off; and the condition of the bus and the uncertainty about the Intourist arrangements made us fear for her and the other twenty-nine hardy souls' lives. Lady Diana ran back to her cabin and returned with an inflatable cushion and a rug. "At least take these," she begged.

Dame Rose rejected them. "I'll be like the others," she said, placidly resigned to whatever fate held in store for her.

The bus departed in a cloud of foul fumes and we went to a restaurant in Yalta, where the ladies Diana and Juliet had invited the members of the charmed circle to dine and for which the Intourist people had, after a great deal of absurd fuss, furnished the necessary prepaid vouchers covering the cost of the meal, wines, and "entertainment."

"You must consider yourselves very lucky that we were able to secure these vouchers for you, at such very short notice," they said. "It is the best restaurant in Yalta." A meal there was the highlight of their holiday for the workers who filled the sanatoriums.

There had been discussions about appropriate attire for this dinner ashore, and the ladies had rightly refused to "dress down." "Why should we? Let them see us as we are," they said; and the entry of the Romanovs with their court could not have created a greater sensation than our arrival at the restaurant. The ladies' hairstyles, their maquillage, their pearls and diamonds, silks and satins, the high-heeled evening shoes, all were studied with avid and generally approving attention.

The restaurant was as big as an airplane hangar. Thousands of holidaying workers sat at large tables, waiting patiently for their big treat to be served to them. An orchestra of octogenarians in peasant blouses ground out sad peasant tunes. Our vouchers were scrutinized with great care and at length at a barrier. We were then conducted to a table where, after half an hour, a waiter collected the voucher stubs, counted them three times, counted us three times, appeared satisfied with the result of his calculations, and produced a basket of hard rolls and carafes of water.

Then two *Hermes* passengers, timid ladies who had also purchased vouchers to dine at the restaurant and whom the management mistakenly assumed to be members of our party, were shown to our table, which had several empty places. The members of the charmed circle froze into haughty stares, but Lady Diana jumped up, gave each of the ladies a hug, and cried, "Oh yes, *do* join us! Sir Colin, please move down one place—Simon, take the chair at the end—there! Oh! What fun we'll have!"

Half an hour later a big tureen of tepid soup was placed before Lady Diana, who sat at the head of the table, and a stack of soup plates. "These plates are icy-cold!" she called out. "They must be breast-warmed." And she took up two of them at a time, pushed them under the top of her low-cut dress, and gave them each a brisk rub. What fun we were having, indeed!

An hour later thin slices of cold gray meat were brought to us, beside congealed mashed potatoes and cabbage. Only the champagne was warm.

"And now," said Sir Colin Anderson when the plates were being removed, "we have only another hour to wait for the ice cream—for surely dessert must be the ice cream of which we have heard so much but still not seen."

He was correct about the further hour's wait, but surprise! surprise!—it was not an ice that was ceremoniously placed before each of us, but a fresh banana. A fresh banana! No wonder that a meal here was the culminating joy of the workers' holiday. "At last, at long last, a dream has come true," said Stewart Perowne. "I am having a banana with Lady Diana." And we all rose, banana in hand, and chanted the World War I music-hall ditty:

> *I had a banana—*
> *With Lady Diana—*
> *I'm Burlington Bertie from Bow!*

✧

An excursion in a fleet of antiquated open-sided buses was arranged into what was described as "the frosty heights of the Caucasus" while the SS *Hermes* sailed along the coast from Sochi to Sukhumi. The large number of vast, gaunt sanatoriums for workers in these Black Sea resorts suggested to us that Soviet workers must be very prone to illness or that they were made to work too hard.

A surprising number of male passengers did not accompany their wives, mothers, aunts, and female travel companions on this adventurous foray into the Caucasus. They preferred to remain on board and would take the opportunity, they explained, to catch up on the office paperwork they had brought along, to write letters, or to bring their journals up to date; but the ship had barely pulled away from the dock at Sochi when many of these gentlemen lingered furtively in the corridors outside their cabins. Soon the bathrooms were all mysteriously occupied, and the most attractive members of the crew were conspicuous on deck by their absence. Never, at any other time during the cruise, did the obliging bathroom stewards earn so many tips in so short a time.

Next day we arrived at Trebizond. After the drab, antiseptic, institutional Soviet Union, what a relief it was to see picturesquely ragged people on the quayside, moving about freely as they wished; to marvel at the charmingly disorganized efforts to bring our ship alongside; to hear the cries of vendors offering fresh fruit, *loukoum,* iced drinks, imploring us to have our shoes shined the moment we stepped ashore; to hear people laugh. In the middle of this jolly crowd of photogenic Eastern comic characters stood a lone English gentleman in a neat gray suit, a tie that those passengers who knew such things recognized as that of a prestigious university college, and who leaned elegantly on a tightly furled black umbrella. This incongruous figure was Mr. David Winfield, the archaeologist in charge of the restoration of the Byzantine church of Santa Sophia, who had come to greet us. Without any of the officious fuss to which we had become accustomed at the Soviet ports, we disembarked. There was no transport for such a crowd, said Mr. Winfield; we would have to walk two miles to the church.

We welcomed this, for we were now in fabled Trebizond, that remote and romantic outpost in Asia Minor through which so many interesting travelers had passed on foot en route to Central Asia and India. Here, when they crossed the mountains beyond the town, Xenophon and the band of ten thousand lost Greek mercenaries returning from Mesopotamia in 400 B.C. had seen the Black Sea far below them, embraced one another with joy, and cried, "The sea! The sea!" Here, as Stewart Perowne reminded us, the emperor Hadrian had come to beautify the town in his elegant style. After the fall of Constantinople it had become for a time the capital of an isolated Christian state deep within the Ottoman Empire; then, when it, too, was conquered by Islam, its many churches had been converted into mosques, their frescoes obliterated. Massive Turkish walls and towers contained it. Here that most eccentric of travelers, the Reverend Joseph Wolff, a German Jew who became an Anglican curate, stayed at the British consulate on the hill in 1843 and 1845, both going to and returning from Bukhara to ascertain the fate of two British soldiers who had been imprisoned and killed by the emir. We were at last in Trebizond, which Dame Rose's book had made into a household word.

Stoutly shod, we followed Mr. David Winfield up the steep street from the harbor, through the town, past the crumbling walls, and then over a bridge into the fields to Santa Sophia, the Church of the Holy Wisdom. One incident somewhat marred our progress, when some angry women in black gowns who stood outside their hovels with their children threw stones at Professor Lavender and Professor Lacey, the sight of whose bare legs and arms deeply offended them. On his visit in 1951, Patrick Kinross had found the church being used as a military storehouse; in 1954, when Rose Macaulay went there, the army had abandoned it and it was filled with refuse. Now it was in the process of being restored by Mr. Winfield and his team, and he showed us the stern, narrow faces of aesthetic saints with golden halos that had been hidden from view under thick layers of plaster during the five hundred years when this thirteenth-century church had served as a mosque. Set among fields with wildflowers and bright red poppies, on a hill overlooking the sea, it was to become a museum.

Dame Rose and I decided to escape for the rest of the day from our shipmates, even from the members of the charmed circle. She wanted to go back to the Hotel Yesilikoy, where she had stayed four years before and which featured in *The Towers of Trebizond.* It was a basic, down-at-heel establishment occupying the upper floors of a seedy building, and no one in it remembered her—maybe none of the staff remained there so long as four years. Multiple-bedded rooms led off the central reception hall, and in an attempt to create some ventilation the doors were left wide open, revealing the guests—all male—taking their siesta in the stifling afternoon heat. They looked at Dame Rose and me with astonishment: we must have seemed a very curious pair to them, this desiccated old lady with her long, old-fashioned dress and straw toque, and the young man, not at all the usual couple who came here to rent a room for an hour's tryst. Dame Rose was not even sure, she said, that we were in the right hotel; perhaps it had been less sleazy, more respectable, four years before. She took the opportunity to use the bathroom, and while I waited for her the men in one of the bedrooms beckoned to me and made room for me to sit on a bed. They were traveling salesmen and wanted to find out who my companion and I were. In a mixture of German, English, a little Italian, and sign language, I attempted to explain our reason for looking at the hotel. Then a group of *Hermes* passengers entered the reception hall—they, too, had come to see the Hotel Yesilikoy of which Dame Rose had written in her book. The sight of me in conversation with the disreputable Turks in their underwear seemed to disconcert them, and they hurriedly left.

Then Dame Rose and I went to a workmen's café in a side street, which she pretended to remember and where we had tea and many rich, sticky cakes. Two youths in black leather jackets, obviously inspired by having seen films starring Marlon Brando and James Dean, were having their shoes shined while keeping an eye on their motorcycles parked outside; and Dame Rose noticed that I could not avoid looking at them. "Very well, so do tell the fascination of those leather jackets; so many of my young men friends are addicted to this odd cult."

I was embarrassed. The gender gap, the age gap—both were too wide to be crossed. "It is a secret which I cannot divulge," I said.

"Like Freemasons?" asked Dame Rose, but she was far too wise to be taken in by my evasive response.

Our departure from Trebizond was a spontaneous, happy event—one of those unrehearsed, unexpected occasions that make travel so memorable. Half the population of the town, it seemed, had come down to the quay to see us off. Mr. David Winfield stood surrounded by men, women, and children who screamed and shouted and waved handkerchiefs, tablecloths, and bed sheets. Boys turned somersaults, blew trumpets, banged drums; lovely naked youths dived into the harbor for coins, and when the SS *Hermes* was untied and moved slowly away from the quay, they frolicked in the water all around the ship and like dolphins escorted us out into the open sea.

✧

Then we cruised along the Turkish coast and dutifully attended lectures on the history and art of Turkey (by the genial Dr. Geoffrey L. Lewis of Roberts College) and on Greece (by the obnoxiously condescending Mr. A. R. Burn) and on Russia (by the charming and suave Prince Dimitri Obolensky). As Lord Kinross had predicted in *The Queen,* when Simon Fleet sunbathed on deck, I now had an opportunity to observe some tattoos. There were four on his left shoulder, all rendered in the sentimental style so dear to the best tattooists, and they perpetuated his beloved ladies: a rose for MOTHER, a swallow for DIANA, a pierced heart flanked by roses for JULIET, and a heart with a star above it for SOPHIE—Sophie Fedoro-vich, the stage designer, who had left her pretty house on Bury

Walk, London SW 3, to him in her will. The red of the designs had faded over the years, as in most tattoos; and Lady Diana touched up the roses and the hearts with her lipstick before photographing them in color.

This was the time, too, for shipboard gossip. There are few secrets aboard a ship, and things seen or heard are often misconstrued. "We must have a cozy tête-à-tête after the cruise, if your enslaved Stewart will permit it," Sir Colin Anderson said to me. "You must tell me all about your adventures in the stews of Odessa, and with the two Russian ruffians whom you hid in your cabin all the way from Odessa to Sukhumi, and your orgiastic *cinq-à-sept* with the four Turks in the Hotel Yesilikoy."

Trivia assumes momentary importance at sea. The whole ship buzzed with excitement—the news was flashed from table to table at breakfast: Professor Lavender and Professor Lacey had been seen wearing striped pink shorts! It was true—here they came, oblivious of the sensation their entry into the dining room created. "The Dolly Sisters really are too shamelessly Harry's Bar–ish for words today," said Stewart Perowne.

After dinner, when the charmed circle was assembled on deck, Simon Fleet urged me to give them another tale out of school he had heard me tell, of my teenage pupil Carol Whitney, poor, neglected, and confused, who was laughed at by all the other children for believing that a prince would come and marry her and lavish riches upon her. She ran away to London, and a month later she had met and married her prince and her dream had come true. But he was an African prince, black as ink, and the British government, which provided him with a pension, disapproved of the hasty *mésalliance* and promptly shipped him back to Uganda without her. Six months later, poor Princess Carol again made headline news in the English tabloids when she committed suicide in the flat of a bandleader with an unsavory reputation.

This story, too, was well received despite its tragic ending. My reputation as a storyteller was firmly established. "Oh, Hanns, I am so proud of you," Stewart Perowne told me, as if he were Pygmalion and I his Galatea.

❖

In Istanbul, the passengers pursued their own interests with Baedeker's *Konstantinopel und das Westliche Kleinasien* or Murray's *Handbook for Travellers in Constantinople, Brusa and the Troad* in hand. Stewart Perowne took me off in a taxi as promised and guided me beneath the giant dome of Santa Sophia and through the treasure chambers and pavilions and seraglio of the Topkapi Palace; and this long day made me realize what rich rewards can be reaped by being associated with a cicerone who is possessed of such scholarship and who is, at the same time, so witty and enthusiastic and imbued with such zest. Even the best guidebook is only a very poor substitute when one is fortunate to be instructed by the "tutor or grave servant" whom Sir Francis Bacon recommended nearly four hundred years ago to young men on their travels.

Apart from short stops at Lemnos and Aegina, this was the end of our cruise. At Aegina, Lady Diana Cooper left the ship grandly in the grand manner to return to Athens in an open caïque, hoisting one of her sandals on her shepherd's crook and making a farewell sweep round the SS *Hermes,* waving and blowing kisses, which were rapturously returned. Preparations for the traditional last evening's speeches, recitations, and comic songs kept the passengers occupied as the ship sailed back up the Adriatic to Venice.

Lady Diana sent a telegram for it, which was read out: "SHIPMATES! DESPERATE YOUR LOSS!" What a giver she was, what a heart she had, how she enriched all who traveled with her.

What shall we tell them when we get home?
What shall we say we've seen?
Shall we give lectures
On strange architectures,
Or shall we say archly, "It's all in The Queen"?

Thus recited Stewart Perowne on the last evening's festivities, in a very slow, sad voice, with an arpeggio accompaniment on the ship's ancient piano, for we all knew that Dame Rose had been commissioned to write about the cruise in our favorite magazine and looked forward to "The New Argonauts" in its next issue and wondered which of us would be featured in the photographs. "There was no dull moment, even at sea, since we had among us scholarship, wit, beauty, and zest," she wrote.

Naturally enough, it was the *bon gratin* of whom photographs were included; but the picture the *Queen* photographer had taken of Stewart Perowne facing, and me with my back to, the camera in the prow of the SS *Hermes* appeared in several other publications and caused considerable comment. A friend of mine, who had long been anxious that I make a suitably advantageous ménage, wrote, "That photograph! So right not to be able to see your face, quite Garbo-ish, all that mystery in the prow of the ship sailing to the promised land; you look so right together: I do hope it means great happiness."

For some months it seemed as if, almost against my inclinations, it might do so. While Stewart traveled for the next six months and wrote me almost daily on the thick embossed writing paper of great English country houses, castles in Ireland, and Government House, Cyprus—where he had been summoned to avert civil war and feared for his life—he let me know that he had changed his will, gave me the name and address of his lawyer, sent parcels containing handmade shirts, his inscribed books, and a rug that had been a present to him from the king of Iraq. "It was pleasant down in Kent," he wrote, "tape-recording my memories of the past for a radio programme and dreaming dreams of the future for you." He was not anti-Semitic but abhorred Zionism. My Jewish heritage was distasteful to him, and he preferred to call me his *habiby* and wrote my name in Arabic script and claimed that my physique and my features proved that I was of the finest ancient Nabataean stock.

His overly effusive, faintly silly attentions fortunately never turned my head. After six months his letters became fewer and he adroitly transferred his platonic adoration to a young man in the diplomatic corps—and presumably altered his will once more. But we kept up a spirited correspondence and remained friends until his death twenty years later.

He was unable to attend the black-tie reunion that Lady Juliet Duff arranged for selected SS *Hermes* passengers in October, although Simon Fleet wrote, "I do wish he'd come—please use your influence. Lady Diana is coming over from Chantilly for it."

On October 28, 1958, the members of the cruise's charmed circle occupied a row of seats in the stalls of the Hammersmith Theatre to see *Valmouth,* a musical based on the decadently alluring novel of Ronald Firbank; and it struck me how much those eccentric highborn ladies on the stage, who were the chief characters and whose zany conduct caused such mirth, resembled the ladies among whom I sat and whom, as we remained in our seats during the interval, many acquaintances and autograph hunters approached to pay homage for a few moments.

It was the nearest I have come to being in public with royalty. After the theater we drove to Simon Fleet's house in Bury Walk for a buffet supper. I told Lady Diana how envious I had been of young Dimitri Limberis, the director of our Greek shore excursions, who had left the SS *Hermes* with her at Aegina to return to Athens. "Four hours in a caïque, sailing across the Saronic Gulf, alone with the legendary Lady Diana Cooper—what a story for him to tell his children and grandchildren," I said. "What did you talk about?"

"Talk? Not a word. The wretch slept all the way," she said.

Sir Colin Anderson took me aside. "Had plenty more adventures since the cruise? Seen many tattoos lately?"

I had collected Dame Rose at her flat and driven with her to the theater, and after supper I escorted her home. She drove her tiny car like a demon, quite unconcerned about other traffic, regardless both of pedestrians and traffic lights. It was a terrifying experience to sit beside her. At every intersection I was afraid that she would crash into an oncoming bus like the heroine in *The Towers of Trebizond* and kill me.

"Oh, but he was a married man, and her *lover*," she reassured me. "I had to end the book that way. *You're* quite safe with me."

Next day she wrote me a gracious letter to thank me for having seen her home after the reunion; the postman delivered it to me on the following morning, just after I heard the news of her death on the radio. She had carefully planned her Christmas card for that year and Simon Fleet had drawn it; and he had it printed and hand-colored it to her specifications and sent it out to all her friends.

Lady Diana Cooper's Christmas card was a pretty picture of a unicorn carrying a tiny fairy-tale princess on its back. With it she sent me an inscribed copy of her book *The Rainbow Comes and Goes*:

To dear Hanns, on whom we most relied on my first cruise, that encourages me to cruise again—thank you so much— be indulgent with my book.

Diana Cooper

6

FIRST

NIGHT

IN THE

PROMISED

LAND

MY ARRIVAL in the Promised Land was not very promising.

Plowing through high seas and winter fogs for four days and nights in November 1965 on the Zim Line's MV *Moledet* had been uncomfortable and dull. The Israeli government had used part of its German reparations to have a fleet of passenger ships built with which it planned to compete in the lucrative transatlantic and Mediterranean vacation markets, but had failed to realize that neither American nor European tourists wanted to be transported like immigrants—six to a cabin, a bathroom along the corridor, dismal meals, and no entertainments. The only pleasantly appointed room was a nursery reserved for children under the age of twelve, of whom many dozens ran screaming and shouting all over the ship and made life hell.

The smaller the country and the more recent its creation, the more complex and tiresome are its entry formalities. Endless forms had to be filled out, and long lines of fretful passengers formed in the lounge as the ship approached Haifa.

My passport and tourist visa were in order, but the immigration officer was not happy with my form. It had been foolish of me to have facetiously entered "Human" against "Race." My interrogator did not consider this amusing. Worse, "Religion: Christian" and "Place of Birth: Hamburg, Germany" gave him cause for concern.

"Where are parents?" he asked me.

"Dead."

"Any relatives living in Germany?"

"Yes, an uncle."

"His profession?"

"Colonel in the army."

This incongruous truth was clearly most unpalatable. A considerable delay ensued as others in line behind me were processed, until, after a whispered discussion among three officials, one of them led me away to a distant cabin. A security officer, wearing a short-sleeved shirt and with an impressive diver's watch on his hairy wrist, made me stand awkwardly before him as he lounged in an armchair, legs wide apart and crotch thrust aggressively forward, enjoying an obnoxious cigar while he flipped slowly through the pages of my passport and surveyed me.

"You have an uncle in the German army?"

"Yes, my mother's brother," I admitted.

"Other relatives in Germany?"

"No."

"They live elsewhere?"

"No. My father's relatives all died in concentration camps."

This was reassuring at last. Scrawling something on my form, he slipped it between the pages of the passport and handed it to me. "Enjoy your visit."

I thanked him and walked down the gangway to face the customs officials ashore.

The Israel Government Tourist Department had invited me to visit Israel's part of the Sinai Peninsula and make recommendations

for tourism there. (It was not until 1984, when the whole of the
Sinai Peninsula was Egyptian territory, that I led my first group
across the peninsula in the way I had planned to do it more than
twenty years before.) I had learned on previous visits that although
the country was striving to attract not only pilgrims but tourists,
Israelis were too busy with more important problems and projects
to spare the time and make the effort to cosset visitors. Israel is very
high on history, but sadly short of charm.

A representative of the Tourist Department met me outside the
customs area and took me to an impressive car; it was to drive me to
Tel Aviv, where I was to spend the night and meet my official hosts
next day—but first, he said, we would make a little deviation to
pick up some friends of his in order to give them a lift.

We drove north instead of south for more than an hour toward
Safad and collected two women and three noisy, unruly children,
who crowded into the back of the car and removed my suitcases
from the trunk and filled it with their parcels and packages. I was
not introduced to them, and no one spoke to me during the long
drive back to Haifa and then to Tel Aviv. I sat between the driver
and the government representative, who both smoked cigarettes
and talked to each other in Hebrew as though I did not exist. It was
almost midnight when they dropped me off outside the Dan Hotel,
the pride of Israeli tourism.

The listless doorman made no attempt to carry my luggage into
the lobby. The receptionist did not disguise his contempt. "Only
one night?" he asked. After a great deal of searching in drawers and
turning of ledgers, he found my reservation and handed me a key.

With a suitcase in each hand and my overnight bag tucked
under one arm, I took the elevator up to my room—and was amazed
to find that it was not merely a bedroom but an exceptionally grand
suite on the top floor of the hotel, taking up the entire width of the
building.

There was a huge sitting room filled with sumptuous furniture and a long terrace overlooking the Mediterranean; a corridor led to a magnificently appointed dressing room and bedroom, beyond which I found another balcony overlooking the city. Elaborate floral arrangements graced every table throughout the suite; there were lavish pyramids of fruit under cellophane and a box of chocolate mints and a bottle of water on a bedside table; books and magazines were neatly set out as in a library; on the writing desk stood a model of what looked like a town development.

I was bewildered. This display of luxury seemed most unsuitable for a single, unimportant guest. Why, I wondered, am I being treated like a visiting cinema actor or an expensive whore?

I walked from room to room, from the ocean view to the city view, and felt sad and lonely. Then I unpacked, tried out different light effects, and counted a total of twenty-three lamps, including four ceiling chandeliers that were fiendishly ornate, nibbled at the fruit and gorged on the chocolate mints, and went to sleep.

✧

"Breakfast 7:00 to 10:00 A.M.," stated the hotel information sheet in my suite; but when I entered the dining room at five minutes past seven, I was not welcome. Waiters made ineffectual gestures to lay tables in a parody of slow-motion-movie style, and the members of a tour group filed into the room and settled down with resignation to await events.

After twenty minutes, a waiter approached me. He was an elderly Central European and doubtless possessed the highest qualifications to perform brain surgery or judge a court case, but he resented having to wait at table. He was unshaven and sickly pale.

I asked for tea, toast, and honey.

"*Toast?* Toast must be made; rolls are ready," he admonished me.

"But I prefer toast, please—"

"Why make me troubles? I give you rolls."

He also brought two kinds of jam, artificially colored red and green like traffic lights. I reminded him that I had asked for honey.

"I give you jams; why make me troubles and want honey?"

"But isn't Israel the land of milk and honey?" I asked him. "And I prefer honey."

"You *prefer*!" His whine rose to an anguished scream. "*Toast* you want! *Honey* you want! Who do you tourists think you are?"

After breakfast I went back to my suite, laid out my clothes for the luncheon meeting with the officials of the Tourist Department, put on my swimming trunks, and took a towel, a book, and my room key to the hotel beach.

It is always fascinating to arrive at a beach very early in the morning and watch as it becomes animated. I was the only hotel guest at that hour; the few other people were hardy year-round swimmers and gymnasts going with intense concentration through their morning gyrations.

Israeli women do not exercise—they become trees, tenderly putting out springtime buds, swaying in the summer breeze, shedding leaves with calm acceptance in the fall; they are lotus flowers, opening their dewy petals to welcome the sun; they are birds, free as the air, fluttering to and fro. Old ladies without an ounce of excess fat on their trim bodies, with sun-scorched skin like leather, and with their hair pulled back from their faces like a ballerina's, twisted slowly this way and that, raised arms to heaven, moved fingers like Indian palace mimes, stood for amazing lengths of time like storks on one trembling, varicose-veined leg. Old gentlemen ran up and down the beach, singly and in packs, encouraging one another and puffing with pleasure and exertion. Tough young men pranced and postured and turned somersaults, raced one another into the ocean, swam vigorously, then changed to go to work.

Later, as the December day became warmer and when the good people of Tel Aviv were at their toil, less energetic women arrived. They greeted one another with screams of delight and rubbed one another's beautiful bodies with pungent oils. Their swimsuits were extremely abbreviated, and necklaces of bleached seashells or of gold set off their impeccable suntans. They flicked their fingers to the rhythms of portable radios, posed on bright towels, and hid their roving eyes behind dark glasses.

Later, a stunning tall man appeared on the beach and spread his towel near mine, pulled off his trousers and shirt, and surveyed the scene around us. He was very blond, muscular, and deeply tanned. Occasionally our eyes met. "English?" he inquired. I told him that it was my first day in Israel and asked him whether he was Scandinavian.

He was deeply offended.

"Me—Scandinavian? You think I am tourist? I am Israeli, born here, a Sabra."

I apologized for my blunder but said that I had been misled by his blond hair.

"So you think all Israelis must be thin little men with white skin in black suits and hats like in the old Polish ghettos?" he said. "We are a nation now; we have everything other nations have." He looked toward the young women in their bikinis, soaking up the wintry sun. "Even prostitutes: in the day they come here outside the Dan Hotel; at night they are in the coffeehouses and bars on Dizengoff Street." He seemed proud that Israel was so advanced as to have ladies of easy virtue, yet disapproving.

Presently he leaned back onto his elbows and gave me a very meaningful look. "I wish—" he said.

"Yes?"

"I wish to go with you."

"Go with me?"

"Oh, you know what I mean. But I cannot take you to my house. My wife did not go to work today; my daughter is home sick with ear infection."

I told him that I had a place to go and showed him the key of my suite, with its massive metal Dan Hotel tag.

He was delighted and immediately began to pull on his clothes and roll up his towel. *"Maher, maher,"* he cried, "I have only forty minutes; I must be at work at one o'clock." It suited me fine—I, too, had only forty minutes before my luncheon meeting.

We walked through the underground passage from the beach into the hotel basement and took the elevator to the top floor. How impressed he will be with my opulent suite, I thought, with its flowers and fruit baskets.

We came out of the elevator and I began to lead him toward the suite at the end of the corridor; but there was a soldier sitting on either side of its door, and as we approached they rose, grim-faced, and pointed their automatic rifles at us.

"Hara!" shouted my golden Sabra, and ran back to the elevators.

I was totally bewildered and, barefooted and wearing only swimming trunks, felt extremely vulnerable and intimidated.

"That's my room," I said, and showed the key, but I did not take a step nearer.

A chambermaid came running up behind me. "Please, mister—other room for you!" she called out.

"But *that* is my room—"

The Sabra was frantically pressing all the elevator buttons; one of the doors opened and he disappeared.

The maid led me back along the corridor to a small room, where I saw my clothes neatly laid out on the bed, my teddy bear propped up against the pillow; my books and maps lay on the dressing table. I found my shaver, my toothbrush, my 4711 eau de cologne, and my bottle of Dr. J. Collis Browne's Chlorodyne on the bathroom shelf. The maid handed me the key of the room in exchange for that of the suite from which I had been evicted.

✧

At the luncheon meeting, my government hosts explained to me what had happened. They thought it a great joke. I was not, happily, no longer a welcome guest in Israel, as I had feared. The night clerk had made a monumental error and had given me the key of the suite that had been prepared for Mr. Levi Eshkol, Israel's prime minister, who had arrived from Jerusalem early in the morning.

The mistake had been noticed when the day staff came on duty, and the hotel management had tried all morning to contact me. Unable to find me, they had removed my belongings—and, presumably, had quickly repaired the damage I had inflicted on the splendid fruit basket and the box of mint chocolates.

"We hear you travel with a teddy bear," my hosts said. I blushed.

They drove me up to Jerusalem in the afternoon, and before taking me to the King David Hotel made a detour through pretty, tree-lined suburban streets and slowed down the car outside a modest villa behind a high wall.

"We thought you might like to see where our prime minister sleeps when he is in Jerusalem," they said.

7

THE

MYSTIQUE

OF

MUSTIQUE

"SEND ME some *nice* Americans, dear boy," said the Honorable Colin Tennant.

It was 1972, soon after I had opened my travel company in New York; he was the owner of the island of Mustique, one of the lovely Grenadines between Saint Vincent and Grenada in the Caribbean, which he had bought from the French government. It was an exclusive and carefully guarded private retreat for a handful of his friends whom he had encouraged to build villas there, and he had created a casually elegant ten-room hotel, the Cotton House, as a focal point and social center for these members of the smart and rich international set.

I did not have to ask him what he meant by *nice* Americans. It was obvious that he had little liking for Americans, whom he considered with few exceptions to be hopelessly crass and uncouth; but the bedrooms of the Cotton House were sometimes empty, and he hoped that I could fill them with American guests who had plenty of dollars but manners that at least approximated those of his European friends. His wife was lady-in-waiting to their friend, Britain's Princess Margaret, whom he had given a house on Mustique as a wedding present; he had to take care with whom Her Royal Highness would mix when she was in residence on the island. He had heard that I had a reputation for being able judiciously to vet prospective hotel guests. "Not just *anyone* must be given the opportunity of dining with the only sister of the queen of England," he told me.

He was quite unaware that there were Americans of distinction and wealth who had their own estates and private islands and for whom it was not necessarily the ultimate idea of bliss to dine with a princess and meet raffish albeit titled European villa-owners on Mustique.

I offered to do my best to send him only nice Americans, but explained that if he was going to advertise his hotel, I could not guarantee that all the reservations I accepted would be from people who were to his liking. "Oh, one can advertise in such a way as to attract only the people one wants," he said. "It's quite easy: we will print the advertisements in ancient Greek, or in Latin; that will keep away the hoi polloi, dear boy. There's a phrase in Horace's *Epistles* which will be ideal for the purpose." I pointed out that practically no one in the United States understood ancient Greek, and only lawyers knew some Latin. "All the better: it will show how exclusive we are and make the nice people all the more keen to come to us."

✧

And so the advertisements in *The New Yorker, Gourmet,* and *Town & Country* magazines, whose readers Mr. Tennant believed to include *nice* Americans, were set in classical Roman letters and headed:

NON CUIVIS
HOMINI
CONTINGIT ADIRE
CORINTHUM.

Horace:
Epistles XVII.35

This was eye-catching, and the small type explained that just as in classical times, when not every man could visit Corinth, so today not everyone can get to Mustique, "the aristocrat of the Caribbean," to be pampered there in sinful luxury.

Mr. Tennant's scheme worked—he was, despite his flippant, occasionally almost clownish manner, an extremely shrewd businessman—and soon I had the satisfaction of making many reservations for the Cotton House from people whom I felt he would consider entirely *nice.*

"I have the Marcuses booked in for Christmas and New Year's," I proudly told him when he next passed through New York. The Jewish name clearly worried him. "You know," I explained, "the owners of Neiman Marcus, the big department store in Dallas."

He was not impressed. "Oh, dear," he said, *"shopkeepers,"* and, after a dramatic pause accompanied by the raising of one mischievous eyebrow: "and from *Texas!*"

Nor were my trump cards, the Johnstones, more to his liking. I told him that Mr. Johnstone had recently retired, having been chairman of the board of Bethlehem Steel. It meant nothing to him. "Is he a little man living on a pension or does he have *money*?"

The Marcuses changed their travel plans and never did go to Mustique. The Johnstones quite endeared themselves to Mr. Tennant—"Such a *nice* old couple!"—and when I sent Ambassador Bernard Zagorin to the Cotton House, Mr. Tennant praised me with a telegram: "DELIGHTED WITH AMBASSADOR PLEASE SEND REST OF UNITED NATIONS."

It was difficult, if not impossible, to understand by what test if any he judged the hotel guests and whom he found acceptably *nice* or considered persona non grata. He doted on the foulmouthed Mr. Mick Jagger, but when a respected Boston lawyer stayed at the Cotton House for ten days with his male companion, Mr. Tennant complained that I should have known better than to have accepted that reservation. "Please don't take offense, dear boy, I've no objection to homosexuals per se; but if you *must* send me one with his little friend, at least let it be Gian Carlo Menotti or Lenny Bernstein."

It was hard to please him, but an interesting challenge.

His personal assistants—who never stayed long with him—were the personable but unemployable sons of millionaires or, in one case, of a famous World War II general—highbred arrogant minions who pranced around him ineffectively and were aware of their shortcomings. "Colin is very difficult; but who else would ever give me a job?" one of them admitted to me.

He was a remarkable living example of an eccentric but benevolent eighteenth-century British landowner. When he bought Mustique in 1958, and before he built any of the pretty villas and the Cotton House and filled it with antiques and amusing pieces of furniture made of seashells, he moved the indigent island population of about eighty persons from its ramshackle homes to a new, well-planned, attractive model village for them and the villa and hotel staff, on a low hill overlooking what he named Britannia Bay. The Mustique over which he reigned was unique in having none of the squalor, the heaps of garbage by the roadsides, the tin shacks, the abject poverty, the hideous advertising signs and neon lights, that disfigure all the other Caribbean islands—none of the antagonistic black natives who despise the white tourists on whose money they depend, the surly hotel servants, the overzealous immigration and customs officials who make the visitors' arrival so unpleasant.

He gave the island a rare style, and if it did not always appeal to every visitor, it was unquestionably personal. Guests at the Cotton House were sometimes distressed by his autocratic ways; the beach in front of the hotel had to remain littered with rotting fish heads and hooks and tackle because he insisted that this provided authentic local color—besides, the hotel made a charge for driving guests in jeeps to the island's other, pristine beaches. He permitted Mr. Mick Jagger to monopolize the only tennis court, so that guests who waited for their promised game had to listen to him call out "shit" and "fuck" every time he missed a ball, which he did frequently. Guests were disconcerted when Mr. Tennant's teenage son, dressed in ominous black from head to foot like Hamlet, crept about silently in a drugged daze.

But there were considerable compensations. One never knew what celebrity or luminary might descend when a private plane touched down or whether the yacht at anchor had brought in a member of the British Royal Ballet Company, the owner of a chic brothel in Hong Kong, or a Saudi prince of incalculable wealth and power with his entourage. And in which other hotel did the manager walk from table to table at dinner and spoon a great dollop of fine caviar into each guest's plate of Brown Windsor soup, explaining that "it needs a bit of a lift"? Where else did a hotel pay the airmail postage for its guests' letters and cards to anywhere in the world? "I wouldn't *dream* of charging them for stamps," Mr. Tennant told me when I expressed my surprise. "It would be so vulgar, dear boy."

There were managers at the Cotton House, but like Mr. Tennant's assistants they never stayed long. These professional hoteliers tried to but could not adapt themselves to Mr. Tennant's unconventional ways of doing things. He often managed the hotel himself, as he did everything else on his island, in the manner of a feudal lord. "There's nothing to running a hotel," he said. "It's quite easy. After all, I seldom have less than forty weekend guests at my house in Scotland in the summer." Nothing troubled him. When the French cruise liner SS *Antilles* went aground on the rocks off Point Lookout in 1971 and its four hundred passengers were brought ashore on Mustique, he quickly provided shelter and a splendid luncheon for them, although the Cotton House kitchen had never previously catered for more than thirty persons. Nothing he did was mundane. When he built a swimming pool for hotel guests, it was not placed on the large lawn in front of the Cotton House, where a less inspired entrepreneur would have put it, but he caused an artificial hill to be raised and had his pool up there, surrounded by mock ruins. He was very conscious of guaranteeing privacy for the villa owners and hotel guests; when a plane approached the island with passengers whom he suspected of being members of the press, he hurried to the little airstrip and warned it off with a shotgun.

Although his abhorrence of Americans grew less over the years as he met many delightful people—even from Texas—he never became reconciled to what he considered vulgar American habits. "Why do they insist on talking about their bowel movements and how much money they have?" he complained. And he despised the use of credit cards. He refused to accept them at the Cotton House. The preferred, nicely civilized method of payment was by personal cheque—always spelled in that way.

✧

The presence of Princess Margaret on the island during the high-season winter months added considerably to the attraction of Mustique as a resort destination. It had been a masterstroke of adroit public relations by Mr. Tennant to give her Les Jolies Eaux, the pretty pink villa high above Gelliceaux Bay at the southern end of the island. Her Royal Highness was not averse to making money by letting her villa, and despite its remote location and hideous furniture, there were always vacationers eager to rent it; and when she was not in residence, she stayed in Room No. 1 at the Cotton House. Pieces of her luggage, bearing long, slim, heavy cardboard labels reading "H R H PRINCESS MARGARET," were always standing about on the island's airstrip and on the terrace of the Cotton House, carefully placed there as if by chance.

The princess spent most evenings at the Cotton House, and guests occasionally complained that they had to wait for dinner until Her Royal Highness had made her late arrival——but there was, after all, nothing else to do on Mustique in the evenings but await the appearance of its regal star; and how effective it was, back home in Essex, Connecticut, or Shaker Heights, Ohio, to be able to talk about having dined with Princess Margaret and, after coffee, listened to her sing to the accompaniment of a guitarist or a steel band.

Although it was supposed to be a closely guarded secret, there was widespread speculation in the press both in Europe and in America that the princess and her husband were estranged. Rumors persisted that she had formed an attachment to a young playboy, but there was no proof. Then, toward the end of January 1976, a shabbily dressed young couple came to my office in New York and asked to make a reservation for a week's stay at the Cotton House on Mustique. Mr. Ross Waby identified himself as a New Zealand businessman on his way back to England——"But first me and the wife need a week in the sun," he said. It was obvious to me that they were not ideal Cotton House guests, but the hotel had just sent me a telegram urging me to try and fill some rooms that were unaccountably still free for the prime winter period, so I accepted the booking, though with misgivings. It was strange that Mr. Waby made a point of showing me his passport, to prove that he was a

New Zealander. There was no need for that. His accent was common and not that of an affluent businessman who could, as he did, unhesitatingly pay cash for first-class air tickets to Barbados, charter planes to and from Mustique, and a week at the Cotton House. I thought that his very pale, undernourished appearance was due to having been recently discharged from prison—but his demure little wife was very pregnant, and nothing makes a man seem more respectable than to be traveling with a pregnant wife.

At the Cotton House, the couple bought some pretty resort clothes and acquired suntans and were soon not too embarrassingly out of place. Alas, a week after their departure, Mr. Waby's identity was revealed in the London *News of the World*—he was a journalist and, pretending to snap pictures of the beach and by the hotel pool with his Instamatic camera, had taken photographs of Princess Margaret holding hands with her dashing young swain, the ex-model Roddy Llewellyn; and his article described the couple walking together arm in arm on the beach and noted that "Roddy rubs suntan oil on her bronzed shoulders."

Whether the cunning Mr. Waby had hired a pregnant woman to give him "cover" for his coup I do not know; but the enormous publicity of his revelations caused a scandal in England and around the world and brought about the princess's divorce. Mr. Colin Tennant blamed me for the entire disaster. "You have ruined Princess Margaret's life," he said.

✧

The brochures of the Cotton House were very curious. Mr. Tennant had personally designed them. He never knew, or I believe he never knew, and I was much too embarrassed ever to tell him, that many people who received the brochures asked whether the Cotton House was a gay hotel—a misconception of which I had to disabuse them. On the cover was a color photograph of an exceptionally handsome young black man, smiling invitingly from behind the hotel's bar. This was Basil, whose position in the island hierarchy was viewed by residents and visitors as being most ambiguous. Although he was posed as the hotel barman, in reality he acted as a general factotum for the whole island and all its activities, with such inexplicable powers that Mr. Tennant's assistants and most residents deferred to him. It was not in the role of a barman that he attended dinners and parties in the private houses on the island, but as an honored guest; and all the men and many of the women rose from their seats when the gorgeous Basil made his entrance in a flimsy shirt open to the waist, and trousers so tight as to leave no doubt about his spectacular manly endowment. It was said that titled ladies journeyed from Europe to Mustique more for the sake of Basil than for the pleasure of swimming off its nine glorious sand beaches.

It amused me to fantasize that this stunning black man with his commanding manner really owned the island, that one day there would be a coup d'état and Mr. Tennant and his yes-men and his friends would be banished and King Basil would take rightful possession of his ancestral island home.

There was a dreamlike and frivolous quality about Mustique in its heyday in the 1970s and in the early 1980s, when Mr. Tennant succeeded to his family title and became Lord Glenconner and built himself an Indian pleasure palace there in which he entertained on the lavish scale and in the style of the Moghul emperors. When he sold the island, the ambience altered. His benign reign gave way to that of a resort island operated on strictly commercial lines, like many others in the Caribbean, not for amusement and fun but only for profit. Venezuelans with dubious sources of money were much in evidence; cruise ships were permitted to call, so that their passengers roamed the island, indulged in sex among the dunes behind Macaroni Beach, and gaped at the houses of the celebrities. Basil put on weight and ran a beach bar. The island's new owners dismissed me curtly, and instead of having a representative who personally answered each telephone call and written inquiry and knew every room in the Cotton House and provided intelligent information, reservations for the hotel were handled by a large organization; those who inquired about Mustique were put on hold a long time before they could talk to an agent who had never been there and cared nothing for it.

It was, in a way, the end of an era. Anyone with the necessary money cavorted where formerly only *nice* people had played at being simple folk under the sun.

I remember Mustique's crazy but enchanting period with nostalgic regrets. I only stayed once at the Cotton House—on all my other visits, arrangements had been made for me to be accommodated in one or another of the nearby private houses whose owners were not in residence. Mr. Tennant found my services useful in New York and approved, on the whole, of my ability to send him guests who were to his liking; but on Mustique he preferred to keep me at a distance. I was not what he referred to as "people like us." I knew neither Greek nor Latin; I had been to no prestigious school or university; I lacked any grand social connections, had no money, was not good-looking. I had never murdered anyone and did not take drugs. Not even my single gold earring redeemed my dullness. I was too boring for Mustique.

On the one occasion when I did stay at the Cotton House as its guest, I was given the highly prized Room No. 1, which Princess Margaret had vacated a day or so before. It was a gracious honor, and I appreciated it. The room was not particularly grand—none of the Cotton House guest rooms was luxurious; they had been well described as being *"merveilleusement confortable, raffinée, et cosy"*—and I was intrigued to see that most of the books on the shelves and the bedside table were recently published novels with homosexual themes. I did not inquire whether they had been hurriedly and thoughtfully placed there for my delectation, or constituted the favored reading of Her Royal Highness, or merely formed part of the normal furnishings of the Cotton House bedrooms, to titillate its worldly guests.

I had made this visit in order to see the hotel's four new guest cottages, replicas of slave quarters on Martinique that Mr. Tennant had admired; and when I flew back to New York, by the time I reached Barbados I began to itch all over. This was strange, because I had not sunbathed; but when I arrived home, I found that my body was covered with a nasty rash. Happily, some household remedies reduced and soon cured it, but I enjoyed the notion that the staff at the Cotton House had failed to change the bed linen in Room No. 1 and that I had caught the Royal Itch, which has been attributed to various ancestors of Princess Margaret. I was not serious in this suspicion, of course, but when I later foolishly tried to amuse Mr. Colin Tennant by regaling him with this flippant thought, I failed dismally. He was greatly displeased. I had failed him. "*Nice* people don't make jokes about Her Royal Highness, dear boy," he said.

8

HOW THE

GRAND

CANYON

WENT

GAY

IN THE 1960s, after having spent more than a year traveling around the world, my friend Brian Kenny and I lived frugally but very happily in London and did not expect ever to live anywhere else; but when Lindblad Travel, Inc., in New York offered me a job I could not refuse, it was, in many ways, a dream come true: four times the salary I was earning in London, the prestige of working for the most inventive and famed travel organization in the world, in the most glamorous and exciting city in the world, which we had visited several times and with which Brian and I were both enchanted.

Mr. Lars-Eric Lindblad and his wife, Sonja, were soon not only my employers but became friends, and invited Brian and me to their New York apartment for dinners and to their house in Connecticut for weekends. When Brian suddenly became very ill, they telephoned their physician in Washington, D.C., to fly to New York with his nurse to take charge of him and fly him back to Washington the same day for an emergency operation at Doctors Hospital; and later Brian recuperated for six weeks in their house in

Wilton. Mrs. Lindblad and I drove there every Friday afternoon, and before we returned to New York on the Sunday evenings she cooked five tempting and nourishing luncheons and five dinners and put them in plastic containers in the refrigerator, which he had only to warm up until we returned the following Friday to check on his recovery. I am indebted to her forever for that kindness.

We felt wonderfully welcome and at home in New York, with its cultural attractions and its unlimited wickedness; and for our first vacation in our new country we wanted to take part in the most thrilling experience it has to offer: to travel through the Grand Canyon of the Colorado River, with its formidable rapids, and see the most fabulous place in the United States, maybe in the world.

We had worked in the travel industry and escorted tour groups in many countries most of our adult lives, so the last thing we wanted to do for our annual vacation was to travel with strangers and feel compelled to make ourselves agreeable to them; but one cannot go river-running down the Grand Canyon alone. Mr. Buddy Bombard, the balloonist, introduced us to Mr. and Mrs. Ron Smith, the Mormon river-running outfitters, and we joined one of their trips.

When we boarded the bus at dawn outside the hotel in Las Vegas for the four-hour drive to Lees Ferry, our worst fears were confirmed. Could we, we wondered, bear to spend the next nine days and nights with these ghastly fellow travelers at such proximity, crowded together on a rubber raft all day and camping out with them at night? It was what is known as a family group: a garrulous divorcée with her eight-year-old daughter, a pastor with his two prim sisters, a painfully square airline pilot with a domineering wife and three unruly children, two fun-seeking widows with no previous outdoors experience, two earnest, ecology-minded women, and an old doddering alcoholic who hoped on this adventure trip to relive the days of his youth. They were all far worse even than we had feared. At Lees Ferry, a Californian university professor with his petite, ebullient, and sparkling French wife joined us: we disliked them on sight.

We attended the briefing by the park rangers and were given our life jackets, and with grave forebodings we floated some miles down the river to our campsite for the first night. The Colorado is not particularly exciting below Lees Ferry, merely a river running beneath a high bridge through a wide gorge—all the drama one expects, and more, comes later during the trip. As I lay in my sleeping bag after dinner, I wondered how I would be able to survive using the portable toilet and listening to the incessant inane chatter of our fellow travelers. It was not what I had hoped for and anticipated. Before dinner by the campfire, the professor's wife gave her husband a bottle of wine to chill in the river while she changed into a gingham dress; then they sat side by side on the rocks at the river edge and toasted each other with crystal glasses. It seemed incongruously pretentious.

But next day, although most of the other rafters remained anathema to Brian and me, the canyon became narrow and everything we had expected it to be: magnificent and grandiose to a degree that cannot be described and must be experienced, surely the most spectacular geological exhibit anywhere on earth. And with all that stunning scenery all around us, plus the thrill of negotiating the rapids, everything else also altered. We began to appreciate the expertise and knowledge and patience of our riverman crew, who steered the large raft, cooked three tasty meals for us each day, and took care of all the camp chores. They were handsome fellows and always cheerful, even when the divorcée's daughter, everyone's least favorite trip member, took no interest in the canyon and its ever-changing shapes and colors, or in the sighting of a bighorn sheep or a wild burro or an eagle, but whined over and over again, "When are we stopping for *lunch,* when are we stopping for *lunch*?" How clever, we now realized, had it been of the professor and his charming wife to bring along those two elegant glasses and a bottle of French wine for every evening on the river. At the end of each day, during which we had all been in turn either too hot or too cold or too wet, how sensible it was of Catherine to change into her light summer dress and look cool and refreshed. Why should one not make oneself as comfortable (and as pretty) as possible at the end of an adventurous day on the river? We admired her for it.

Indeed, Professor David Colburn and his wife became good friends of ours and have remained so for twenty-five years. Both David and I are early birds, and we went to sleep immediately after dinner; but Catherine and Brian (who had studied at the University of Besançon in France) found much in common and sat up by the campfire talking about Molière and Colette and *la civilisation française* so late, and so often, that some of the other rafters warned me, "We don't want any trouble here; David is sure to get jealous; you'd better tell Brian to cool it." I assured them that David had no cause to be alarmed, and knew it.

At the end of the trip came an unexpected and astonishing moment. When the raft was pulled up on the shore and all the gear had been unloaded, the river crew deflated it; and within minutes the strong, safe, and sturdy vessel that had carried us down three hundred miles of turbulent river became a pathetic thin shell of gray rubber, which the crew members neatly folded and tossed into the back of their van, to drive it back to Lees Ferry, where they would inflate it again and start the next river-running trip.

It was the identical procedure that the Greek historian Herodotus described twenty-five hundred years ago when the Armenians built boats by stretching animal hides over thin wood frames in which they floated down the Euphrates River from their mountains to take wine in palm-wood casks to the city of Babylon (in what is now Iraq). The Euphrates, like the Colorado, has a strong current and they could not sail their boats back against it, so each boat carried one or more donkeys, and on arrival in Babylon they dismantled the boats, sold the cargoes of wine, and loaded the animal hides onto the backs of the donkeys, who carried them back to Armenia, where new boats were built for the next journey to the market in Babylon.

There is indeed nothing new under the sun.

Despite the good company of the Colburns and the pastor's moving Sunday service in that vast cathedral of natural rock, and although we had become far less critical of the amiable widows and the dedicated ecologists by the end of our trip, Brian and I much regretted that we had necessarily had to make it in the company of many people who were not congenial to us. How much more wonderful and more meaningful and really enjoyable those nine days and nights would have been, we thought, if we could have shared this experience with a group of like-minded men who would be able to wear their boots, Levi's, and cowboy hats in the setting for which they had been designed, instead of to the bars.

It was unthinkable then for me to propose to Lindblad Travel, my prestigious employers, that they offer an all-men river-running trip, so I wrote to the Mattachine Society about it. It was at that time the only organization that might sponsor such an event, and I had met its president. To my surprise, he dismissed the suggestion as totally impractical and unsuitable. Gay men did not want to rough it and camp out and endure days and nights of discomfort, he said. "They want to go to the opera and musical concerts in the best seats; they enjoy dining in fine restaurants and going on to elegant piano bars, not risking their lives going over dangerous rapids."

I felt that he was quite wrong, but there was nothing I could do to prove him so.

But when I started my own travel company in 1972, I decided that I would offer some travel programs for gay men, and one of the first of these was what has become my annual Grand Canyon Expedition in the summer, still operated for me by the same Utah river-running outfitters.

Friends and business associates thought it was foolish and demeaning of me to attempt to cater to this special clientele. Former colleagues at Lindblad Travel avidly spread the news. "Hanns Ebensten has set himself up in a hole-in-the-wall office on West Forty-second Street," they announced, "and oh, boy, we didn't think he'd sink *that* low—he's arranging tours for *homosexuals*!"

But my ex-boss, Mr. Lars-Eric Lindblad, the respected doyen of the North American travel industry, thought otherwise. "He'll do it with style, and it will be extremely successful," he predicted.

As usual, he was right. The Grand Canyon expeditions were a great success from the start, and attracted men ranging in age from early twenties to late sixties from all over North America—and soon also from Australia, New Zealand, and many European countries whose visitors often found the canyon more awesome even than Americans, who are apt to take things on a vast scale for granted. The Mattachine Society's president had been out of touch with reality—my friend Brian and I were not the only homosexual men in the world who had no interest in elegant piano bars and preferred to travel down the Colorado River and sleep at night under the stars. The Mormon outfitters at first had reservations about handling a group of gay men, but I assured them that these river-runners would be as well behaved as any others—maybe more so—and after the first trip they welcomed us back enthusiastically each year. Their guides and crew enjoyed the easygoing camaraderie of our participants, and some of them put in their bids a year ahead to be assigned to our groups.

A man who reserved a place on one of the first gay Grand Canyon expeditions was married and as closeted as most homosexual men were at that time (and as many still are today). He lived in New Jersey and asked me never to write or telephone him at home or at work, and as a matter of course I respected his privacy. He came to our office in New York to make his trip payments and later to pick up his travel documents; and he told me that in the belief that if one must lie, it is best to keep as much as possible to the truth, he had told his wife that he was going on a raft trip through the Grand Canyon organized by his factory. Then, two weeks before the trip, his wife returned home on Saturday afternoon from her weekly visit to her beauty parlor with news of a weird coincidence. "You won't believe this, but Bobby, my cute gay hairdresser, is also going down the Grand Canyon, exactly the same week as you, and with a group of gay guys—maybe you'll see them!" Then, as her husband's face turned deep red, she stared hard at him and said, "Oh, my God—it's the same group. *You and Bobby are in the same group!*"

When the unfortunate man later told me about this, I sympathized with him; but he explained that having hidden his sexual orientation from his wife for almost eight painful years, it had in fact been a relief to him when the truth was so unexpectedly revealed to her. I have often wondered whether his marriage survived the shock and if he and Bobby became friends.

✧

More than any conventional tour, more than other tours for gay men, the trip down the Colorado River from Lees Ferry to Lake Mead is a great bonding experience.

A young man for whom this trip was particularly meaningful has written of his "joy of lying naked next to a kindred spirit in the heated air along a roaring river, counting the shooting stars, watching the moon become fuller night after night, and discussing the day's events, life's hopes, past experiences, and dreams." He poetically described his favorite moments of each day, when "after the first early-morning chilly splashes with yelps and screams," after hiking and picnicking, after the heat of the day had subsided, after having safely negotiated thrilling rapids and explored Indian caves, when the group was gliding along a smooth stretch of water to the campsite with the outboard motor of the raft turned off, there would be "no conversation, no jokes, no songs. I would slowly look around at the faces of my companions—all staring off in different directions, spaced-out in their own little worlds of thought. How beautiful each man looked, and how proud I was to know each one of them in that time and space and frame of mind. Each of us discovered a lot of things about ourselves on this expedition. Most of us found hidden physical strengths we didn't know we had or hadn't used in a long time. There were strengths of compassion and tolerance. And there were strengths of daring and character that each man summoned out of those dark recesses that are sometimes hidden in our city lives."

It is not unusual for men who have made the trip to repeat it a year or more later, occasionally to bring along a friend; but when one man signed up for it for his third time, I was curious what attracted him so much. "I want to go for the ride again," he said.

Yes, more than anything else, it is the exhilaration of riding almost two hundred rapids between Lees Ferry and Lake Mead that is the biggest attraction. Although the dangers the early rivermen encountered have been overcome by modern techniques and safe equipment, the thrills remain. The rapids are officially graded from 1 to 10 for height and difficulty; trip members study their river-runners' waterproof guidebooks eagerly each day, and there is tremendous anticipation when the raft approaches one of the biggest rapids. Then, when it is sighted, the guide in the stern of the raft calls out, "Lava Falls ahead—that's a number ten—I want you all on the deck!"—whereupon the men are only too anxious to crouch down low in the raft and clutch one another as they go screaming through the frothing waters and over the thirty-foot drop.

No one who travels down the Grand Canyon of the Colorado River can fail to be moved and touched by its amazing beauty and peace, but what makes the river-running trip for men so rewarding is the companionship that is absent in the mixed groups, where diverse people are haphazardly thrown together. It is the gay men's eagerness to learn and enjoy, their infectious spirit of wanting to share a great experience, that the dedicated river guides and crew appreciate so much on the all-male trips and that have made them so outstandingly successful. On the last night of these expeditions there is rarely a dry eye in camp after the toasts to the river crew, the farewell speeches and awards, and the "Grand Canyon Follies" of skits, parodies, and songs.

Now, twenty years since I started these trips—and tours and expeditions for men to many other places in the world—there is no longer any novelty, oddity, or surprise in seeing gay men on the Colorado River each summer. Many people who remember the general attitude of suspicion and disdain for homosexual manifestations in the early 1970s tell me how audacious, bold, and courageous it was of me to have innovated these tours, and they praise me for the service I have rendered the gay community. Not so. I cannot accept such accolades, because it seemed to me simply that the time was ripe for gay group travel, and I seized the opportunity. Gay publications of merit, other than the sexually oriented magazines for "one-handed reading," were beginning to appear; two men kissed in a major movie; there was a gay radio program in New York, and plans for a gay television program. Opinions were changing: an extremely influential lady who was informed by a former colleague of mine, in order to discredit me, that I was offering tours for "confirmed bachelors," replied: "How clever of him; that's where the money is." Although Pan American World Airways persisted in refusing to carry gay groups, other airlines were happy to accept reservations in the name of the National Gay Task Force. I had nothing to lose by arranging and publicly promoting travel programs for gay men, and I never considered it as a charitable service. I thought it would be interesting and satisfying.

And that is how it has turned out to be.

9

VOLLEYBALL

WITH THE

CUNA

INDIANS

"FIRE ISLAND, move over!" said the advertisements for a series of tours to "our own island paradise in the Caribbean" in 1973 and 1974. I had arranged for an entire uninhabited tropical island, for the first time, anywhere, to be reserved exclusively for groups of gay men, who would not only be able to enjoy a week in the sun but to take part in an historic event.

The island was one of the four hundred San Blas Islands off the Caribbean coast of Panama, many of which are uninhabited, where a genial Californian genius named Roy Stewart had come ashore in his trimaran *Tontine* at the end of a voyage around the world. He had fallen in love with the tiny island, which consisted of nothing but sand and palm trees, grandiosely named it Isla de Oro, and put up a main hut with a kitchen and dining room and some basic thatched shelters with hammocks for guests. Two wooden toilet seats were located at the end of a long catwalk built over the ocean.

I had visited Roy Stewart there some years before and been enchanted with the total simplicity of the island and impressed with its possibilities as a vacation haven for anyone willing to dispense with modern comforts and amenities. Now, Roy, surprisingly in those days when one barely dared to mention the word "homosexual," was not only agreeable but enthusiastic to make his hideaway available for my groups of men. I was able to offer the tours—a night at a hotel in Panama City, a week on the island, all meals, and the airfare to and from the island—for $175 per person, which was a very, very affordable price, even in 1973. The maximum number of guests for which Roy could cater and for which there was room to sling hammocks was thirty-six; and the tours were soon fully subscribed, some of the participants coming all the way from Europe.

Tours for gay men were a new concept then, and I believed—erroneously, as it soon became apparent—that in order to have appeal, a somewhat racy, salacious element had to be incorporated into a travel program. Through friends at Colt Studio, the leading purveyor of male photographs, I arranged for each Isla de Oro tour to be accompanied by one or two of their well-known models, who would pose with tour members among palm trees, on the beaches, and in canoes during photo sessions. They were amiable young men, but many of the tour members were no less muscular, handsome, and photogenic, so that the models contributed little to the success of the tours—except Val Martinelli, who later starred as the leather-clad master in porno films, a good-natured and warmhearted Brazilian who could identify all the tropical plants for us on our nature hikes along the rivers of the nearby mainland; and Richard Trask, a mischievous imp with an infectious sense of fun whom providence had compensated for his short stature with a truly prodigious male endowment. This no doubt caused his overwhelming urge to discard all clothes at almost any time and in any circumstances; when he accompanied one of my nature tours to see the seals on the ice pack in the Gulf of Saint Lawrence, he was immortalized there by Mr. Fred Bruemmer, Canada's greatest wildlife photographer, streaking among the astonished seals. The picture of this muscular, suntanned young man running over the ice, wearing only a red wool cap, my borrowed wristwatch, and boots, appeared in newspapers and magazines all over North America and became an extremely popular postcard.

✧

The Isla de Oro, as well as two other uninhabited islands that Roy Stewart planned to develop for tourism, were owned by the Cuna Indians of the nearby village of Aligandi; each palm tree was by tradition the property of one of the ninety families of the village, who alone had the right to pick its coconuts and sell them to the Colombian trading boats that plied the coast. Roy Stewart could not buy the islands, but he made a treaty with Chief Johnnie Goff, the largest landowner, and the other caciques, allowing him to bring in a limited number of visitors, with the understanding that the income derived from them would be shared by him and the Indian landowners.

The Cuna Indians do not physically resemble any of the Indians of North, Central, or South America, and there is a theory that they came to the islands off the coast of Panama from Mesopotamia—but how they did so, and when, no one can say. It seems romantically farfetched, but the little Cuna women, with their curiously mannish hairstyles and their many rings on fingers, ears, and through the nose, bracelets, anklets, and massive breastplates of gold, do look amazingly like the jewel-bedecked female statuettes that were excavated at Ur in what is today Iraq.

Wherever they came from, the Cunas are an oddity, a matriarchal society, semi-autonomous and only nominally under the control of the Panama government, with village parliaments, the *congresos,* where their rights are fiercely debated.

The women at this time still produced handmade *molas,* decorative reverse-appliqué panels, often with delightfully naïve patterns and designs: playing cards, kitchen utensils, clocks, scissors, Santa Clauses—anything that attracted them was represented in a frivolous manner. Soon after our tours, the Peace Corps introduced sewing machines to the Indians, with the sad result that the *molas* began to be mass-produced and lose all their charm and individuality. The Cuna men carved *uchus,* stern-faced wooden ceremonial male figures, sometimes representing white men in fantasticated garments of the colonial period, others crudely daubed with industrial paint and adorned with nails, bottle tops, and pieces of wire. These, too, are no longer made, and have become museum pieces.

Our tours began at Miami Airport, where we assembled for the Braniff flight to Panama City; and there were always a number of tour members who failed to identify themselves, afraid of being seen to take part in a tour for gay men. I had to locate them on the plane or on arrival at Tocumen Airport in Panama City, from where we drove to a modest hotel for dinner and the night. When I checked in there with the first group, I was somewhat apprehensive about the reception we would receive, but my fears were groundless, because the whole hotel was filled with men—three other male groups were lodged there, firemen from Bolivia, Ecuador, and Venezuela who were attending a *congreso de bomberos.* They were almost as athletic and rugged as most of my tour members, and wore similar blue jeans or work pants, T-shirts, and boots. My tour members thought they, too, were gay, and the firemen thought we were a contingent of United States fire fighters. From our separate tables in the dining room, we viewed each other with considerable interest.

Early next morning, when we arrived at the downtown Paitilla Airport, from where small charter planes were to take us over the mountains to the Aligandi airstrip on the Caribbean coast opposite the Isla de Oro, Roy Stewart met me with a very dejected face. "We have a problem," he said.

Because of an acute shortage of aircraft fuel in Panama, all nonessential domestic flights were temporarily grounded. The owner of the company whose planes had been chartered to take us to Aligandi had applied for fuel to be able to operate our flights, and the form of authority had to be signed by three members of the committee that controlled the use of the diminishing fuel. A government official and a lady of the prominent Arias family had signed, but the third member of the committee, an army officer, had delayed, not apparently in order to extract a bribe but to demonstrate his power.

While my tour members and their baggage were being weighed, and lists of their names and weights were being slowly typed in quadruplicate with many erasures and revisions, the owner of the charter air company and Roy had planned to drive to the home of the officer, who had been informed the previous afternoon that they would call on him to obtain his signature. They asked me to accompany them. "It will prove to the colonel that we need the fuel for foreign tourists," said Roy; and on the way to the colonel's house he briefed me on the short, appealing speech I was to make to him. The colonel, he said, did not speak or understand English well but would know what I was saying.

His home, not far from the downtown airport, was quite unpretentious, in a middle-class suburb; two or three soldiers lounged outside the gate, and the small, unkept garden was littered with plastic children's toys and tricycles. Roy rang the bell, and two slatternly women in dressing gowns opened the door. Roy asked for the colonel.

"Still sleeps," said the women. "Is Sunday!"

The owner of the air company explained that he had made an

appointment—our business with the colonel would take only a minute or two—it was an important matter. The women went to the back of the house and banged on a bedroom door. "Manuel! Manuel!" they called out.

We waited on the porch.

After some time the colonel appeared, sleepy and in a foul mood, wearing a pair of soiled striped pajamas. He had woken with an erection and made no attempt to hide this condition from us. Despite his ugly, puffy face and short, stout body—or possibly because of the lack of any normally acceptable physical assets—this ithyphallic colonel exuded sexuality like a randy beast. I sensed the same powerfully intoxicating masculinity I had felt emanating from the similarly ugly but suave Mr. Aristotle Onassis when I had sat next to him on an Olympic Airways flight from Paris to Athens—but Mr. Onassis had made an effort to be agreeable to me, while this boorish colonel did not disguise his contempt for us three humble petitioners. His cunning porcine eyes darted from the air-company man to Roy Stewart to me. He knew quite well why we were there, how important his signature was to us, but he made the owner of the air company explain again at length why he needed the fuel. He accepted the form of authority that the airline man handed to him on a clipboard, but did not look at it. He scowled at us.

When Roy nudged me to say my rehearsed piece, I found it difficult to raise my eyes from the man's erection under his pajama pants to his horribly pitted face.

"I apologize for disturbing you at home so early on Sunday morning, Colonel Noriega," I said, as deferentially as I could. "I am the leader of a group of thirty-six tourists who have come a long way to visit the San Blas Islands, and we will appreciate it highly if you can very kindly make it possible for us to do so today."

Colonel Noriega gave no sign that he had understood my plea, but he held up his right hand; the airline owner put a ballpoint pen in it; the colonel signed his name, returned the clipboard but not the pen, turned abruptly, and went back into his house.

We had not been well received, but we had accomplished our mission. Half an hour later the little single-engine planes started to take off with my tour members.

But other problems with the flights to and from Aligandi were to plague each of the groups. The air company did not own enough planes to handle efficiently the transportation of thirty-six passengers with their luggage, and only their two smallest planes could touch down on the short airstrip at Aligandi. There were long delays, waiting for planes to return and pick up more tour members; six or even eight passengers were crammed into four-seater planes, sitting on one another's laps—"Oh, that is quite normal here; we always do it for these short hops," I was told—and once, an emergency landing had to be made for unexplained reasons at an airstrip that had not been used since World War II and was heavily overgrown by the encroaching jungle. A tour member's scarlet shirt was attached to a pole to attract the attention of the other planes, one of which returned after several hours to rescue the stranded passengers just before darkness fell.

These delays were particularly worrying on the return journey from Aligandi to Panama City, where connections had to be made to the Braniff jet flights to Miami. I sat for many hours on the Aligandi airstrip, anxiously looking into the empty sky and silently praying for the sight of an approaching plane, making everyone stop talking whenever I thought I could hear the noise of an engine. Then, when one or two planes did at last touch down and I had to decide which of the impatient tour members were to take their places in them, the planes merely carried them to another, longer airstrip along the coast, where they were ordered off with their baggage and told that a larger plane would come and take them on to Panama City. But the logistics of planning these arrangements and seeing that they were carried out was something quite beyond the capabilities of the little air company's staff, so that frustrated tour members were left for many hours, sitting without food or water in the shade of trees at airstrips all over Panama, uncertain whether they had been forgotten and would have to spend a terrifying night, a week, or the rest of their lives lost in the jungle. Somehow, everyone always reached Panama City and returned home safely, but participants in the tours have dined out for many years on dramatized accounts of their chaotic flights over the mountains of Panama.

✧

The airstrip at Aligandi ran along the shore, amid a profusion of lilies, and from there canoes with outboard motors—which frequently failed—ferried passengers to the Isla de Oro, half a mile away. The tour members jumped ashore and ran from one shelter to the next, selecting their hammocks so that they would be under the same thatched roof as their friends, or away from cigarette smokers, or with the Colt models.

Sleeping in a hammock is an easily acquired art; the descriptions of the simplicity of the island in the tour brochures had prepared most of the men for something even more Spartan, so that they were pleasantly surprised by such amenities as the Isla de Oro did possess; and they settled in contentedly. "I can't remember when I was happier or more relaxed," one of the men in the first tour told me, and that was to be the reaction of the members of all the groups.

Roy Stewart had set up a volleyball net, and when the Cuna Indian boys from Aligandi came in their canoes to play with the tour members, the men looked with pity at these stunted little Indians whom they would easily annihilate—but not so: in game after game, the short, nimble urchins triumphed seemingly without effort over the frantically battling six-footers, who were so upset and distressed by their humiliating defeats that when the boys sailed back to their village, the tourists practiced for many hours to be able to acquit themselves better next day. But not a single game did the mighty North Americans ever win.

Apart from taking part in or watching the volleyball games, there was blissfully little to do on the Isla de Oro except to enjoy the sea, the sun, the meals, and the fellowship. We swam, we ate, we gossiped, we dozed in our hammocks during the hot afternoons. We walked along the reef, where some of Roy's Cuna helpers often caught iguanas and cruelly killed them and cut up their flesh. "They use it for bait when they go deep-sea fishing," said Roy. But we never saw a deep-sea fish.

There was no discord, never an acrimonious argument, not a voice raised in anger. Occasionally, one or two men were strangely moody and irritable when they came to breakfast, or wandered about the island in a disoriented manner, or sat gloomily staring out to sea; I thought they were suffering from sunstroke or heat prostration and wanted to give them first-aid treatment, but the other tour members were amused by my naïveté. "Just leave them alone," they said. "They're happy—they're just stoned out of their minds."

I was then, and have remained, totally ignorant about drugs and their effects.

One morning, the plane from Panama City brought us an unexpected visitor. He was a young engineer from Düsseldorf who worked in the Canal Zone; he was looking for *molas* and wanted to spend the night at the Isla de Oro. Roy asked me whether he could stay with us. I told the German that we would be happy to have him join our group, but explained the sexual orientation of the tour members. He was delighted. "I expected this to be an adventure, but oh, boy, a night with thirty gay guys makes it even more so!" he said, and an extra hammock was found for him. Next morning, before he took a canoe back to the airstrip, he thanked me for our hospitality. "I'm not in the least that way," he said, "but if I were—I am speaking strictly theoretically, of course—but if I were—well, in that case I might feel tempted to try it just once—to see what it is all about, you understand—with that guy over there in the yellow T-shirt—or the big guy with the long blond hair— yes, that one getting his back rubbed with suntan lotion—or those two who are always together, with the same tattooed panther on their shoulders and the same swim trunks—or the one with . . . Well, I'd better go across and wait for the plane."

On Christmas Eve, after dinner, and without any preparation, verse after verse of "Jingle Bells" and "White Christmas" and "Rudolph the Red-Nosed Reindeer" rang out over the ocean—and these thirty talented men did not merely *sing,* they gave a brilliant performance in full harmony that brought tears to Brian Kenny's and my eyes. What a joy it was, we felt, to have brought these men together, to be that night in their company—we few, we happy few, we band of brothers.

Alas, the arrival of the next group was marred by an unpleasant and disconcerting incident. As we assembled on the jetty by the airstrip to embark for the crossing to the island, we noticed that many of the canoes had large hand-lettered banners with words in the Cuna language. The illiterate Cuna boatmen could not tell us what the banners said and did not seem to understand their purpose; they welcomed us as cheerfully as always and laughed and joked and stowed our luggage and set off with us. It was only when we reached the Isla de Oro that Roy explained that the banners, which we had assumed to bear expressions of welcome, said something to the effect of "PERVERTS GO HOME!" and had been lettered by the Baptist missionaries in Aligandi, who had been told about the nature of our groups.

The demonstration was particularly inappropriate because during the previous tour, Roy had introduced me to the Baptists at their pathetically ill-equipped hospital at Aligandi, and at his suggestion I had given them a contribution.

Fortunately, they were not able to turn the villagers against us. The Cunas invited us into their homes for cold drinks and fruit when we went to Aligandi to buy *molas* and *uchus,* the volleyball players continued to visit us daily to beat our groups' teams, and on the last evening of each tour a flotilla of festively lamplit canoes brought Cuna girls in their finest clothes and all their gold jewelry to the Isla de Ora, where they danced and sang their Cuna songs for us, and Chief Johnnie Goff's wife settled herself into a hammock between two palm trees on the beach and sang lullabies to her baby.

Roy Stewart ran the whole island establishment almost single-handed, with only three or four untrained Cuna boys to assist him in an ineffective way. He organized the volleyball games and gave prizes, he arranged canoe excursions, crab races, sing-alongs, crossed to the mainland at least once each day to pick up the bottled water and beer and soft drinks that the planes from Panama City left for him at the edge of the airstrip, and, in the evenings, when we sat after dinner under an oil lamp swinging between two palm trees, kept us all enthralled with his stories about the Cuna Indians. He had studied everything that is known of their history, he knew their myths and their beliefs, he understood and admired and respected their way of life; and if he embellished his talks with his own inventions, he did so in a well-meaning effort to keep his audience dramatically entertained. He had cast himself in the role of the Cunas' protector and benefactor; and he held forth so eloquently about his Cuna Foundation (which existed only in his mind) that many of the tour members were quite carried away with enthusiasm and pressed cash contributions for it on him.

How convincingly he explained that he would send selected Cuna youths to the Hotel El Panamá to be trained in the rudiments of operating a tourist resort—cooking, serving, cleaning; that he would purchase carpenter's and shipbuilding tools to enable the idle men of Aligandi to engage in useful work in which they could take pride and that would benefit the whole community; that he was taking a group of pretty Cuna maidens Stateside to give promotional performances of their traditional dances—and as he spoke of all this, he had every intention of doing it, but somehow none of it ever happened.

Meanwhile, no one knew better how to keep a group of men happy and content. He did all the cooking himself, in a small, dark space behind the dining room, and refused all offers of help.

We ate bananas from morning to night, and although this became a joke among the tour members, no one seemed to mind. For breakfast, Roy served bananas either whole or sliced in bowls of rich, refreshing cream; for luncheon, we had fruit salads that consisted of sliced bananas with a few pieces of coconut and a raisin or two and lemon juice, accompanied by chilled chocolate or coffee-flavored milkshakes—"to build up you growing boys," quipped Roy. With drinks before dinner there were always large platters of deep-fried crisp banana slices, more delicious than potato chips, very salty in order to encourage the guests to run up sizable tabs at the bar; and dinners always included more banana chips or bananas sliced lengthwise and fried in batter. Desserts were milky banana puddings or, as a special treat, bananas flambéed in local rum. And great bunches of bananas were hung daily from a tree outside the main hut, so that anyone who had not enjoyed enough bananas at meals could pick one for a snack.

These bananas came from the mainland, where Roy said he owned a plantation; but often, when the canoe returned that he sent there each day with two Cuna boys to cut down and bring the bananas, we heard angry voices and saw Cuna women on the mainland shore running to and fro waving their arms. It seemed that Roy's boys had raided their plantations.

Each afternoon, after his nap in what he called his "stateroom" aboard the derelict trimaran, Roy sequestered himself in his kitchen to prepare our gourmet meals—and truly splendid they always were, consisting of rice or spaghetti or beans with some pungent, tasty, richly spiced meat or fish sauce, topped with finely chopped onions or cheese. We ate like kings on the Isla de Oro and were always hungry after the day's swimming, snorkeling, volleyball games, hikes on the reef, and jungle excursions. There was always plenty of food, the hot coffee and cocoa that followed the dessert were excellent and creamy, and Roy was smug in accepting the many compliments on his catering and, on the tours' last evenings, the applause when we toasted him.

His most-acclaimed dish was what he called Chicken Supreme, a pilaf of rice with chopped peppers and onions and many spices, and chicken breasts cut into small, narrow strips, served under a creamy sauce. "Can we have Chicken Supreme again?" I would ask Roy.

"You all really go for that, don't you?" he said. "Sure, I'll fix it again for dinner tomorrow."

The tour members asked him where he bought the chickens. We saw none in Aligandi. Roy said that he bred them at a farm of his some miles up one of the rivers on the mainland; but I never saw a live chicken, or a dead one. "You don't really have a chicken farm, do you?" I asked him one day when he and I were alone.

He laughed. He was so proud of his deception that he could not resist confiding in me. "Don't tell any of the guys," he said. "Chicken Supreme is iguana, cut up so small that no one knows the difference. It tastes the same, with all those spices, but the guys wouldn't eat it if they knew."

I was amused. After all, the iguana meat was always fresh.

But then, toward the end of our fourth tour on the island, when I was looking for Roy and ventured into his kitchen and found it empty, in the semidarkness I saw some curious packages; I lifted a lid, and another, and a third, and I gasped with disbelief when I saw the contents: all those delectable meat and fish dinners we enjoyed so much were made of canned dog food and cat food; the bowls of rich cream at breakfast, the milk shakes, the tasty sauces, and the puddings were all created with the powder from a large tin container labeled ANIMAL FEED ONLY: DILUTE WITH WATER; the "freshly ground Colombian mountain-grown coffee" and the "cocoa which my people pick in the hills" were dark liquids of industrial flavoring in two large bottles. Only the bananas were bananas.

I was truly appalled and ran to confront Roy in his "stateroom" aboard the *Tontine.* "Oh, take no notice of all that," he said, smiling happily. "I have it all labeled like that to avoid paying the high Panamanian import duty for bringing in gourmet foods from Stateside. I wouldn't dream of serving my guests pet food, would I?"

Not for a moment did his usual aplomb fail him; but he did not convince me. For two months, before the next tour to the Isla de Oro, I was deeply troubled every day by the thought of knowingly sending my tour members to a place where they would be fed animal food; but I knew that it would be useless to beg or order Roy to use anything else. He would simply adhere to his fairy tale of having gourmet foods hidden under spurious labels. And I assuaged my conscience with the thought that a total of 144 men on four tours had eaten offal and cattle feed with considerable relish and no ill effects.

As it turned out, I need not have worried about Roy's cooking ingredients. Fate intervened, and the members of the fifth (and, regrettably, last) tour to Panama did not eat canned pet food, did not stay on the Isla de Oro at all.

❖

When my fifth tour group arrived in the morning at the Paitilla Airport in downtown Panama City, Roy Stewart confided to Brian Kenny, who was the leader of the group, that during the night he had received news that the Cuna Indians of Aligandi, in a drunken rampage, had raided the Isla de Oro and completely wrecked the resort and his beloved *Tontine.* The efforts and hopes of ten years had come to nothing, and his paternal trust in the Cunas had been shattered. He said he knew of no reason for the Cunas' action, but it was not difficult to suspect that he had failed to pass on the promised or expected share of the income he had derived from the groups, which Chief Johnnie Goff and the people of Aligandi had clearly regarded as fabulously profitable windfalls. In frustration, they had destroyed what was partly their own property.

This unexpected development, which might have caused the immediate cancellation of the tour, instead provided a challenge for the adroit and inventive Roy. "We have to make a small change," he announced to the tour members after consulting Brian Kenny. "Instead of going to my island on the Caribbean side of the isthmus, we'll go by boat to a far more interesting island I own in the Pacific." And appearing quite unruffled by events that were so ruinous for him, he drove the group to the Balboa Yacht Club for luncheon and gave orders that the men were to be plied liberally with aperitifs, wines, and liqueurs while he dashed all over Panama City and the Canal Zone to buy blankets, cutlery and crockery, glassware, cooking utensils and fuel, and food—and this time not cans of dog food and cat food but fresh meat, eggs, vegetables, fruit, butter, milk, and staples.

Nothing ever dismays or worries Brian Kenny, and although some of the tour members were bewildered by and uneasy about the change of plans, Richard Trask, the Colt model, kept up spirits with his infectious cheerfulness and comic antics. By the time Roy returned to the yacht club in a truck with the provisions, the motorboat he had chartered had arrived there; the tour members helped to load his purchases onto it; and they set off to sail past the many ships anchored while waiting their turn to go through the Canal, along the coast past the former leper colony at Palo Seco—"I'm going to convert that into a luxury resort hotel," said Roy—and across the Bay of Panama for the ninety-minute cruise to what Roy referred to as the island of Taborcillo, a name found on no map.

The sun had set when the boat arrived, and its draft prevented it from drawing up on the beach. It anchored about fifty feet off, in three feet of water, and in the fast-approaching darkness the tour members waded ashore, carrying their belongings and all the blankets, cooking and eating utensils, and provisions on their shoulders. It was a real Outward Bound experience. As soon as everyone and everything was on the beach, Roy lit an oil lamp and began to cook dinner, while the tour members staked their sleeping places and made bivouacs with palm fronds and grasses. It was a pleasantly warm night, the only sound was that of the sea lapping the beach, and it was high adventure—but even the normally unflappable Brian Kenny wondered, before he fell asleep, how he and the others could stand a week under conditions that by contrast made the Isla de Oro a luxurious resort.

Next morning, when the tour members awoke—the blankets were a great boon during the chilly hours before dawn—the admirable Roy had already made coffee. Eggs and bacon, toast with jam, and fresh fruit soon followed, and the men began to take stock of this strange island to which they had been brought in the dark.

Beyond the beach was the island's only structure, a small and ruinous wooden house built on stilts, unsuitable for habitation but with a ladder up to its deck. This became the group's social center, where the tour members gathered in the evenings and talked long into the nights. "I'll meet you for a drink before dinner at the Club," they said.

Nearby, Brian Kenny, who can exist only if he takes a shower every day before breakfast (and who contrived to have one even during the Battle of El Alamein and when chasing the Japanese out of New Guinea), had discovered a freshwater well and an old bucket that leaked only slightly and, elsewhere, a serviceable length of rope with which he hauled up the water and sluiced himself. Several tour members followed his example.

The island proved to be surprisingly large. Those energetic tour members who set off to walk around it along the beaches only returned after two hours, and others who explored the interior, forcing their way through dense tropical growth, were astonished to come upon the skeletal wreck of a World War II twin-engine U.S. Air Force fighter plane, which provided them, and the others who later went there, with fascinating photo opportunities.

There had been no alternative the first night except to accept the situation and make the best of it; but by daylight the island appealed so much to the tour members, was such a perfect place on which to relish this rare opportunity to live out the universal fantasy of being marooned on a Pacific island with only a few basic necessities and in congenial company, that it never occurred to a single member of the group to leave and return to civilization before the end of the week.

It was a tropical idyll; it was paradise without troublesome animals or insects; it was the Garden of Eden with no snake and no Forbidden Fruit. The men sunbathed and swam and snorkeled, collected seashells, searched for old bottles and other jetsam, found bits and pieces of rusted machinery dating from days when there had been aborted attempts to cultivate parts of the island. For nocturnal privacy, some of them built sleeping shelters of driftwood and palm fronds and vied with one another in decorating them to best effect.

Roy's meals were as excellent as at the Isla de Oro, with the bonus that here all the ingredients were intended for human consumption. He had chartered the motorboat for the whole week, so that it went to Panama City every evening and returned next day with ice, water, beer and soft drinks, and fresh provisions.

Tour operators are inclined to claim that any unavoidable change in a travel program is for the better, but the week on Taborcillo was in all respects an enormous success and the most enjoyable of the tours to Panama. It was an unrehearsed, spontaneous happening that those who shared remember with pride and pleasure. A month after the group's return, I flew to Panama to visit Taborcillo with Roy and consider it for future tours; and then, when I walked barefooted along its beaches, and sat on the rickety deck of the Club, looking over the ocean, and paid my respects to Brian Kenny's well and the old leaking bucket, and saw the remains of the driftwood-and-palm shelters with their shell decorations and colored ribbons, and made my way through the thick foliage to the wrecked plane, I fully understood why I had received all those gratifying letters of appreciation from the tour members. One wrote of "this disaster averted in the most beautiful manner," that "everyone profited by contact with the untouched surroundings, the freedom of the total situation, and the implicit call to creative ingenuity." Others described the tour as "one of the most memorable weeks of my life," "certainly the most fantastic enlightenment of our years," "probably the most unusual vacation I shall ever take."

They wrote affectionately about "the great cast of characters," "the unbelievable scenery," "the great direction by Messrs. Stewart, Kenny, and Trask," "the great show," and formed an association,

Los Amigos de Taborcillo, which sent out newsletters and organized a reunion.

But the astonishing success of the tour to an island that had been quite worthless had given Roy Stewart ideas that were not only wildly impracticable but repellent to me. In his ebullient way he urged me to send monthly groups to Taborcillo—"It's so big, I can easily handle a hundred, even two hundred, guys here," he said—and he proudly showed me a big map of the island on which the little wooden shack on stilts appeared grotesquely transformed into a complex with restaurants, bars, and a gambling casino. A narrow-gauge railroad encircled the island and would take vacationers to the tennis courts, the mini–golf course, the yacht marina, and to cottages built all along the beaches. It was quite appalling, and I realized that the tour that had been diverted at a moment's notice to Taborcillo was unique and could never be repeated.

It was time to bid a fond farewell to Roy with his megalomaniac project, to forget the treachery of the Cuna Indians and the bigotry of the Baptists, to allow Taborcillo to return to oblivion or become commercialized and ruined, and to go on to other ventures.

10

GAYS

IN

THE

GALÁPAGOS

I FIRST HEARD about the strange Galápagos Islands, six hundred miles off the coast of South America in the Pacific, when I was a child, because an acquaintance of my father's, young Dr. Karl Ritter, left Germany to live on one of these dismal uninhabited islands. He was a vegetarian who believed that teeth are unnecessary and potentially harmful, and he had his own and those of his mistress removed before they sailed away to Floreana. It had been the sensation of Berlin in 1929.

Not until 1967, when Brian Kenny and I settled in the United States, was I made aware of the islands again. At the end of my first week at Lindblad Travel, Inc., Mr. and Mrs. Lindblad took me to a gala fund-raising dinner in a New York hotel at which the naturalist Dr. Roger Tory Peterson gave a talk and showed his film on the Galápagos Islands; and he mentioned the privations that the crew of a freighter had endured when their ship had sunk there and they had managed to swim ashore at one of these uninhabited, stark, sunbaked, and treeless islands, and survived for several months without shelter and fire by killing and eating the indigenous booby birds.

At the end of the presentation, the plight and resourcefulness of these seamen were discussed at our table. I turned to the lady next to me, and intending to dazzle her and the others by my European wit and sophistication, I loudly said, "It must have been dreadful for those seamen all those months. After all, how many ways of serving booby birds can there be? There is *booby à la broche,* roasted on a spit, but how often can one eat that? And to prepare the proper stuffing for *booby rôti à la normande* is so time-consuming. *Booby au porto* is good, but with all that rich red wine and cream and mushrooms it might not be the ideal dish for such a hot climate. No doubt they preferred the simpler *booby au vin;* but to ring the changes they probably had *booby en cocotte bonne femme,* so delicious with the tiny sweet onions and crisp bacon slices, and the hearty *booby sauté chasseur,* and *booby Mornay gratiné* with its delectable coating of cheese, and *booby grillé à la diable* with that wonderfully zesty mustard sauce and covered with bread crumbs, and that perennial favorite, the fine old-fashioned *fricassée de booby à l'ancienne.* But on extremely hot days they doubtless preferred to enjoy a cold dish—chilled aspic is always most acceptable—like *booby en gelée,* with crusty bread and a tossed green salad—but no matter how they prepared it, booby, booby, booby, day after day, must have been terribly dull for those poor men."

No one at the table laughed.

"But, Mr. Ebensten," said the lady next to me, appalled by my evident ignorance, "you don't understand: they had no cooking utensils on that island to roast and grill and boil—they had no fire—no sauces and wines and cheeses and spices—they only had the booby birds!"

I decided never again in America to be flippant and facetious. Irony is not generally appreciated or admired in the United States.

❖

Mr. Lindblad became so enthusiastic about the Galápagos Islands that he was determined to operate the first tourist cruise there. He put me in charge of it. When he had an idea for a new venture, nothing deterred him from putting his plans into effect. Those inhospitable islands were too remote, their wildlife was not spectacular enough to appeal to the traveling public, he was told. There was no ship to take tourists there—only a government vessel that transported convicts in chains to the prison on one of the islands. There were no guides; the Ecuadoran government would never grant permission for tourists to go; and even if a ship could be found, costs would be prohibitive. But Mr. Lindblad took no notice of all these objections. He heard of a forty-passenger ship in Chile, and we flew to Valparaíso and looked at it and chartered it to sail empty to Guayaquil, where the Galápagos cruise was to begin. The Ecuadoran government reluctantly granted permission to proceed. Naturalists who had visited the islands on yachts were enrolled to act as guides. The cost of the cruise was indeed very high, but Mr. Lindblad understood the growing interest in and demand for wildlife and nature vacations, and believed that there had to be at least forty people in the world who wanted to explore those fascinating, unique islands that Charles Darwin had visited in 1835 during his cruise in HMS *Beagle* and of which he had written in *On the Origin of Species* that they were the origin of all his views: "Here we seem to be brought somewhat near to that great fact—that mystery of mysteries—the first appearance of new beings on earth."

Mr. Lindblad relished the tales about Dr. Ritter, and about the self-styled baroness and her two young lovers and other eccentric early settlers, some of whom, like the indomitable Mrs. Margaret Wittmer, still lived there; but he realized that it was not the prospect of being able to wander among the lava rocks and cacti where these quaint characters had made love and quarreled and died mysteriously, or of meeting their surviving relicts, that was the irresistible attraction of the Galápagos Islands, but their great importance to anyone with a feeling for nature, the strangeness of their flora and fauna, and the tameness of the animals and birds, which are without fear of man there.

As usual, he was right. The cruise was quickly fully booked; and in the following year we organized three cruises on a larger ship. "But everyone who wanted to see the Galápagos Islands went with you last year!" cried the Cassandras. We held our breath, and soon *those* cruises were fully booked. The Galápagos Islands, of which few people had heard, had become a major tourist destination.

When I left Lindblad Travel to open my own travel company, I operated Galápagos Islands cruises in a traditional three-masted schooner, the *Golden Cachalot,* which its British owners had handsomely converted to accommodate a dozen passengers. It provided the best and a truly civilized way for discriminating travelers to cruise among and explore the islands at leisure, and did least to harm their delicate environment. Rockefellers and Roosevelts, senators and socialites, saw the islands on these cruises; but by 1975, when my travel programs for men were becoming extremely popular, I felt that the time had come to be more ambitious. The sixty-eight-passenger MV *Iguana,* an old and hurriedly converted ship, had been positioned at the islands, and by chartering it for eight days I was able to offer a Galápagos Islands cruise for men at remarkably low rates. Mr. Lindblad had proved right when he predicted that there must be at least forty people who wanted to see the wildlife of these islands with him; I hoped that now there would be sixty gay men who wanted to see them with me.

Brian Kenny and I went to see Mr. Eduardo Proano, the owner of the MV *Iguana* and of Metropolitan Touring in Quito, Ecuador. He had practically the monopoly of tourism to the Galápagos Islands, and I had known him many years. I explained that I wanted to charter his ship for a cruise and that the passengers would be men—homosexual men. He had heard that I was operating travel programs for such men but was considerably astonished. Were such men interested in seeing wildlife? I told him that I believed that many of them were. He was reluctant to fill his ship with passengers of this kind; but I assured him that the men would be just as eager to see the birds, animals, and marine life of the islands as any other travelers, and be equally or more appreciative, that they would include teachers, doctors, lawyers, professors, all eminently respectable men, that we would even have a naturalist lecturer with us.

"I will have to warn Captain Ayala about these special passengers of yours," he said. "He will not like it, nor the officers and the crew. We are a very Catholic country, you know."

I refrained from pointing out that many of my men would doubtless be Catholics, but assured him that my cruise members' conduct would not offend the susceptibilities of the captain, officers, or crew. "But you must tell them," I said, "to be prepared to see some of the men holding hands"—and to illustrate this possibility I reached out and took Brian Kenny's hand as we sat side by side in front of his desk.

Mr. Proano went scarlet with horror, as shocked and distressed as if we had defecated on his fine office carpet. He looked with great fear at the closed office door. "Please, please—*no!* Someone might come in!" he cried.

I hurriedly released Brian's hand. I should have heeded Mr. Proano's reaction as a warning; but in my eagerness to arrange the cruise I dismissed it as insignificant and thought it merely amusing.

The Galápagos Islands were an established tourist goal by then and the men's cruise in the MV *Iguana* was soon fully booked. Our naturalist lecturer, Justin Aldrich of the New England Aquarium in Boston, prepared a fine dossier of notes on the history, geologic structure, and appearance of the islands, with checklists of the animals, birds, and marine creatures, and charts showing their distribution at the different islands, which we sent to the cruise members so that they could properly prepare themselves.

There was something odd about the reservation of one of the passengers. His index-card record indicated that he had responded to us as a result of an advertisement in *Natural History* magazine for the *Golden Cachalot* schooner cruises that were *not* for gay men; and when he sent in his application for travel insurance, he listed his wife as beneficiary. This was not unusual, but when his wife telephoned twice to check on his travel arrangements, and when a daughter sent a check to cover the cost of putting a bottle of champagne in his cabin, together with a "Bon Voyage" card handpainted by his twin grandchildren, I became uneasy. I telephoned him on a pretext and asked him whether he understood that the cruise for which he had booked was for men only.

"Yes," he said. "I understand that."

"And these men are—well, homosexuals."

"Oh, I know all that. I was in the navy. I'm not gay; but my wife and family are urging me to go—I'm losing my eyesight fast and have to see those islands before I'm quite blind. I've shopped around, and your cruise costs less than any of the others, and I don't care with whom I see those islands as long as I see them soon. I take it you're not going to discriminate against me and cancel me off?"

I assured him that I was of course delighted to have him with us.

✧

Mr. Eduardo Proano had told me that his company's guides in Quito refused to be assigned to my group when he explained the nature of it; finally he had managed to persuade one of them, a married woman, to take on the job. "But at the first sign of any impropriety, I'll leave them," she had told him.

She was at the Quito airport to meet us. "Are these the homos?"

she asked me, incredulous. "But they are all *men*!" She had expected to see sixty-eight freaks swishing off the plane, heavily rouged, their lips bright with lipstick, hands on hips—the South American conception of homosexuals. Instead she saw many tall, rugged, bearded men in blue jeans and boots and chunky sweaters. "Are they all really homos?" she asked.

"All except one, María," I told her. "But I will not tell you who he is."

She immediately relaxed, and within a few hours loved the entire group; and because she was efficient, knowledgeable, and also a very funny and amusing lady, the cruise members all loved her.

Next day we drove with her in two motor coaches to the Equatorial Monument some miles out of the city, where the men arranged themselves around her and posed for the traditional group photograph. "This picture will ruin your reputation, María," someone said.

"No, it will ruin *yours*," she promptly replied.

It was there that one of the cruise members, an accountant from Virginia, took me aside. It was apparent to me that he was considerably agitated. "You must get me home," he said. "I've got to get away from here."

I asked him what had happened—had he received bad news from home? Was he ill? Was there anything wrong with the tour arrangements? Had anyone upset him? No, he said, nothing like that—"But all these guys are *queers*! I had no idea it would be like this—you never told me!"

I tried to calm him and asked where he had heard about the cruise. "In your ads, in *After Dark*," he said. *After Dark* was a glossy monthly magazine that covered New York opera, ballet, and theater, reported on chic discos and bars and fashionable restaurants and elegant men's fashions. Its readers were gay men who could safely leave it on their coffee tables for mothers and cleaning ladies to see and think that their son or employer was interested in New York's nightlife. I advertised my gay travel programs in it with great success, and I explained to the accountant that when we received responses from *After Dark* readers, we automatically assumed them to be gay and issued a blue index card for them. People who responded to our advertisements in *Natural History, Audubon,* and *The New Yorker* magazines were given white index cards.

"I am truly sorry for the misunderstanding," I said, "but you seem to have the distinction of being the only nongay reader of *After Dark.* Didn't you suspect anything when you saw that the cruise was for men only?"

"I had no idea that the men would all be *queers,*" he said. "I subscribe to *After Dark* because I'm keen on the theater."

"But you are obviously also keen on seeing the wildlife of the Galápagos Islands," I said. "And you *will* see it with us—so does it matter who the other passengers are? After all, no one is going to molest you."

"I can't stand their attention-grabbing attitude, all that posturing and giggling," he said.

I had an inspiration. "It so happens that we have another cruise member with us who is not gay. He knew it was a gay group, but our dates and the price suited him and he had no hesitation in joining us. We match up cabin mates according to age, and he is quite a bit older than you; but would it help if I changed the cabin assignment and put him and you together?"

"Well, yes, that would help," he said.

On the first evening of the cruise, as the light was fading, I saw him on deck still with his checklist in his hand, peering through his binoculars and trying to identify the seabirds. "Is everything all right?" I asked.

"Yes, I think so. I'm glad you persuaded me to stay. This is a learning experience for me in more ways than I had expected," he said. "But when you get back to your office, please be sure to change my index file to a white one." (I did, and he later joined several of my wildlife tours that were *not* for men only.)

✧

During dinner, the ship's naturalist guide played the guitar. Michel Kaisin was a stunning-looking big blond Belgian, and he had never had an audience as appreciative as this. On other cruises, the passengers ignored his background music as they ate and discussed the flora and fauna they had seen that day; but the gay men responded enthusiastically, banged spoons, stamped feet, noisily sang along with him, and demanded he play favorite songs. Michel was mightily pleased with their admiration and attention; but Captain Ayala, at whose table I sat, was far from happy. He was accustomed to gentle, docile passengers; he had been led to expect that this week's passengers would be soft, timid creatures, and easily cowed by his authority. Instead, all these boisterous, uninhibited men worried him. They could so easily, if they chose to do so, take over his ship. His twenty stunted little crew members were no match for these big tough-looking gringos. He scowled.

After dinner, there was taped music in the lounge; and some of the men began to dance—not cheek to cheek, naturally, but alone and in twos, threes, or more, stomping and swaying and gyrating sensuously. The barman looked on, at first with fascination, and then, clearly disconcerted, left the lounge and returned after a while with one of the officers. Some of the dancers attempted to persuade him to dance with them. He fled, and came back with Captain Ayala, who took one look at the activities and pulled a master switch that plunged the lounge into darkness and stopped the music. The party was over. The men were less chagrined than amused, and made their way to their cabins. It was, in any case, time to sleep—we were to go ashore at eight next morning at Punta

Espinoza to see the marine iguanas swarming in their thousands on
the black lava rocks.

The Galápagos Islands lie on the equator, and it was customary
during the cruises on the MV *Iguana* for passengers to be subjected
to a "Crossing the Line" ceremony at which the guides, assisted by
crew members, humiliated the passengers in varying degrees. I disapproved of this degrading practice, but I realized that many cruise
members enjoyed it in a perverse way. Instead of the usual, tasteless
ceremony on board, I arranged with the gorgeous Michel that on
the day when the cruise members were on the beach at Sullivan Bay,
he would be rowed ashore from the anchored MV *Iguana* in his King
Neptune cloak with his crown and triton, officially to greet and
welcome the passengers to his realm and to accept their homage.
Brian Kenny and Fred Clayton, dressed as pirates, accompanied
him in the boat and waded ashore and beckoned to the men to come
and kneel before him; Michel looked most impressive and played
his role well. The cruise members were very pleased with this unexpected and decorous ceremony. "I will give you all your certificates
tonight!" called out King Neptune as he was rowed back to the
ship.

These certificates had been designed for the occasion by A. Jay,
the creator of the "Popperman" cartoon strip, and they featured a
naked, muscular, and extremely well endowed Neptunus Rex with
an anchor tattoo on his shoulder. After dinner, when I called out
each of the cruise members' names and Brian and Fred distributed
the certificates, Captain Ayala showed great displeasure and pointedly walked out of the room to avoid being contaminated by them.

No other incidents occurred to cause me uneasiness. The cruise
was a success. The men were thrilled to find the wildlife as tame and
easily approachable as it had been described; they began to identify
the different varieties of finches, were vastly amused by the courting
dance of the quaint blue-footed boobies, by the pathetic flapping of

the flightless cormorants' rudimentary wings, by the sexy big scarlet neck pouch of the male frigate birds, excited by the sight of pink
flamingos rising from the crater lake on James Island, and by the
cute penguins. They swam with the seals and snorkeled among
dolphins; they hiked along the beaches between dozing sea lions;
they climbed the five-hundred-foot tuff cone on Bartolomé Island
and then, screaming, slid down its sandy sides. They attended Justin Aldrich's lectures, and many of them were the most-interested,
best-informed passengers Michel Kaisin had ever conducted on his
field trips. He felt flattered by their attention and was indulgent
with those of them who insisted on sitting down on the backs of the
giant tortoises—the *galápagos,* who had given their name to the
islands—and being photographed as they were carried about by
these slow-moving, lugubrious beasts.

At Academy Bay on Santa Cruz Island, the small settlement and
site of the Charles Darwin Research Station, where we were to be
received and shown around, the entire population was out to see us
come ashore. They had been led to believe that they would see a
collection of a weird species of *Homo sapiens* unknown to them, but
as we were dressed and behaved much the same as other tourists and
were only a little more animated and noisy, they were sadly disappointed in us. We were not the circus they had expected.

I was well satisfied with the success of the cruise and gratified
to receive many testimonials from its participants. It was especially
delightful to hear from my favorite among the cruise members, a
spectacularly good-looking and much-admired long-haired construction worker from Kokomo, Indiana, who had discovered his
true sexual orientation only a few months previously and was outrageously promiscuous. "You and Mr. Kenny and Mr. Clayton were
very tolerant of 63 queens, 2 straights, and 1 stud who is looking
forward to new adventures with you," he wrote.

It was all most encouraging.

But then, two weeks later, when the leader of my latest schooner cruise group returned from the Galápagos Islands, she reported that in Quito, in Guayaquil, at Academy Bay, and when talking with the skippers and crew of other yachts that were moored close to the *Golden Cachalot,* she had been told that the men's cruise in the MV *Iguana* had been a total disaster. No one had been specific, but all agreed that a cruise with gay passengers would never again be permitted to operate.

I was amazed and perplexed. I had not forgotten Captain Ayala's displeasure at seeing our mildly erotic "Crossing the Line" certificates and his abrupt turning-off of the lights and the music in the lounge; I remembered that I had occasionally detected the smell of marijuana and amyl nitrite emerging from a cabin or on the top deck at night, and that some of the younger cruise members had sometimes seemed strangely disoriented and, with glazed eyes, had had to be helped by their friends out of the dining room or lounge to their cabins, and that a few others had astonished me when they appeared oddly aggressive and loud from their preprandial nap but a few minutes later became quiet and as amiable as before.

I had not forgotten, but could not believe that these unimportant and rare incidents, which might have been grossly exaggerated in the telling, were causing my popular and profitable cruise to be denounced in Ecuador and at the Galápagos Islands as having been a *disaster.* Had something else occurred, of which I was not aware?

Six weeks later, Mr. Eduardo Proano came to see me in New York. He was embarrassed but told me that he would never again charter his ship to me for a group of what he called "this special clientele of yours."

"You told me," he said, "that these men might hold hands in public—but they did much more than that. They were seen to put arms around each other, even to *kiss*! When music was played in the lounge, some of them *danced* together! Dear Hanns, I like you, I like doing business with you, but I cannot permit such behavior on my ship. Captain Ayala will not tolerate it again."

"But, Eduardo—" I began.

"And something more: the captain reports that many of these men smoked cigarettes which were not normal cigarettes—something with a strong smell, a drug—and some of them had small metal tubes hanging on chains around their necks, and they inhaled from these—again a very strong, bad smell—another drug. We cannot permit this; the crew has protested—they will not serve such special clients again."

It was a shock to me to hear that the underpaid Ecuadoran crew members, who depended so desperately on their tips for survival, would rather go on strike than clean cabins and serve meals for passengers whose sexual orientation was repellent to them. But it was, at the same time, humbling to be reminded that acceptance cannot be bought, that respect must be earned by good behavior. No matter how loudly the marchers in the parades down the streets of New York and San Francisco chanted "Gay is good! Gay is great!" the Ecuadoran seamen did not hear it.

I am not a prude, and believe that every man and woman must be allowed to do in private what he or she desires; but I had to admit to myself that there had been something not quite right, something faintly unsavory, about my gay cruise. It seemed, in retrospect, almost as if I had used the attractions of the Galápagos Islands, with their unique wildlife, as a spurious enticement to gather together a group of men for a week of dissipation aboard a cruise ship, that it was not the sight of the iguanas, the thirteen varieties of finches, the booby birds and the flightless cormorants, and swimming with the seals that appealed chiefly to many of the passengers, but the opportunity for sharing illegal substances and for illicit couplings below-decks.

I did not like it. I was in the business of planning and conducting interesting, meaningful travel programs, not promoting hedonist excursions, either for gay men or for anyone else.

"You cannot control a group of sixty men," said Mr. Proano. "You cannot keep your promise to vouch for their good conduct. If you want to cater to such men, take a small ship—we have many fine yachts available—bring ten such men, a dozen, and then there will be no objection."

He was a good businessman and did not want to lose me entirely as a customer; but I realized that he was right. I never again handled a group of more than two dozen travelers. The cruise in the sixty-eight-passenger MV *Iguana* taught me a salutary lesson not to cast my net too wide. Twelve, eighteen, even twenty-four people who have the desire to see the same places, at the same time, in the same way, can be brought together and with adroit leadership formed into a journeying group of friends, considerate travel companions, a family party. A larger group remains a vulgar crowd, an unwieldy horde, a common herd. To fill a ship with sixty or six hundred or three thousand people and organize them every minute of the day from morning to late at night, feed them five enormous meals each day, entertain them with gambling and stage shows, and set them down for a few hours at some port of call for a little superficial sight-seeing and a great deal of shopping is exceedingly profitable for the shipping companies, and popular, but is a travesty of what travel should be.

Even on the historic SS *Hermes* cruise to the Black Sea in 1958, it was only the members of the snobbishly exclusive circle of a dozen friends and their acquaintances who traveled in style. The other passengers, though never herded together and processed as those on today's pleasure cruises, seemed to be a race apart.

Even the hundred rich passengers of the world's most choice cruising vessel are a pathetic lot when I see them being herded like sheep around the ruins of Delos in the Aegean, proudly wearing shirts and hats and carrying tote bags with their prestigious ship's name and emblem. "There's nothing to buy here except postcards!" I hear them complain.

My Galápagos cruise in 1975 decided me not to expand my business, not to follow the pattern set by Mr. Thomas Cook, the inventor of commercial tourism, not to emulate even the inventive tours and cruises of Mr. Lars-Eric Lindblad, which, in order to be profitable, had to be planned for ever increasingly large groups. Mass tourism repelled me; I would be more selective and try to find travelers who were interested in wildlife and archaeology, who wanted to climb mountains and cross deserts and jungles, who were not seeking to have what others consider having a good time. I would remain a maverick and plan travel programs the way I wanted to travel, to the places I wanted to see, and hope that there would always be a small number of compatible people who would join me in these endeavors.

11

WHO

WAS

NICK?

THE SOVIET UNION—that "evil empire," as President Reagan called it—held a sinister fascination for the Western traveler who was reared on sensationalized spy novels and films. During my many visits between the 1950s and the 1980s, I never found it as spooky as many people imagined it to be; nor was the tourist as regimented and restricted as those who were never there insisted that he or she was. It was strange, certainly, and therein lay much of its appeal; but the people were invariably welcoming and always ready not only to give lost travelers directions back to the hotel but actually to go far out of their way and take them to it, always eager to link arms and drink to friendship. Their country had been invaded and ravaged by Sweden in 1709, by France in 1812, by Germany in 1914 and 1940. They had enough of war and feared it; they wanted only peace, peace, peace. Had they and America not fought together against a common enemy in two world wars?

All visitors, in varying degrees, felt an uncomfortable but exhilarating atmosphere—a mixture of suspicion, fear, distrust. There were rumors and substantiated reports of horrible Gulag detention camps and torture and assassinations, but the tourist was given a very good time. Everything worked. The waiters in the hotels knew that if one was going to the ballet, the first dinner course had to be on the table at 6:40 P.M., the bus left promptly at 7:40 P.M., and the curtain rose exactly at 8:05 P.M. And despite all the reservations one may have had about communism and the Soviet régime, one had to admire a nation that in the face of overwhelming odds had taken infinite trouble and spared no expense to meticulously, lovingly rebuild and restore to their former splendor the palaces of the past rulers whom they despised.

What the majority of tourists saw in the Soviet Union was neither exotic nor very different from anything in Western Europe. Leningrad (as it was then named) is an entirely European city, and a very lovely one, built largely by Italian architects; Odessa could be mistaken for Brooklyn, and Kiev for a cathedral city in Bavaria or Austria; the resorts in the Crimea and in the Caucasus are plebeian versions of those along the coasts of Spain and Italy. Only Moscow comes up to expectations, is indeed the Third Rome, is, as Napoléon said of it, "the Asiatic capital of a great empire with its innumerable churches in the form of Chinese pagodas."

In 1983, when I was in Moscow with one of my groups of men, the state travel organization, Intourist, had begun to understand that foreigners came to see the fifteenth-century icons in the Tretiakov Gallery, not the display of farm tractors in the Park of Economic Development, that they wanted to visit museums and ancient churches and elegant palaces, not shoe factories, that they expected to be provided with tickets for opera and ballet performances, not for amateur folk-dance events. But in those days, before the freedom that Mr. Gorbachev brought about, long before the demise of the Soviet Union, it was still officially frowned upon—if not actually against the law—for a foreign visitor to speak to Soviet citizens or to stray from the regulated tour program or to make any purchases except in the government-owned dollar stores. Soviet people were not allowed to enter the tourist hotels; and it was almost incredible to me, having been accustomed during thirty years to be strictly separated from Russian people, when after *perestroika* and *glasnost* the invisible barriers were suddenly down and the hotels filled with adroit young Russian entrepreneurs who circulated freely in the lobbies at all hours of the day and night and invited tourists up to their rooms, which they had turned into emporiums stocked with everything that was previously forbidden or unobtainable: the best caviar and champagne, watches, jewelry, and furs. They spoke half a dozen languages, and their manner was so streetwise that it was assumed that they were quite willing to sell their bodies, like their merchandise, to both male and female tourists.

Prostitutes were even bolder. They plied their trade in the hotel elevators, wearing provocative, abbreviated Western-style clothes and covered with Estée Lauder makeup. It was a revival of the decadent but entertaining days of Berlin in the permissive 1920s.

But in 1983 all this was unknown and could not be envisaged. The Soviet Union, if not an evil empire, was no place like home. Two members of my group, American physicians, had for years corresponded with a Moscow lady doctor in their field, and telephoned her. She was terrified to hear that they were calling her from their hotel room. "Never do that again! Always only from a public telephone!" They suggested a meeting in the hotel, but she was amazed at their lack of taking proper precautions. "It is strictly forbidden. It would cost me my job." She told them to meet her in the subway station opposite the hotel, from where they took a walk in the bitter cold in the Park of Economic Development.

On our first evening in Moscow, we were taken to see a performance of three ballets at the Moscow Art Theater—the Bolshoi, as always at that time, was "impossible"; worthy Soviet workers were given all the tickets. We did not sit together; instead of supplying a block of tickets for a group, Intourist provided one, two, or three seats in different parts of the house for all opera, ballet, and circus performances, and I did my best to arrange for friends to sit together, and always took one of the tickets for a single seat, which on this evening was in the third row of the stalls.

At the end of the third ballet, as I made my way up the aisle, someone asked me in perfect English, "Did you enjoy it? Was *Les Patineurs* not the best of the three?"

I looked up. He was a magnificent creature, a man well over six feet tall, very blond, tanned, with dark eyes and eyebrows, wearing that prized status symbol of the Soviet Union, a pair of bleached, tight, button-fly Levi's, and a sweater that had a Western and most expensive look to it.

The crowd was dense, and progress up the aisle and to the vestibule was slow. How surprised my tour members will be, I thought, when they see me with this wonderful-looking man—and I was gratified by the appreciative looks on the faces of the first members of my group when I introduced my acquaintance to them.

"This is Nick," I said, "and these are my friends Tom and Jim from San Diego in California."

Nick went to claim his parka at the cloakroom. "My God, Hanns, your beau is gorgeous; you've hit the jackpot, haven't you?" said young Tom and sweet Jim. I told them it was all part of the tour; he was my gift to them—a real, live, big Russian.

When we were all assembled with our topcoats in the theater vestibule, Nick announced that he would come to the Hotel Cosmos with us. No one had mentioned the name of our hotel, and I wondered how he knew where we were staying.

The bars of the Cosmos were by that late hour unattended and in semidarkness, but bottles of champagne could be bought at inflated prices in the hotel lobby; and although all the glasses were locked up, I found thick coffee mugs hanging in rows behind the bar counter, so we drank the warm champagne out of them.

Nick had thrown off his bulky ski parka and sat well back on a settee with his long legs stretched out and thrust far apart, one fly button of his Levi's tantalizingly undone in the approved American manner, and pushed up the sleeves of his sweater. I felt certain that he was quite aware of the sensation this seemingly simple action created: every member of the group almost gasped at the enticing, provocative sight of those gloriously muscled forearms, which held out the promise of equally sensuous upper arms, shoulders, torso, legs. Every one of us, young and old, fantasized to be held close and tight in those superb suntanned arms—suntanned, in *Moscow,* in *November,* when every other Russian was sickly pale and flabby on a diet of potatoes and cabbage!

Who was this godlike creature? He was too good to be real—he was a fictional hero, the stunningly handsome Russian with whom James Bond battled to the death on the ski slopes and at five hundred meters below the surface of a shark-infested tropical sea; he was a wildly idealized Quaintance painting, an impossibly erotic Tom of Finland drawing come to life. He told us that he was a gymnastic instructor, and a ski teacher in the winter, that he was twenty-eight years of age and unmarried, that he had learned his excellent English "here and there." I wondered which of my tour members would try to entice him to bed—and might even succeed—and then, to my astonishment and considerable confusion, I felt his large brown hand press harder and more firmly against my thigh and to my crotch. It was not unwelcome, far from it, but it was so unexpected, so incongruous, as to make me flush not with pleasure but with acute embarrassment. I was, after all, sixty years old!

Despite the gloom in the bar, my dear tour members may have noticed Nick's roaming hand, and ever so politely, diplomatically, no doubt with great regrets, one by one and in pairs they left us, so that presently Nick and I sat alone on the settee in the deserted bar.

"Now we go to bed," said Nick.

But common sense and experience and inclination all combined to convince me that we would do nothing so foolish or potentially dangerous. First of all, I viewed this stranger's intentions with great suspicion. Why had he selected me? Why had he not taken advantage of the openly expressed admiration of the other tour members—of one of the attractive young men like Tom or Jim or, if he intended to be paid adequately for his favors, of the older men with hundred-dollar neckties and ten-thousand-dollar wristwatches? His air of assurance and sophistication, his fine command of English, all indicated that Nick could surely recognize such signs of wealth. Why did he wish to become involved with me—the tour leader, always the least-affluent member of any group?

Second, even when I was young I had felt that it was simply not worth it for a moment of pleasure or a brief thrill to make myself vulnerable, to place myself in a situation where I could be overpowered and robbed, beaten, injured, even killed.

And third, in the Hotel Cosmos—in the heart of the Soviet Union—in the enemy's camp—in the evil empire—it was out of the question for a tour leader who wanted to be able to return again and again to take such a chance.

Last, and most persuasive of all, was the abhorrence I felt for taking a stranger to my neat room, a man who would throw his clothes onto the floor and onto chairs, and use my bathroom, maybe even turn on the radio. I wanted to go to bed quietly and without complications and eat a piece of chocolate to calm myself and turn out the light and hug my teddy bear and fall asleep.

I thanked Nick for his offer and told him that I felt highly flattered but that it was impossible. "The floor lady will not permit it," I said.

"Oh," he said, "the floor lady on the right side on the twenty-fourth floor is my friend; there will be no problem. Come, we go up!"

How did he know my floor? No one had mentioned it. My suspicions increased. Despite his sensuous grin and the suggestive way in which he thrust his hands between his thighs, I remained firm. It was not easy, and he was so persistent that at one moment, when he took my hand and hooked his large, spatulate fingers through mine, and with their tips pressed hard into my palm, I almost succumbed to temptation; but I insisted that he must leave. I walked across the hotel lobby with him and watched as he slowly, slowly pulled on his parka; I shook hands with him passionately, cursed myself for being so stupid, and bade him good-bye at the guarded glass door of the hotel.

✧

Next morning my tour members wanted to hear all the details of my tryst with the irresistible Nick, and did not believe me when I described how we had parted in the lobby.

"How *could* you, Hanns!" they cried.

That evening, as we arrived at the Hall of Congress in the Kremlin for Prokofiev's opera *War and Peace*, they called out delightedly, "There's your beau, Hanns!" And it was true: there was Nick, in his tight Levi's and sweater, a foot taller than anyone else, waiting for us in the lobby and grinning at me. He walked me to my seat. "I cannot sit with you, but I will meet you in the interval and we go for champagne and caviar up to the restaurant," he said.

There is always a mad rush by the thousands of members of the audience to reach the restaurant on the top floor during intervals— it is very much the thing to do, in Moscow, to drink a glass of champagne and eat a caviar sandwich there—but although Nick raced me up the series of escalators and most of my tour members followed close behind us, the restaurant was already packed when we reached it, with long lines formed at the bar where the obligatory treats were for sale.

Nick took one look at the situation. "Wait here," he told us, and with a great air of command walked boldly behind the bar, gave a brief order, and instantly, glasses of champagne were placed on a silver tray, caviar sandwiches on another, and both were brought to us. It was an amazing and highly effective coup de theatre, but perplexing. No one asked for payment.

"My God, Hanns—your beau is KGB!" whispered the tour members.

It seemed to me a ludicrous, terribly farfetched explanation of Nick's authoritative action, but in the highly charged atmosphere of the Soviet Union, anything was possible—and it was certainly odd, to say the least, that Nick knew that I lived in Key West, since neither I nor any of the tour members had mentioned this, and that he was so fascinated with the place. "It is your great naval base facing Cuba—so close also to Nicaragua—you send up spy balloons from there," he told me. How well informed he was, even if everything was not quite as he imagined it.

After the opera, when he had again waited for me in the lobby, he invited me to go with him to what he called "a theatrical café." I told him that as I was the tour leader, I could not leave the group and had to return to the hotel; but hoping to make at least one of my fellow travelers' cup of happiness run over, I asked Nick whether he would instead take with him the youngest member of our group, a Californian art historian who spoke some Russian and who was always ready for an adventure.

Next morning we others were all intrigued to know what had occurred. In the dim corners of the café some men had been petting, but Nick had shown himself more interested in asking questions about the United States and in finding a taxi to take our tour member back to the hotel than in any action. "But at least I got him to put his big red Russian tongue deep down my throat," said the disappointed art historian.

"Oh, poor Hanns," sighed my tour members in mock commiseration. "Your beau has been unfaithful to you. Those KGB men are so fickle!"

This was our last day in the Soviet Union, and we had our tour farewell dinner at the Slavianskii Bazar, a favorite restaurant of Moscovites and almost entirely unknown to foreigners. It was opened in 1870, when French décor and food were all the rage, but, as an innovation, was decorated in Russian style and served only Russian dishes, as it has done ever since. It became the meeting place of the intelligentsia; and the writers Chekhov and Tolstoy, the composers Tchaikovsky and Rimsky-Korsakov, and the great singer Chaliapin all patronized it. On June 21, 1898, the theatrical producers Nemirovich-Danchenko and Stanislavsky dined there, from 2:00 P.M. to 8:00 A.M. next morning, and during their long conversation founded the Moscow Art Theater.

The restaurant now seats six hundred people, and to dine there is considered a rare treat by Muscovites; birthdays and weddings are celebrated in the private dining rooms that overlook the large main restaurant below, where the band is; and pitchers of kvass stand on all the tables beside baskets filled with rolls baked in the shape of padlocks, salads in sour cream, and *pirozhki* stuffed with meat. The service is lethargic, and always was—it has been said that the length of Nemirovich-Danchenko and Stanislavsky's conversation was presumably due to other causes than slow service.

One of the private rooms was reserved for us, and I sat next to Olga, the Intourist guide who had looked after us throughout our tour from Leningrad to Kiev to Moscow, and I took the opportunity to ask her—as I had so often previously asked other Intourist guides—to what extent, if any, we foreign visitors were permitted to socialize with Soviet citizens. It had puzzled me for years. "Of course it is permitted!" she cried. "We are a free country!" I mentioned our doctors' colleague, who had been so afraid to come to our hotel and did not want to be telephoned from it; and I told her that a presentable young Russian had come to the hotel with us for drinks, and had met us again at the theater next evening, but that we sensed something forbidden, something secretive, in these meetings, as if either he or we were doing something wrong, which we certainly did not wish to do, although that young man had not wanted to change money or buy blue jeans, which we knew to be illegal activities.

"Of course you are permitted to meet!" said Olga indignantly. And at that moment, as in a play, the door of our private dining room opened and Nick stood before us, smiling at us.

I was disconcerted, to say the least. I was certain that no member of the group had told him where we were having dinner.

"This is the young man I mentioned," I said to Olga, and had a chair pulled up for him between her and me, and offered him fruit and a glass of wine. The tour members were very surprised to see Nick again, for the third time, so unexpectedly. He and Olga chatted away in Russian; he seemed to be asking her what theatrical performances we had seen in Leningrad and Kiev.

The door of the dining room was thrown open again, and two burly men in dark suits walked fast around the table.

"Police," Nick hissed to me as they expertly grabbed him and led him out of the room—so quickly and efficiently that most of my tour members, engaged in conversation, did not notice the incident, and the others assumed that two unusually heavy waiters had summoned Nick to the telephone.

I begged Olga to go after them. I assured her again that Nick had done nothing wrong, nothing illegal, had neither offered to change rubles into dollars nor wanted to buy blue jeans. She shrugged, as though she had seen it all before. "I could do nothing," she said when she returned. "They have gone."

There was nothing further to be said.

After dinner, as always on the last evening of my tours in Russia, I led the group out of the restaurant along the quiet lanes of the Kitai Gorod, the oldest part of Moscow, and then around a corner and, to the surprise of all those who had lost their sense of direction, into Red Square, which is so large that it can accommodate two million people but is almost deserted at night, with only some dozens of old women in white overalls sweeping it clean with birch brooms, and the Red Army guards outside Lenin's Tomb. The massive walls and Gothic towers of the Kremlin and the multicolored cupolas and spires of Saint Basil's Cathedral were floodlit, the huge red-crystal stars on the turrets glowed like vast jewels in the sky. To make the scene quite picture-postcard perfect, snow fell in gentle, soft flakes. It was, as always, a stupendous, magical sight. We were indeed at the very heart of that ancient and sacred Asiatic capital of a great empire that had enticed Napoléon so disastrously to it.

"What are we here for?" asked one of my tour members querulously. "We've been here before."

"But not at night," I pointed out patiently. "And not on our last evening in Russia."

"It's cold here," said my tour member.

We walked out of Red Square to our bus, which was waiting for us outside the Kitai Gorod wall, and drove back to our hotel around Dzerzhinski Square and past the tall, unpleasantly mustard-colored building of the Lubyanka, the headquarters of the dreaded State Security Committee of the Soviet Union, the KGB, with its prisons and interrogation rooms.

"That's where your beau is, Hanns," said my tour members. "In a cell, for not getting you into bed with him. Now they'll have to get another spy to count the sailors in Key West!"

✦

So what was it all about? Did the KGB, in the paranoiac way that has been attributed to that organization, learn from Intourist that I was bringing groups of homosexuals to the Soviet Union; and were they really so naïve as to try to compromise me in order to have someone pliable in Key West—that "great naval base facing Cuba—so close also to Nicaragua"—in case one day, if war broke out in the Caribbean, they needed him to tell them if there was an unusual number of sailors in Key West—more naval vessels—more planes at the Boca Chica Naval Air Station—more spy balloons taking off into the blue sky? Were they so well informed about my tastes that instead of tempting me with a pretty boy, the stereotype imagined to be the old homosexual's dream, they had assigned this mature, almost menacingly athletic gymnast to recruit me?

Or was my tour members' talk of the KGB a fantasy induced by reading too many spy novels, seeing too many spy films? Was Nick merely a charming and unusually attractive man who happened to speak impeccable English and attended ballet and opera performances and wanted to make himself agreeable to an elderly foreign tourist? But if so, how was it that a gym instructor/ski teacher had the authority to give an order to provide us with instant service, free of charge, in the restaurant of the Hall of Congress? And who had briefed him about me, so that he knew that it would excite me so to have my fingers pressed hard? Was a hidden camera directed onto the bed in my room on the right side of the twenty-fourth floor in the Hotel Cosmos? Who were the two sinister men who had hustled Nick away in that melodramatic way from our farewell dinner, and why had they done so?

Why had this whole elaborate charade been arranged to snare a totally insignificant, useless old tour leader? Was I astute or foolish to have rejected my last chance of an illicit romance—and with the most gorgeous man in all of Russia?

Can someone please tell me what it was all about?

Who was Nick?

12

STAYING

WITH

THE

MONKS

FATHER PETROS LAVRIOTIS, the old guestmaster of Pantok-ratoros, had not been pleased with us the evening before. He had sternly reprimanded Mr. Bryce Carver and Dr. Earl Miller for sitting after supper in the courtyard under one of the orange trees and *talking*, and had been quite outraged when he saw Mr. Gordon Roland remove his shirt in order to wash his neck and chest. "You are not here in a hotel!" he cried. "This is a monastery. Saint Jerome tells us, 'He who is once washed by Christ need not wash again,' and the good Saint Anthony never changed his vest or washed his feet all his long life!"

But next morning he was most genial again; and when he brought us our tiny cups of thick, sweet coffee before we hiked away, he also proudly produced a large pile of warm toast. We greedily cleared the platter in no time. Each piece had a curious, semicircular portion cut out of it; and I asked him whether this had a religious significance.

"Oh, no," said Father Petros. "We monks are old, have no teeth;

last night we have bread with our soup, eat only the soft middles. I keep the other parts and toast for you."

✧

These most acceptable pieces of toast were one of the unexpected bonuses during my first visit in 1982 to the celebrated Mount Athos in northern Greece, the *Ayion Oros,* or Holy Mountain, of the ancients. It is a theocratic republic that occupies the easternmost of the three promontories of the Chalcidice Peninsula of Macedonia, forty miles long, where females—including female animals—have been forbidden since the edict of the emperor Constantine IX Monomachus in the year 1046. The edict is strictly enforced, but each time I visit Mount Athos I see cats—and kittens!

After the death of Jesus, the ship in which his mother, the Virgin Mary, was traveling to visit Lazarus in Cyprus was driven far off its course during a storm and cast ashore at a distant and incomparably lovely green coast with which Mary was delighted. "Let this be forever *my* country," she decreed, and so it is today; the visitor who arrives at the "Garden of the Blessed Virgin" as a traveler leaves it a humbled pilgrim and is not, as elsewhere in the world, looked upon as a walking wallet. Wealth and status are meaningless to the monks; religious belief is the only criterion by which they judge men. The brain surgeon with an income of a million dollars a year is seated with the other heretic visitors at the back of the refectory, and it is the poorly dressed merchant seamen from Chios who, being orthodox Christians, are given places of honor at the monks' tables.

To dine with the monks in their candle-lit Byzantine refectories and to attend the long and formalized services in their Byzantine churches, surrounded by frescoed saints whose gold-leaf halos glitter up high, by icons filling the walls and hanging from every pillar, must be a wonderful and spiritual experience for anyone who is religious. Even I, a Christian merely in name and not Orthodox, so that I am not permitted to enter a church there during a service but must witness the dawn Liturgy and Vespers as best I can from the back of the *leti,* waiting there for the great moment when the Holy Door in the glittering iconostasis is opened to reveal the altar beyond—even I understand the awe that the pagan emissaries of Vladimir, prince of Kiev, reported to him on the identical ceremonies in the seventh century: "We know not whether we were in heaven or on earth, for surely there is no such splendor or beauty anywhere upon earth. We cannot describe it to you: only this we know, that God dwells there among men, and that their service surpasses the worship of all other places."

The twenty monasteries of Mount Athos and their dependencies, the little toy-town capital of Kariés, the tiny port of entry, Daphne, and the scenery of the Holy Mountain have remained unchanged for many centuries, so that the glowing descriptions of early travelers are as valid today as when they were written. One of the first lay visitors to Mount Athos was the Honorable Robert Curzon, in 1837, whose chief interest was in the libraries of the monasteries, which housed thousands of manuscripts and early books and of which he bought as many as he could carry away, paying a pittance for them to the monks, who were ignorant of their value. He published his *Visits to the Monasteries of the Levant* in 1848 and described the scenery as "the most beautiful imaginable . . . the dark blue sea in the distance . . . odoriferous evergreen shrubs all around me . . . lofty hills covered with a dense forest of gigantic trees which extend to the base of the great white marble peak of the mountain . . . a succession of narrow valleys and gorges, each more picturesque than the other."

The Reverend H. F. Tozer, who visited Mount Athos in 1869, wrote of it that "nowhere in Europe can such a collection of jewelry and goldsmiths' work be found as is presented by the relics preserved in the different monasteries; nowhere can the Byzantine school of painting be studied with equal advantage; and some of the illuminated manuscripts are inestimable treasures of art. . . . The buildings of the monasteries are the most ancient existing specimens of domestic architecture; and within their walls the life of the Middle Ages is enacted before your eyes, with its manners and customs, dress and modes of thought and belief, absolutely unchanged. And it is no slight addition to the pleasure of a visit, that, in passing from one monastery to the other, you are surrounded by scenery unsurpassed, and hardly equalled, by any in Europe."

In this century, when travel to the Holy Mountain became less of an arduous undertaking, visitors still felt so special that most of them wrote books about their experiences, ranging from salacious tales of perversity among the monks to pedantic hour-by-hour accounts to the fine travel books of Robert Byron, in 1929, and Lord Norwich, the son of my old shipmate Lady Diana Cooper, in 1966. The latter wrote of his visit that it was one of the most memorable travel experiences of his life—as it was to be for me, sixteen years later—and that there, in the "Garden of the Blessed Virgin," nature herself seems virginal: "The entire peninsula has preserved a richness and luxuriance unique in Greece and perhaps in Europe. For nearly ten centuries, perhaps longer, the fields have lain ungrazed by cattle, the trees have escaped the ravages of goats, the flowers have had no children to pick them."

Only the venomous Australian novelist Mr. Patrick White found nothing to praise when he went there with his Greek lover, Manoly, in 1960. They were ignorant and quite unprepared; instead of carrying backpacks they brought along masses of bulky, heavy luggage, including a typewriter, and were shocked that no one would carry it. Nothing pleased this bitter man: the gorgeous Russian *skete* of Saint Andrew was "an inflated Fabergé object in chipped viridian"; failing to arrive at a monastery before sunset, they almost had the door slammed on them by "a big black bearded monk-queen." White complained endlessly about a fellow traveler's smelly socks. "We could not wait to get away." Why do the wrong people travel?

In the past nine hundred years, only two women have been granted the privilege of visiting the monasteries: a Byzantine queen, and Lady Stratford de Redcliffe, the wife of a British ambassador in Constantinople in the early nineteenth century (and of whom it was said that she ought to have known better). A French writer claimed in the 1920s to have cut off her breasts in order to visit the Holy Mountain, and wrote a book about her experiences, but was generally thought to have been an imposter. The closest that women may approach the Holy Mountain is on the excursion ships from Ouranoupolis, which must keep five hundred meters offshore and from which, with binoculars, they can inspect those monasteries at or near the shore.

Before boarding the daily small boat from Ouranoupolis to the Athonite entry port of Daphne, the port master confiscated my tour members' passports and our permits to visit the Holy Mountain; they would be returned to us at the government building up in Kariés. We found ourselves among a group of diverse men: a dozen or so monks, returning to their monasteries with bundles and packages; a Greek Orthodox bishop from Australia, on a pilgrimage; four Greek firemen looking forward to a free vacation—the monasteries make no charge for overnight accommodations and meals; and two beautiful youths from Athens who, they told us, had been invited by the monks of Stavronikita Monastery to stay with them and help with the grape harvest.

At Daphne, a small bus was waiting; it was at that time the only motor vehicle on the Holy Mountain, and its license plate read AO 1. There was a scramble for seats, and monks were given preference. Forty minutes later we were in Kariés, the small capital of this religious Ruritanian country, with a few shops selling provisions and religious handmade souvenirs, a rudimentary inn, a post office and a police station, and the impressive mansion of the government, above which fluttered the yellow flag with the double-headed eagle of the Byzantine Empire, which is also the flag of the Orthodox Church. Although the Holy Mountain forms part of Greece, it enjoys a considerable degree of autonomy, and the entire peninsula is the property of its twenty ruling monasteries. Seventeen of these are Greek, one Russian, one Serbian, and one Bulgarian; and they all have many dependencies, sketes and kellia, some of which are extremely large and at their period of greatest importance housed thousands of monks. In remote, wild mountain areas and in steep sea cliffs live hermits whose huts or caves can be reached only along precipitous trails and by means of wooden ladders.

While our passports and permits were being scrutinized at length by the authorities, we went to a workshop where monks made painstakingly accurate reproductions of Byzantine icons, which are sought after by Orthodox churches and museums all over the world. A magnificent visitors' book was presented to us. I signed my name immediately below the arrogantly large Gallic flourish of President Mitterand of France, who had recently placed an order for three paintings.

Our passports were returned with an impressive-looking document for each of us: the prized *diamonitirion,* duly stamped by four of the monasteries' representatives; it allowed us to spend four nights on the Holy Mountain as guests of the monks. By now it was late afternoon, and we had to set off at a brisk pace to reach our first monastery before sunset. Hiking on Mount Athos is a delight, for the trails are through forests of ancient oaks and walnuts and other trees, and during the next four days we all relished the unaccustomed ease of walking among lovely scenery, with the sea in view, and the towers of the monastery that was our goal growing nearer.

How soon we all forgot our past existence, how quickly we adapted ourselves to local conditions and were not twentieth-century travelers but medieval pilgrims; what simple, prosaic thoughts occupied our minds as we walked: What sort of meal would we receive? Would there be any fresh fruit? Would there be a mirror, enabling us to shave? Would the toilets be Western or Oriental? Would "the tray," with which visitors are welcomed on arrival at every monastery, have not only the tiny cups of thick coffee and glasses of water, but also little glasses of ouzo and the sweet *loukoum* for which we quickly acquired a craving?

There is no restriction on male Greek nationals visiting the Holy Mountain, but few take advantage of this opportunity, and only ten foreign visitors are granted permits for any day. Although most of the monks were welcoming, some questioned our presence and our intentions.

"Why have you come here?" asked the guestmaster at Koutloumetsou.

"To see your way of life," I replied through Adam, our guide and Byzantine expert.

"In four days you can learn no more than I can understand a book by looking at its cover," said the monk.

I told him that one can often learn at least something about a book by its cover.

In all the monasteries, the monks are much concerned that visitors adhere strictly to the regulations of this theocratic state. We were reminded again and again not to cross our arms behind our backs, not to put our hands in our trouser pockets, not to smoke except in the guest rooms, neither to laugh nor to sing, not to swim within sight of a monastery, not to play cards—I unknowingly caused great offense one afternoon before supper, while waiting outside a monastery on its belvedere overlooking the sea, when I played solitaire, that most innocent of pastimes.

I had briefed my nine tour members carefully to wear clothing that would be acceptable to the monks; and we were all appropriately dressed and somewhat startled at Stavronikita by the appearance of a young German who was garbed in what looked like a black sailor suit. He told us that he had made it himself. "You get better treatment on Athos if you wear black," he said. "Sometimes, even if you are not Orthodox, they let you into the church during the service and even show you some of their holy relics." He had made several visits and complained vehemently of the accommodations, the food, the sanitary conditions. "I threw my filthy pillow on the floor at Iveron and demanded the guestmaster to bring me a clean one."

I doubted that he had in fact spoken thus to the monk, but sympathized with him—Iveron's guest quarters were horrible, a penance to endure in order to see the superb library, the icon of the Virgin of the Gate (which the sea had miraculously deposited there), and the silver lemon tree with its thirty gilt lemons in the church, a gift from the czar of Russia in the 1820s. Elsewhere we did not encounter the hardships and tribulations of which the early travelers had written—the bigoted monks, verminous beds, foul food, and obnoxious insects.

On my first visit, my tour members and I were all prepared for such privations but pleasantly surprised to find conditions far less Spartan than the reports of earlier travelers had led us to believe; and on subsequent visits, we were astonished by the improvements of the guest quarters almost everywhere we went. At Great Lavra, at Xenophontos, at Dionysiou, we found cheerful guest rooms with such previously unknown luxuries as soft beds and tiled washrooms with spotless toilets and washbasins, hosed down twice daily by a rubber-clad attendant monk, which Tim and Tom, that clean-living pair from Minnesota, praised as being "as good as a country club."

On later visits, meals sometimes were culinary delights, particularly at Stavronikita on the north coast, the youngest of the twenty monasteries—it dates from A.D. 1533—which, with its neatness, orderliness, and ambience of a peaceful, tranquil university college, has become my favorite. We were always very happy there, and I regret that because this monastery is so small, it has no overnight accommodations for visitors. Most of its monks are young and hardworking, and one day they served us the most delectable ratatouille I have ever eaten, on fine pewter plates, accompanied by perfect goat cheese, excellent bread, and the monastery's own chilled white wine. Coffee was brought to us on the terrace in the shade of a giant grapevine, and then we were conducted to view the church with the holy mosaic icon of Saint Nicholas, which was found in the sea with an oyster shell stuck to the saint's forehead.

The greatest changes during the ten years of my visits have taken place in Dionysiou, perched on a steep rock some three hundred feet above the south coast. It looks forbidding from below, but it is inside its thick walls that its full solemnity is felt. The gaunt church fills the courtyard, leaving only a few feet—in some places, merely inches—between its blood-red walls and the surrounding buildings. It is a terrifying place, and on my first visit, in 1982, we were all frightened and repelled by the stern monks who moved about with downcast eyes deeply set in their emaciated faces and who seemed to us to be crazed by their fervor.

By 1992, the formerly dismal guest quarters had been transformed into comfortable, attractive lodgings. A new guestmaster was the driving force behind these welcome innovations: he greeted us warmly, served us delicious crystallized figs he had made, and offered to give us a guided tour of the church—an unheard-of act of kindness, for elsewhere we always had to rely on our guide, the excellent Adam, to show us the monasteries' treasures—and hearing from the others that I was not feeling well and had gone to bed early, he came to me and asked whether he could bring me a cup of hot tea. The monasteries of Mount Athos have a long tradition of hospitality to pilgrims, but this was an unusual gesture, and one which, on my fifth visit, I knew how to appreciate.

Dionysiou contains the famous frescoes depicting scenes of the Apocalypse, which in their horror resemble atomic warfare and destruction, and one of the richest libraries of the Holy Mountain. When the guestmaster showed us some of the hundreds of early manuscripts and books, another, older monk rushed in and angrily pulled the cloth covers back over the glass cases. "They are unbelievers! Their eyes do harm to our treasures!" he cried. It was not a good moment for us, but nevertheless an impressive demonstration of faith and devotion.

At dinner in the dramatically gloomy refectory, with hideous devils pitchforking sinners into a fiery hell on the frescoed walls, during which a monk read from the Bible while we sat in silence and ate soup, fresh tomatoes, olives, and bread, a visiting bishop was the guest of honor. When the abbot stamped the floor with his staff to announce that the meal was over, the reader-monk instantly stopped. Led by the bishop leaning on his gold-tipped cane, the monks filed out. We followed timidly behind them. Outside the refectory, the four cooks were fully prostrated on the floor, their cowls over their heads, like great black groveling rats, two on each side of the doorway, to ask forgiveness if the meal had not been satisfactory. Then they crouched low, kissed the bishop's ringed hand, were blessed, and scuttled away to eat the leftovers. It was a most sinister spectacle.

Next morning, as we assembled outside the gate before walking down to the quay to take the boat to our next monastery along the coast, a big monk exposed his revoltingly inflamed belly to me, where the wound of a recent hernia operation had turned septic. He had heard that I was a medic and that I carried a small first-aid kit.

My tour members included two doctors, who urged me strongly not to touch his wound. I told them that Athonite monks did not sue for malpractice and set to work with iodine and Band-Aids while they watched me with fascination and terror in their eyes.

✧

One year, during our hike from the north coast up to Kariés, we stopped at the Russian skete of the prophet Elijah, a vast church built in A.D. 1913, when the Russian influence—then much frowned upon and feared by the Turkish and Greek governments—was at its greatest on Mount Athos. The enormous golden iconostasis in the serenely unadorned white church is one of the most impressive sights on the Holy Mountain. A handful of American monks resided there, and we spent a pleasant hour with them, sipping coffee under an arbor. I asked one of them why he had chosen a life so removed from the world. "I could not stand it any longer, outside," he replied. I casually mentioned to him that the tenth number of our party had not been feeling well the day before and that the abbot of Stavronikita had kindly loaned him a mule to take him up to Kariés, where he spent the night at the inn and we were to rejoin him. When we left the skete, the monk produced a basket of peaches, which he had picked for us from a tree in the court-yard—and there were ten of them. "This one," he told me, "is for your sick friend. Give it to him with my best wishes."

In Kariés, I went to see Father Petros Lavriotis, who had given us toasted bread on my first visit to Mount Athos. He now lived in retirement in a twelfth-century villa just outside the little town, overlooking the sea two thousand feet below, with a grapevine and chestnut trees. He hugged me to his ample chest and invited me to return next year and stay a month with him—the whole summer. "But you must bring an umbrella if you live with me," he cried. An umbrella? He showed me his bedroom, where he had rigged up two old black umbrellas over the bed to keep out the rain. "My roof is eight hundred years old, has never been repaired."

How his offer would have tempted me, had it been made when I was twenty or even thirty years old, a single man without ties, uncertain of my future! Now it was too late. The same invitation had thrilled the Austrian traveler Jakob Fallmerayer, an unmarried man who visited Mount Athos in 1841 at the age of fifty. The monks had recognized his longing for and appreciation of the solitude they knew so well and the magical influence of nature. "Forsake the world and join us," they said to him. "With us you will find happiness. See there the well-built hut, the hermitage on the mountainside; see the westering sun flashing on its windowpanes! How charmingly the chapel is situated in the rich green of the chestnut grove, among the grapevines, laurels, valerian, and myrtle, how the water bubbles forth as bright as silver from under the rocks amid the oleander bushes. Here you will find the greatest of all blessings: freedom and peace of mind."

Fallmerayer found fame at home and never returned. For him, as for me, the offer had come much too late.

✧

Later that day we had another pleasant encounter, with two merchant seamen from the island of Chios, handsome young men and fast hikers, who stopped in a forest clearing with us between Xenophontos and Saint Panteleimon, and lit incense wafers. That evening we were surprised to see that they had put their shoes outside the door of their cell in the guest quarters, but learned that they did not expect the monks to clean them during the night: it is simply a Greek custom.

"Men seldom make passes at girls who wear glasses," wrote Dorothy Parker; but the monks of Mount Athos are not so particular. Girls do not desecrate the Holy Mountain, but men come a-visiting, and any man who is not entirely decrepit, with glasses or without, soon finds a monk beside him, touching him, in the gloom of the churches. There, during the interminable services, while the non-Orthodox visitor humbly stands in the stalls at the back of the narthex or the *leti,* a monk approaches softly, silently, and takes up his position beside him. Eager fingers run up and down the visitor's thigh and soon come to rest on his crotch. *"Americani? Protestanti?"* the monk whispers. Oh, the thrill, the wicked thrill, of fondling a Protestant, no matter how old or bespectacled he be! Even I have been, on more than one occasion, the object of a monk's attention in the darkness of a church. No doubt my blue jeans, which to them are symbols of all the forbidden sexuality of the world, suggest to the naughty monks that I am a somewhat less ancient traveler. Not wishing to upset someone who is, after all, one of my hosts, I gently remove the groping hand, then press his shoulder in a comradely manner, and move away. But I cannot deny that the furtiveness of these encounters in the darkness of these churches, with the splashes of candlelight far off beyond the pillars, which pick out the lean figures of saints and sinners on the walls and show up the gold frames of the icons and the gold chandeliers with their suspended ostrich eggs, the intoxicating smell of incense—all this makes the monks' erotic advances exciting and curiously thrilling.

The monks' gowns and their long hair and abundant beards make them appear like sexless creatures, all formed to one pattern; but this impression is false. They are individuals, many of them much younger than their bearing and beards suggest, and they are men. "All that is going on behind the arched cloisters is not condu-cive to eternal salvation," wrote Michael Choukas in *Black Angels of Athos* in 1934; and he quoted reports of boys being imported to the Holy Mountain for sexual purposes, which I remembered well when I saw the two lovely Athenian youths who had been invited by the monks of Stavronikita to spend the summer of 1982 with them.

My younger tour members take a perverse delight in being approached. "I will show you something special—come!" begged a stately monk who was far from unattractive, a hero of World War II when Greece was occupied by the Germans who had hidden British airmen and taken them by boat to safety on an island. He led his half-willing victim out of the monastery, through the garden, to a small building beside the outer wall. It looked like a romantic pavilion, a perfect and secluded spot for an intimate interlude; but when he opened the locked door, it was the charnel house, filled with the bones of hundreds of monks, their thighbones neatly stacked here, arm bones there, like logs for the winter months, and the skulls of the dear departed arranged on shelves reaching to the ceiling, with their names and dates of death marked on them. It was not a setting conducive to a romantic encounter.

But the amorous monk did not give up. He led the nice young American to his room, poured him a big glass of wine, peeled an apple for him, charmed him with his most winning smile, and tumbled him into his cot.

The Russian monastery of Saint Panteleimon is unique on Mount Athos for being almost modern—it was created in the early nineteenth century and monstrously enlarged between 1880 and 1912, when so many warships of Imperial Russia lay at anchor off its vast barracks-like buildings that there was fear it was becoming a Russian Gibraltar, to control the Mediterranean. In 1903, it housed thirty-five hundred monks—half of all the monks on the Holy Mountain at that time—and many of them were rumored to be soldiers. Dozens of them were known criminals.

Today it looks less like a monastery than an almost-abandoned factory town, and among its ruins we found half a dozen worldly-wise monks from a Russian Orthodox seminary in the United States. When we first met them, and when they climbed up with us to the top floor of their north barracks building to an incredibly vulgar big church, built in 1898 in the most ghastly and ornate style, they wore the same black habits and hats as all monks on the Holy Mountain; but they were dramatically transformed an hour later when they reappeared for dinner in the gaunt refectory that once served eighteen hundred monks at one sitting and where places were laid for less than two dozen. Whether their altered appearance had been achieved in our honor or because, like elegant ladies of a more gracious and leisured age, it was their custom each evening to change into elaborate gowns for dinner, we did not dare to inquire; but to our amazement they made a theatrically belated entry into the refectory and swept, indeed almost danced, past our visitors' table to their own, where they flirted outrageously with Dimitri and Frangoulis, the seamen from Chios. They were now gloriously attired in heavily gilded, stiffly embroidered, jewel-encrusted garments of scarlet, royal-purple, and heliotrope silk, with richly decorated belts tightly buckled. Gaudy veils, which fluttered around them and reached to the ground, had been thrown over their monks' hats. Their fingers were crammed with rings from which flashed impressively large and brightly colored stones; and the crosses hanging on massive chains from their necks and belts were oversized, fit for the stage. At least three of them had bright glossy golden hair and beards, one with a distinctly pinkish tint, which were all too obviously not their natural color; and as they passed us we were overcome by the combined smell of the sickly perfumes with which they had drenched themselves for their evening toilette instead of washing with soap and water.

Their faces were painted; but all the powder, the rouge, the mascara, and the lavishly applied color to their lips could not disguise their dissipated, raddled features. Were they, we wondered, men who had come to the Holy Mountain less for spiritual salvation and in order to serve God than to escape from prosecution for some offense? We were often assured that the monks of Mount Athos number among them criminals of many nations; a monk's habit and hat, long hair and a beard, and a new name are easily acquired and can hide a man's past.

What the nasty Mr. Patrick White would have thought of these fantastic monk-queens in their dazzling drag, I could not imagine; we were less amused by this band of *folles* than astonished, and when our first shock had subsided, we agreed that they were doing no harm to anyone—except possibly in the eyes of God, who is all-forgiving. They were obviously ecstatically happy, swishing amid the faded fin de siècle splendors of their neglected cloisters and churches under the multicolored, barbaric onion domes of this late-Romanov monastery. But we were also agreed that we much preferred monks to be garbed somberly, traditionally, to move sedately with decorum, to act in a pious manner regardless of their hidden proclivities.

During my five visits to the Holy Mountain I have passed through the little port of Daphne so often that I feel quite at home there; and while we sit at the café under the wisteria vine, waiting for a boat to be made ready to take us to one of the monasteries along the coast, I ask for a jug of boiling water and a glass, and Adam goes to the shop opposite the dock and brings me a few leaves of herbal tea. The port master has become a friend. Like all the Greek officials on Mount Athos—the policemen and the post-office workers—he sees his wife and family for only one week in every month. When he invited me and my tour members for coffee on his balcony overlooking the harbor, and while Adam ran to the shop to contribute chocolate cookies, he told us how, when he was first posted to Daphne, he desperately missed his wife and all female company but had become used to the all-male environment. "It is the same as in the army," he said; but when his extremely pretty houseboy brought the tray with the coffee cups, we gave each other meaningful looks and had no doubt that he was consoling himself quite pleasantly during his enforced bachelor existence.

The nineteenth- and early-twentieth-century visitors to Mount Athos all predicted that the Holy Mountain, then sparsely populated and with its monasteries and dependencies in sad decay, would soon cease to exist. They wrote that when the last remaining old monks died and no young ones came to take their places, the peninsula would become a tourist resort with hotels and gambling casinos. They were quite wrong.

There has been a strong spiritual and economic revival on the Holy Mountain. The monasteries in which the number of fathers had for decades been on the decline are attracting many young, vigorous, active men with university degrees, with training in business management, with experience in agriculture, forestry, and fishing, who speak three or more languages. A fresh spirit of progress is evident almost everywhere. Mount Athos is rich—has always been rich—but its wealth has not previously been put to use. Its monasteries own office buildings in Thessaloníki and land on the Greek mainland and on the islands; they have assets in the Balkan countries, in Russia; their huge forests are a source of revenue that has never before been tapped. Now the export of lumber increases so fast that some of the monasteries have hurriedly had to commission new, efficient port facilities to handle their lucrative business. Athos wine, nuts, herbs, and handmade religious objects are shipped not only to Athens but all over Europe and to Australia and America. Electric typewriters hum in monastery offices, and telephone calls are placed to banks and investment firms in Athens and Thessaloníki. Niko, the handsome young boatman in whose small wooden caïque we sailed along the south coast of the peninsula in 1982, of whom the nine members of my group had been so enamored, and of whom Bryce Carver had said, "I'll fix him breakfast any day," had by 1992 become the affluent and paunchy captain of the big motor ferry that transfers heavily laden trucks and jeeps and dozens of laborers daily from and to Ouranoupolis.

Retired bishops and other princes of the Orthodox Church are reconstructing and modernizing ruined Byzantine villas and towers on the rocky shores, and spend the summer months there in blissful solitude surrounded by delectable orchards and cypress groves. The medieval way of life is fast vanishing. We often found it difficult to hike from one monastery to the next because the forest trails have become heavily overgrown and, in some places, have quite disappeared under the rapidly encroaching growth, so that Adam had to scramble around while we waited until he located where the trail continued a hundred feet or so ahead. The monks no longer use the trails, and mules—until recently the only means of transport—have become rare. The monks now travel by jeep on the new roads that give access to all monasteries, or telephone for a radio-controlled and monk-owned taxi-truck. Most of the monasteries are using their own funds and the Greek government's grants to repair ruinous parts of their buildings, to greatly improve and enlarge the capacity of their guest quarters; and water pipes are being laid in Great Lavra and elsewhere. Lavra, the oldest and most revered of the twenty monasteries, formerly accessible only by boat when the sea was unusually calm or by walking there for eight hours, has been linked to the other monasteries on the north coast by a corniche-like motor road. The Holy Mountain has entered the twentieth century at last, much to the regret of travelers who saw it fifty, thirty, even ten years ago, when it was almost as it had been during the previous nine centuries.

After having hiked for several hours in order to reach a monastery in time to spend the night there, only the most aesthetic pilgrim fails to appreciate the comforts provided in the guest quarters; but since Greek men visit the Holy Mountain rarely except at

Easter or to attend special church services on various saints' days, and with only ten foreigners permitted there each day, it is curious to understand why accommodations are being built for such a large number of visitors. Many of the monasteries now have beds for more than a hundred guests. Is it perhaps envisaged that tourists in large numbers will be admitted each day in the future? Already, many monks devote many hours of their days to catering to the needs of the visitors, and they do so with dutiful resignation, although, as some of them frankly say, they did not choose their vocation to be innkeepers but in order to keep alive the two-thousand-year-old traditions, ideals, and ceremonies of the Orthodox Church.

Fortunately, and despite all the changes and the manifestations of modernity, of which by no means all the older monks on Mount Athos approve, time has in many respects stood still. For many who have chosen to spend their lives there, the passing of centuries has no meaning. As we were swimming off a beach on the north shore, modestly out of sight of any monastery, a monk passing on the path above us called out to us in alarm, "Oh, sirs, please do not enter the water there! That is where Father Dimitrios was taken by a shark!"

On inquiring when this frightful event had occurred, he explained, "Oh, in 1712."

13

EASTER

ISLAND

REVISITED

LESS THAN AN HOUR after having arrived at Mataveri Airport we stood on the rim of the Rano Kau volcano among hundreds of petroglyphs depicting birdmen and the god Make-Make and looked across the flat round disk of deep blue that is the Pacific. Twelve hundred feet below us, after a truck had driven up and down the airstrip to chase the straying cows off it, the plane that had brought us twenty-six hundred miles from Chile taxied along the runway, and as it rose steeply into the air and continued its journey of twenty-eight hundred miles to Tahiti, it seemed to us as if our umbilical cord with the rest of the world was cut: we were acutely aware that we were now part of the small community on the most isolated inhabited place on the globe, Easter Island, which its natives call Te Pito o te Henua—"the navel of the world."

When I went to Easter Island with the first groups of tourists in 1968, a visit to the island was a considerable undertaking. The flight by chartered propeller plane from Chile took twelve hours; the tents in which the intrepid tourists were accommodated were rudimentary; water was scarce; the shortage of wheeled transport made visits to the archaeological sites difficult. We found a distressed population living in poor houses, everyone dependent for all needs on the capricious arrival of the annual freighter from Chile. The sides of Rano Kau volcano and other parts of the island were disfigured by the wire fences, iron huts, discarded vehicles, and broken pieces of machinery of the U.S. Air Force then stationed there. The archaeological sites were unkempt. It was the enthusiasm of Father Sebastian Englert, the island's priest, and the knowledge of Dr. William Mulloy, the archaeologist from Wyoming working there, that then made a visit to the island memorable and meaningful.

The introduction of the regular air service and twenty-five years of tourism have happily not made one's stay on the island mundane. Although large cruise ships now call at Easter Island (but rarely manage to get their passengers ashore through the tremendous surf) and the Concorde touches down during some luxurious round-the-world tours, the island has remained almost wholly uncheapened. Due to its remoteness it is still a very special place and one moreover at which it is tempting to linger longer than the few days that most tour itineraries provide. The islanders have sensibly not permitted their roads to be paved or neon lights to ruin the charm of their village.

But tourists now provide the chief source of income for the island. When the jet plane from Chile arrives each week, passengers en route to Tahiti who have only one hour on the island are driven in minibuses to nearby Ahu Tehai to take photographs of the reconstructed statues on that funeral temple, and then on to a souvenir store, before being returned to the airport for their onward flight.

❖

Despite such businesslike enterprise, the sense of mystery remains on Easter Island. No visitor can help but wonder at these hundreds of huge, perplexing statues—the *moai*—on this very small island. Who made them? When? To what purpose? Only about three thousand visitors come here each year, mostly during the summer months of October to March, and there are rarely more than sixty tourists on the island per week, although the hotels, guesthouses, and private homes can accommodate many more.

The population, which was merely 150 persons in the 1930s, and 1,000 twenty-five years ago, is now approximately 2,500, including officials and administrators from Chile who usually serve a year or two on the island and rarely mix socially with the islanders. The local people look healthy, prosperous, and content. Tourists are cosseted at five hotels—the government-owned Hotel Hangaroa has comfortable rooms with hot showers and balconies facing the ocean, attentive staff, and even a swimming pool—and there are several guesthouses. The debris of the former U.S. base has been removed, and the archaeological sites are protected from roaming animals by neat stone walls and well maintained by guardians.

The site that is generally first visited by tourists is Ahu Akivi, where the late Dr. William Mulloy re-erected seven statues in 1960. He had a passion for sticking broken statues together with cement, and this is not a happy reconstruction. Although the *moai* stand in their original places on the *ahu,* or temple platform, they seem awkward there and resemble huge pins in a bowling alley— one expects a giant to knock them down with a big ball. Adding to the unfortunate effect is the approach to this *ahu,* which is from the side, so that the statues are first seen like thin cardboard cutouts. This is the only place on the island where statues were placed on their platforms facing the sea, across a bare field, instead of dramatically with their backs to the ocean at the shore.

Later reconstructions are much more successful. At Ahu Tehai and at Ahu Nau Nau, the re-erected statues have been left picturesquely incomplete, some missing heads, others topknots; heads and torsos remain where they were cast down centuries ago in tribal warfare. Enough *moai* have been re-erected now to provide the visitor with examples of what the *ahu*s looked like originally. It is best, surely, to let the other sleeping gods lie.

Two other places never fail to intrigue the visitor. The stone wall at Vinapu is considered to be the most enigmatic of the island's structures because it resembles the Incaic walls of Peru and has convinced Mr. Thor Heyerdahl that it provides proof that the island was first settled from South America, not by Polynesians—a theory that finds little agreement among Pacific archaeologists—and there is a thrill in picnicking beside the roar of the surf in the sinister Ana Kai Tangate cave, where men were still eaten only 130 years ago.

The most spectacular place on the island is Rano Ranaku. More than a hundred stone figures—the largest measures sixty-three feet in length—stand and lie on the grassy side of the volcano, some still joined by their spines to the rock walls from which they were hewn. Most of them are upright, stalwart sentinels of doom, their empty eyes staring across the ocean, their lips curled up in disdain. An incomprehensible religious frenzy must have gripped the entire population of this small island, driving its members to go on and on to carve these ever-larger statues and transport them down from the quarry across the island to their sites on the platforms of the funeral temples.

While the main reason for a visit to Easter Island is the inspection and study of the statues, temples, and petroglyphs, other attractions contribute to the pleasure of one's stay. Few beaches in the world can rival the crescent of white sand at Anakena, with surf just rough enough to be invigorating—and what a thrill to swim where the legendary King Hotu Matua and his followers, the initial settlers of the island, landed in the fifth century, and where Captain James Cook came ashore in 1774. The island horses, a small, docile breed, provide the ideal way of exploring at leisure and in solitude; they find their own way to the historical sights. Attendance at Mass in the village church, with wonderful Polynesian singing, is a moving experience. Friendly families offer delightful feasts in their homes, with a pig and a fish and taro roots cooked in earth ovens, and singing and dancing and laughter until late into the night.

✧

It was merely by chance that the island became part of Chile in 1888—no other country wanted it—and in many ways it appears less Chilean now than twenty years ago, when it was largely barren and treeless. Now, with many groves of flowering shrubs and plantations of imported tropical trees, it has an attractive South Seas appearance. Anakena beach, fringed by many tall palms, could be in Tahiti. Culturally, too, the island has drawn closer to Polynesia since the 1960s. The planes from Chile bring mostly European and a few American tourists who stay at the hotels for a few nights and take no part in the island life; but when the planes return from Tahiti, the ladies of Hangaroa village assemble at the airport and offer arriving passengers room and board at their homes—and the visitors from French Polynesia are predominantly young, stay on the island for many weeks, and fraternize with the locals. Their conviviality and shared heritage make them highly welcome. French, not Spanish, is beginning to be the second language of the Easter Islanders, whose aspirations turn to Tahiti, not to Chile; and there are far more islanders than twenty years ago who have the bearing, stature, and classic features of the Polynesian.

Twenty years ago the only available evening entertainment on the island was offered in private homes in the village, where everyone who brought a bottle of rum or beer was welcome to join in the lively and unashamedly sensual dancing. Since there were usually a few genial old men and women from the nearby leper colony among the guests—cured, but with pathetically disfigured faces—it was occasionally somewhat disconcerting when the bottles were passed around from mouth to mouth. But this added to the sense of adventure.

Today, Hangaroa boasts two discos and several bars, including an uninhibited *boîte de nuit* whose owner is a transvestite and where the island's raffish elements mingle cheerfully with those tourists who venture there.

✦

On our first evening on the island in 1989, one member of our group walked to the cliff near our hotel, to watch the sunset; twenty minutes later he returned on the back of a motorbike, having met a young islander—it was love at first sight for both of them. It was Christmas Eve, and the islander insisted on taking our tour member to his home, where his large family was assembling for dinner and where the stranger was warmly welcomed and plied with food and drink. "Meet my new son-in-law," called out the mother to relatives and neighbors who arrived, "a doctor from New York!" Next morning she brought the couple breakfast in bed. No wonder that the *South American Handbook* states that the islanders are very warm-hearted, with a quick sense of humor, and extremely hospitable.

This happy doctor was not the only member of our group to make a conquest. A Canadian lawyer soon acquired a young islander friend who conveniently had a romantic little cottage of his own in the village where he could entertain. An extremely handsome youth with long black hair and a headband of chicken feathers tried un-successfully to sell another tour member a carving he claimed to have found in his ancient family cave that day; instead, he adroitly offered him what he termed his "warm brown body" for the night.

Such easygoing ways are traditionally Polynesian. Ever since the 1770s, when Captain James Cook explored the islands of the

South Seas, travelers have commented on the extraordinarily tolerant attitude to sexual matters among the Polynesians, who copulated in public with every evidence of enjoyment, offered the choicest young girls to the visitors, and whose young men were often eager to become the intimate friend of European sailors. Almost every village had—and still has—its honored *mahu,* who dressed as a woman and did women's work. Captain William Bligh of the *Bounty* noted the acceptance of homosexuality at Tahiti.

When the French writer Pierre Loti visited Easter Island in 1872 as a midshipman, a youth named Petro attached himself to the visitor: naked, very lean, and heavily muscled, with a skin of reddish copper color ornamented with blue tattooing—a description that well fits today's pure-blooded young Easter Islanders, except that they wear blue jeans and cowboy boots with brightly colored ribbons around them.

Most remarkable during a visit to Easter Island is to see how fast the island has moved from the Stone Age into the twentieth century. One can now communicate with the island by direct-dial telephone and fax. The entire operation of the airport is computerized and requires only one man to run it. A smart launderette recently opened in Hangaroa village. Our young islander guide, an extremely knowledgeable and eloquent graduate of a California university, had been brought up by his grandmother, who was born and lived most of her life in a cave, and never learned to sleep in a bed.

Thus a visit to this most isolated of all the world's inhabited islands is fascinating, rewarding, and enjoyable for many reasons— and who else on one's block has been there?

14

THE MOUNTAIN OF THE GODS

WHAT DO A PASTOR, a chief of police, a district attorney, an architect, an actor, a funeral director, a Byzantine scholar, a rich playboy, and a florist have in common?

They were the members of my tour to climb Mount Olympus in September of 1990. It is not only the highest mountain range in Greece but the sacred mountain and abode of the ancient Greek gods. Stefani, one of several jagged, dramatic peaks almost ten thousand feet above sea level and usually snow-covered all year, is known as "the Throne of Zeus"; and I had made reservations for us for two nights at the Greek Alpine Club hut at just below seven thousand feet up the mountain.

The pastor was a good man, and a man of good cheer, despite the fact that his lover of more than thirty years had recently died—we scattered his ashes over the waters of the Aegean later during the tour, at a brief ceremony aboard our caïque from Delos to Mykonos. No doubt his faith helped him to assuage his loss; by traveling with us he hoped, perhaps, to find a fresh interest in living. He was the oldest member of our group, wonderfully fit, appreciative, and considerate at all times. It was an inspiration to travel with him.

The chief of police of a large American city was a commanding man in his early forties, and so good-looking that when we walked off the plane at the Thessaloníki airport, Adam, our Byzantine expert and guide, who greeted us, cried out, "Oh, Mr. Hanns, you have brought me a film star!" He was indeed a glamorized movie police officer come to life, but extremely friendly and endearingly shy. With everything apparently in his favor—position, personality, good health, stunning looks—it was a wonder that he had found no one to share his life, and he confided to us that after his TV dinners, he often felt suicidal with loneliness.

The district attorney was rich and, when his children were grown-up, had set up house with his ex-wife's florist, on whom he lavished many massive gold rings, bracelets, and necklaces. "He must be very good in bed," whispered the tour members; and when he overheard this, the florist said, "You bet I am." He was no longer very young but had retained the slim, trim body of a man half his age, and was witty, amusing, and entertaining. I had traveled with this devoted couple several times, and the florist never failed to surprise me—and his fellow travelers—with some delightful, unexpected antics. He had filled his and his lover's room at the Hotel Grande Bretagne in Athens with hundreds of red and white roses; and when they invited the tour members to drinks there, it was like entering an enchanted bower. When we left the hotel to drive to the airport, he carried huge bunches of these flowers with him—"I'm certainly not leaving them for the maid or to be thrown out"—and in the departure lounge for our flight to Thessaloníki he walked from one woman to the next and, bowing politely, gravely presented each lady passenger with a rose. They probably thought it was a gracious gesture on the part of Olympic Airways. His lover, the district attorney, loved it. "Ronnie is playing flower girl again."

The California architect was knowledgeable not only in his profession but on many fascinating subjects—he identified every moss and lichen and knew the names of every star and constellation in the heavens. Unfortunately, after years of living alone, he had forgotten—if he had ever known—that he was not the only human being on this planet. He treated everyone like a robot that could be summoned to do his bidding. He was not a bad man, and not rude, but he either considered politeness to be unmanly or simply did not know that words such as "please" and "thank you" existed and could so easily give a little pleasure to those to whom they are tossed. When he lost his hat and I happened to find it and brought it to him, he took it from me as from a machine that he had commanded to serve him.

The actor was a gem. Although he had starred on Broadway more than once and was constantly working on the stage, on television, and in films, he was not well known to the general public. He was unassuming, entertaining, and rarely talked about his career. He dismissed his greatest successes when asked about them. "That? Oh, yes, that was a fun part to play." He had traveled with me in the Soviet Union and in Egypt and always prepared himself by doing extensive background reading and took a serious interest in what he saw. It was a pleasure to be once again in his company. He was not at all what one expects a successful actor to be, with nothing ostentatious or flamboyant about him. Only by the way in which he sometimes rose sharply to his feet, the brisk raising of an arm, the graceful sweep of a hand, the quick turn of the head, could one see that with makeup and a wig he was indeed the Prince of Denmark and the King of Siam.

The funeral director was the most jolly, easygoing, fun-loving, and universally beloved member of our group. Rotund and happy, at times a little playfully forgetful, looking about himself at all times with shining eyes, taking pleasure in everything, he was an ideal travel companion. Nothing ever upset him or worried him: he had paid for the tour and relaxed to enjoy every moment of it and trusted me to look after him.

The playboy had been spoiled rotten by his parents. He had never done a day's work in his life and knew all too well that he never would have to do so. He was one of those rich young men who fill their idle time by dashing from one of their residences to another in a meaningless and never-satisfied quest for pleasure, but do not make arrangements for mail to be forwarded, so that it was difficult to keep up with his frenetic movements. Letters, bills, and travel tickets mailed to his New York apartment were not forwarded to his house at Southampton on Long Island; by the time they were returned to me, the young man had left for his private island in Maine; then he was taking in the opera in Santa Fe. He had been indulged in every whim and desire, and had until recently been an inmate for several months at the Betty Ford Center in California and spoke of his stay there with as much pride as if he were an alumnus of Harvard or Yale. None of us had known him previously, but we were agreed that his stay at this famous clinic seemed not to have benefited him in any way. Until midday or so he was a reasonably pleasant travel companion, but then, as he began drinking wine and spirits (and, perhaps, surreptitiously taking drugs), he grew first maudlin and then belligerent and finally so obnoxious that I looked forward to every dinner with apprehension. Happily for the other tour members, his outbursts of hate were generally directed at myself, and I steeled myself to suffer in silence. To his credit, it must be admitted that he had great taste in clothes: everything he wore was stylish but of the utmost simplicity, obviously extremely expensive, always a delight to behold. His custom-made shirts of fine pale-ivory or blue silk were the most beautiful shirts I have ever seen.

Adam, our Byzantine expert and guide, was an old friend. This was the fourth time I was traveling with him, and it was the scholarship and enthusiasm he eagerly shared with us that had made three visits with him to Mount Athos so meaningful. He had grown a little stouter since I had seen him last but was also somewhat less what the French call *une grande folle*—the latter was a welcome improvement. His zest for everything—be it a pretty boy selling soft drinks by the road, or the freshly cooked souvlaki at an inn and the walnuts and honey that were our dessert, or attending a candle-lit service in a monastery church—all these delightful travel experiences made him forget completely that although we wished never to be hurried, we did have to adhere to a schedule, had to be at a certain place at a specific time in order not to miss the bus or reach our goal by sunset. As diplomatically as possible, without upsetting him or damping his enthusiasm, with my eyes on my wristwatch, I had at such moments to make him lead us onward.

And then there was I, on duty twenty-four hours of each day, coaxing the sun to rise at dawn and begging the stars to come out at dusk so that my dear tour members would be satisfied with all the arrangements; held responsible for the weather and the air schedules and the state of the roads; leader, counselor, confessor, medic, nurse; encouraging always, advising, admonishing when necessary; pointing out a fine view here, a photo opportunity there; promising the top of the mountain just past the next turn in the trail; turning any disappointment into an added attraction—"Yes, it *is* raining; but aren't we lucky—it makes everything look so beautiful." As always on tours, I had the patience of an angel and the forbearance of a saint until, goaded beyond endurance, I sometimes briefly and monumentally lost my temper, to the astonishment and consternation of my tour members, who referred to me as their Mother Superior. When he was drunk and at his worst, the playboy wounded me by giving me mock Nazi salutes and called me Dr. Mengele.

✧

I had planned for us to begin the climb as early in the morning as possible, but Adam, who had climbed Mount Olympus when he was young and misjudged the time it would take us inexperienced hikers—and who, after so many years and with his added weight, is overly fond of eating—stopped our bus outside an attractive open-air restaurant in the main square of the small town of Litók-horon at the base of the mountain. Knowing all too well how ill-advised it is to climb after a meal, in the heat of the day, I begged him to forget lunch and buy us each a piece of fruit and get going; but it was too late—the tour members were as eager as Adam to enjoy a leisurely meal and sat down contentedly to study their menus. I advised them to eat very lightly, a traditional Greek salad, maybe one portion of spaghetti shared among two or three of them; I warned them how much harder it is to climb after a big meal—but my tour members believe that by my urging them to eat sparingly, I make more money out of them. Nothing could be further from the truth: I simply have their well-being at heart. They ignored my advice and ordered plenty of bread and butter, rich filling soups, meat and fish dishes with vegetables and potatoes, salads on the side, dangerously rich desserts, far too much wine. I foresaw problems ahead but was unable to prevent them.

One of our waiters was a real charmer, and we instantly recognized him as being "one of us"; he flirted with all of us, but it soon became obvious that the one who appealed to him most was our jolly funeral director, who, when the dessert stage had been reached, turned to me sheepishly and said, "You're going to be very angry with me, but I'm not going up the mountain with you. I'm staying here." It was a case of love at first sight.

I assured him that I was not in the least angry or even surprised. We do not all have the same priorities. He took his backpack off the bus and we wished him well and arranged to pick him up at the same restaurant in two days, at one o'clock.

Then we drove up the winding, narrow paved road to where the trail begins; and here Adam, full of food and wine and bonhomie, infuriatingly delayed us still more by insisting on inviting us all for a cup of tea or a cold drink at the little café by the car park, so that it was well after three o'clock when we started the ascent.

The official guidebook described the hike from the roadhead to the Refuge Hut A at 6,890 feet as "a vigorous walk of 2½ hours"; but I had suspected that this applied to young and experienced hikers and that all of us would need considerably longer. I knew, too, that by 6:00 P.M. it would become cold and, soon afterward, dark. The terrain was more taxing than I had anticipated; the substantial luncheon and too many glasses of the heady red wine, added to the unaccustomed weight of the backpacks, soon began to make themselves felt by all my fellow travelers. With my eyes on my altimeter, I realized that there was no way in which any of us would be able to climb almost 4,000 feet to the refuge hut in two and a half hours.

At first we kept together, but as the others stopped for frequent rests, pretending that they did so in order to take photographs, I walked ahead—not because I was more fit than they but because many years of experience in mountain hiking have taught me never to pause but to go on and on at a slow, steady pace. If I stop to rest, I have considerable difficulty in starting off again. No one else was as foolish as our group to hike up the mountain that hot, still afternoon, but we met a number of young people coming down. After two hours of steady walking, with no refuge hut in sight, and with my altimeter still only at 4,600 feet, I asked two youths who were running down the trail how far it was to the hut. "Oh, half an hour," they said, but an hour later, at 5,500 feet, when I asked other descending hikers, they looked closely at me, noted my age and my state of exhaustion, and said, "Maybe an hour, maybe one and a half?" It was not encouraging; and as I trudged on through the dense pine forest and my backpack became heavier and heavier, I wished that Zeus would appear to me in the guise of an eagle and carry me up to the summit, as he did Ganymede, the beautiful youth who replaced his wife, Hera, in his affections and became cupbearer to the gods.

When the chief of police caught up with me, I felt in honor bound to continue with him at his faster pace, but I was somewhat heartened to note that he was becoming as weary as I; and even when we saw the red roof of the refuge hut almost immediately above us, just below the tree line, it still took us half an hour of increasing effort to reach it.

It was almost 7:00 P.M. and the light was beginning to fade when we arrived on the terrace of the hut, to be met by a wonderful and totally unexpected welcome by the lady who manages it for the Greek Alpine Club.

"You must be part of the American group. Take off your boots; make yourselves comfortable. I have warm slippers for you. Come, I show you your beds; dinner is served till nine o'clock and there is a log fire in the eating room."

Mrs. Kostas Zolotas was born in Holland, educated in England and Germany, and married to a Greek mountaineer from Litókhoron. "I am the new Europe!" she quipped. With her husband and daughter and son-in-law she cheerfully operates the hut every year, from May to October, but was quick to ensure that her rules are obeyed: boots were not allowed in the eating room; smoking was not permitted; the gloriously warm blankets supplied in the bedroom could not be removed to the terrace or the nearby alpine meadows. The dormitories accommodated about forty hikers, but Mrs. Zolotas had reserved a private room for us with a raised wooden sleeping platform and ten mattresses on it, a table, one chair, and a very small window. Forty thick wool blankets were neatly stacked on a shelf, and everything was spotless. The other guests at the refuge hut were mostly aged eighteen to twenty-five and mostly from Greece and the Balkan countries. There was only one older hiker—a very small, very feisty lady with her young, personal Greek Alpine Club guide.

By 8:30 P.M. all the members of the group had reached the hut, assisted on their way by the flashlights with which I had supplied everyone. The district attorney, being twice the age of his lover, naturally found the climb much easier than the florist, who had stopped often to pick wildflowers along the way, and he carried both their backpacks. The playboy, as expected, came last (with Adam in the rear, as instructed by me), and was in a particularly foul mood. "I'll kill you for this" were his first words to me when I greeted him on the terrace; and when we showed him our modest sleeping quarters, he was quite disgusted and refused to come to supper, so that the rest of us enjoyed a peaceful and pleasant meal. The actor sang us a song from *La Cage aux Folles;* and the florist, who had numbered many illustrious ladies among his former customers, regaled us with indiscreet tales about Miss Zsa Zsa Gabor. Mrs. Zolotas's son-in-law was greatly admired by all of us. With his long hair and headband he looked like one of the marble statues of classical Greek athletes we had seen in the Athens Museum. He wore a white T-shirt that showed off his muscular build, and the scarlet pants of a warm-up suit—"and nothing under them," said my observant tour members.

Meat-and-potato soup, bread, salad, and cheese were served at the kitchen counter; but Mrs. Zolotas's daughter, sensing that we were tired and not accustomed to stand in line for food, though we were quite agreeable to do so like everyone else there, told us to sit at a table near the fireplace, brought our meal to us, and took orders for hot tea, jugs of resinated wine, and tots of fiendishly potent grape brandy. We were an intriguing novelty to the Zolotases—all of us much older than most of their guests, and they very rarely saw any Americans there. We were soundly asleep by 10:00 P.M., when the electric light and the water were cut off until dawn.

We awoke early next morning and stepped out onto our little terrace to see a spectacular sunrise over the Aegean Sea seven thousand feet below, and after the somewhat disconcerting experience of sharing the basic unisex toilets and washing facilities with dozens of young climbers, many of them totally and unself-consciously naked, followed by breakfast, we set off to climb the formidable-looking summits, which become visible from the refuge hut on days when they are not shrouded in clouds. They are craggy and somber; it is no wonder that the ancient Greeks believed that they protected the immortal gods from the curious eyes of humans. Above the tree line the trail crossed what the guidebook understates to be "unpleasantly slippery shale"; we all found it hard going. Then the final ascent begins, several hours of it, scrambling up the rock face, hand over foot.

None of the members of our group reached the peaks, although I had taken the precaution of handing out plenty of energy-providing ambrosia of the gods, the ancients' mixture of barley, oil, honey, and nuts, today known as granola bars. Even the most determined among us—the district attorney and the architect—turned back after having reached just over 8,700 feet. There is no disgrace in this: Olympus is not very high by world standards, but it is a most challenging mountain to climb; and it was not until 1913 that it was first conquered, by two Swiss climbers and their Greek guide. As recently as 1910 a German climber who made the attempt was held for ransom by an armed gang, of whom many then roamed these wild regions. Inaccessibility and insecurity hampered exploration even in the 1920s, after the region reverted from Turkish to Greek rule; and when the publicity-seeking world traveler Richard Halliburton set out in 1927 to climb Mount Olympus with his friend Roderic Crane and a shepherd youth named Lazarus, the authorities in Thessaloníki insisted on providing them with nine armed soldiers and six dogs to protect them from bandits. Halliburton later claimed that he, Crane, and Lazarus had spent a night on the summit during a fearful thunderstorm.

Hoping that none of the agile young climbers would notice that we had not made it all the way to the top, we returned to the refuge hut and relaxed on its sunny terrace to drink hot tea or wine and play with the Zolotases' enormous, friendly wolfhound. The feisty little old lady with her personal guide returned from the mountain late in the afternoon and joined us there. She was ecstatic. "Yesterday I make Skala; today I make Mytika," she told us, naming two of the highest of Mount Olympus's peaks. "Now I am ready for Everest, I think."

I suggested the Matterhorn.

"Pooh, that one I have made three times already," she said.

The playboy had not attempted to reach a summit but had spent all day drinking and, without any physical activity to compensate for all that intake of alcohol, was thoroughly drunk and belligerent at supper. After tormenting some of the more docile tour members and achieving no reaction from them, he turned his pent-up fury on me. "I paid for a first-class tour," he cried, "and this is a rip-off! This place is a *dump;* I've never been so insulted in my life!" I attempted to calm him by urging him to eat his food. He pushed his plate away. "You call this *food*? You expect me to eat this filthy mess? I wouldn't insult my *dog* by giving her this garbage!" The Zolotases heard and came running in consternation; Adam and I waved them away, but they were deeply offended. The architect took his jug of wine and sat by himself near the fireplace; the rest of us ate our meal as fast as possible and fled to our bedroom, where the playboy arrived later, more drunk and more disagreeable, and continued to abuse me and the refuge hut until he fell into a deep sleep.

I lay near the door and during the night heard someone groan and twice stumble to the door and go outside; he held his flashlight to guide him and I recognized our architect but was in no mood to ask him whether he was ill and needed any of my medications. At first light I pulled on my clothes and stepped out onto the terrace, and there, although the forest was less than six feet away, immediately outside our door, he had opened his bowels and spewed his dinner and wine. The mess had frozen hard during the night.

I could not let Mrs. Zolotas and her hardworking family see this excreta and vomit on our doorstep, so I found an empty bottle and filled it with water and, with some pieces of cardboard, set to work to clean it up. It was not a task I had expected to perform at my age.

I was doing my best to wash and scrape away this evidence of my tour member's disgrace when he made his appearance in the doorway, to greet the new day. He watched me on my knees before him and was not in the least embarrassed or disconcerted. Not for a moment did it occur to him either to apologize and thank me or to throw me a quarter as a tip for doing something that was surely beyond my call of duty. Instead, he rubbed his hands together and then put them into his trouser pockets to warm them, and laughed at me.

I continued to clean up his filth. What else could I do? I ignored his laughter and hoped that I might get my reward in heaven; but

I was not in the best temper when after breakfast and having said good-bye to the Zolotas family we hiked down the mountain. And when we reached the motor road, a new problem awaited me.

The car park, which had been so crowded two days before when we arrived there, was now deserted except for two cars; the place was weirdly quiet. I realized then that, strangely, no hikers had come up the trail all morning while we walked down. In the small café, Adam and I found its manager resting in bed behind the bar; she explained that the road from Litókhoron was closed that day to enable some long-overdue repairs to be made. I hoped fervently that our bus driver would have the sense to have driven up as far as the construction site and wait there for us; but the prospect of having to tell my tour members that we had to walk down another six miles along the paved road was chilling. Fortunately, I spotted the owners of the two parked cars sitting nearby outside their tents; they had driven up the previous day and, when told about the closure of the road, had decided to camp there. They were Hungarians and I could communicate with them in German; they readily agreed to drive us down to the repair site, where I pressed all my remaining dried apricots and trail food on them. The actor beautifully mimed all our thanks for them, and they appeared to appreciate the performance.

We clambered across the road works, and I was much relieved to find our bus and its patient driver waiting for us three hundred feet below.

It was then past three o'clock, and we had arranged to pick up our funeral director at the restaurant in the main square of Litókhoron at one; but he was there waiting for us, his backpack beside him, with sparkling eyes. "No matter how wonderful your climb was," he said, "let me tell you that I made the right decision."

On the drive back to Thessaloníki the climbers told him exaggerated tales of their hardships and privations on Mount Olympus, and he enthused about his Greek god in Litókhoron. I still smarted from the humiliation of the playboy's beastly behavior and the architect's laughter; but by the time we reached the outskirts of the city, neither of these seemed of any importance. After all, I cleaned up after my cats when they were sick; why should I resent doing it for someone I would never see again who believed it was my job to do so and considered it funny?

In Thessaloníki we all much appreciated the Hotel Capitol's hot showers and soft beds; and it was an unexpected bonus when Adam informed us—correctly, as it proved—that the streets outside that hotel, and the adjoining square with its porno movie houses and bars, were "my city's best areas for hunting." We agreed that his word was much more descriptive than our "cruising" for that activity. After dinner in the hotel, those tour members who wished had only to step out onto the busy sidewalk to obtain their reward for having accomplished the challenging two-day mountain climb.

15

MODERN
WANDERERS
IN A
BIBLICAL
WILDERNESS

HOW CURIOUS is the Bible story of Moses leading the Hebrew slaves out of Egypt to the Promised Land.

During the Eighteenth and Nineteenth dynasties, the Hebrews in Egypt were settled mostly in the Nile delta, the Goshen of the Bible: why did Moses not lead them directly along the coast of the Mediterranean to Canaan, or across the flat, easily traversed desert? No canal then separated Africa and Asia, so why did he take the multitude south and far off the route and face the perils of crossing the Red Sea? And why did they wander in the Sinai for forty years— forty *years*—if it was what the Bible calls "the great and terrible wilderness"? They could so easily have crossed it in forty days, or less, to reach the Land of Milk and Honey.

Did they, perhaps, not intend to return to the land of their fathers at all? Were they so seduced by the fertile and beautiful valleys of the Sinai, with their springs of fresh water and palm groves, like the Wadi Feiran, of which there may well have been many more three thousand years ago, that they were content to remain there and beget children and grandchildren until the terrible old man fancied he heard a voice, saw an apparition, and destroyed their pretty Golden Calf and forced them to move on?

But just past Abu Zenîma, after the dreary drive from Cairo across the Eastern Desert and through the tunnel under the Suez Canal and then along the coast of the Sinai Peninsula, with its oil rigs and tin shanties and ugly cafés for truckers, when we turned sharply off the tarmac, we had no more doubts. Suddenly neither the road nor the torpid sea could be seen, nor any sign of civilization. After a mile the dirt road became a track; a little later this ended and our Land Rovers hurtled across the desert—the gaunt wilderness of the Old Testament where only our Bedouin drivers and guides knew (or claimed they knew) the way through the wadis.

We doubted nothing, then, for the next five days. The oasis of Ayoun Moussa, with its acacias and tamarisks and tall date palms, was indeed where Moses and his followers had rested and where he had sweetened the spring by casting a tree into it. The silver plate set into the floor of the Chapel of the Transfiguration in the Monastery of Saint Catherine marked the very spot where in the Burning Bush Moses had heard God's call; and behind the wall in the yard outside it is the bush itself, transplanted there, still alive after thirty centuries. At Nebi Haroun we saw the hill where the Hebrews had worshiped the Golden Calf; Mount Horeb is where the prophet Elijah took refuge; and when we climbed Mount Sinai in the dark in order to reach its summit at dawn and saw all the deep blue mountains of the Sinai far below us, tipped golden and then scarlet by the rising sun, we knew that this was truly *the place,* the place where God appeared and spoke and gave Moses the Tablets of the Law.

The Sinai made believers of us all.

Darkness comes fast here, and the sun had set when we arrived at Sheikh Selim's settlement. It was not the assemblage of low striped goat-hair tents that the early-nineteenth-century painter

David Roberts depicted in his pale, hauntingly lovely watercolors and that, when I had first seen them as a boy, had sparked my lifelong yearning to travel and be welcomed in them. Instead, the sheikhs of the Sinai now live in miserable stone huts, roofed with corrugated iron sheets, and instead of crouched camels, it was decrepit trucks and rusted old cars that we saw nearby. But despite these doubtless unavoidable manifestations of modernization, our arrival resembled that shown in the early-nineteenth-century pictures, with the womenfolk being hurried out of sight at the approach of the male visitors, the many ragged and some tiny naked children crowding around the Land Rovers to watch sleeping bags, cooking utensils, firewood, and provisions being unloaded, and Sheikh Selim in every way as handsome an Arabic chief as portrayed in the most romanticized of films. While our drivers and guides attended to the chores, he invited us to sit with him on carpets spread on the ground, and ordered coffee and dates to be brought.

The seven tribes of Bedouins of the Sinai, each headed by a sheikh, are not descended from the original dwellers; they came here from Arabia during the Muslim conquest. The lowest tribe is that of the Jaballiya, whose members are the descendants of four hundred men whom the emperor Justinian sent here from the Balkans in the sixth century to build the monastery below Mount Sinai and who still do all the work in it; they were converted to Islam and worship in their mosque within the monastery walls.

Of Bedouin women one sees nothing except heavily shrouded figures, hennaed hands, and eyes; but Bedouin men must be the most stunning males in the world. It is not by chance that the legend of "the Sheik of Araby" has fired the erotic imagination of the West. Ever since I heard Miss Marlene Dietrich in her throaty voice long for "the man who takes things into his hands and gets what he demands . . . by moonlight, under a big palm tree," the desert with its regal sheikhs has beckoned. The desert had entered my heart, the glorious sands of Arabia where one has only to call out "*Ana dakhil-ak*" to a hawk-eyed Bedouin at a moment of danger in order to be swept up into his strong, protective arms. Was I, perhaps, after all, of Nabataean stock, as my old friend Stewart Perowne had claimed, and thus drawn atavistically to the Sinai because my people had dwelt there in goat-hair tents two thousand years ago?

Bedouin men are lean, their bodies worn, their legs all sinew and as slender as a goat's. Their eyes are as keen as those of a predatory animal. Their daily lives—despite the substitute of a stone hut for a tent, and of trucks for camels—have not changed in a thousand years. They exist on a few dates, a little corn, and several cups of coffee. They move with great dignity, princes all; and when a Bedouin modestly arranges his white galabiya to sit beside you on the ground, and smiles, you are transported to heaven.

And so, on our first night in the Sinai, we twelve men sat with Sheikh Selim and his young sons by lamplight while our guides prepared dinner, and for me a dream had come true: it was, here on earth, the paradise promised in the Koran, where beautiful youths serve food and drink to the faithful warriors. Even when the sheikh produced his large photograph album and proudly showed us the pictures of all the young (and not so young) German women whom he had entertained there, and who had sent him lovingly inscribed pictures—"*Vielen Dank für die schönste Nacht, meines Lebens!*"—we were only somewhat disappointed.

Early next morning he sent one of his sons to lead us up the steep cliff to Serabit el Khadim, which is on land claimed by his tribe. The temple, on a plateau several hundred feet above the valley, was begun in a cave on a modest scale during the Twelfth Dynasty, almost four thousand years ago, when turquoise was first mined here. It is dedicated to the cow-headed goddess Hathor. For more than five hundred years it grew to include a great court and chambers where many stelae were erected and still stand, bearing reliefs and hieroglyphic inscriptions; they are very impressive, but it is above all the setting of this remote temple that makes the journey to it so rewarding—the view over the rugged granite mountains with their layers of red, black, purple, and yellow rock, and the thrill of having reached an archaeological site so dramatically situated, so difficult of access, so rarely visited. We were alone here with the sheikh's son and our guide, and despite the sign that the Israelis had erected at the entrance to the site during their occupation of the Sinai in the 1970s, we felt as though we were the first travelers to have made the arduous climb up to the temple since Karsten Niebuhr discovered it in 1762. Except for the earliest alphabet carved in the rocks—Canaanite pictographs of the eighteenth century B.C., which ultimately developed into Hebrew letters—Serabit el Khadim is not a site of major importance, but for the traveler who has shuffled with hundreds of other tourists through the crowded great temples of ancient Egypt, it is a welcome relief.

Our Land Rovers awaited us in the shade of acacia trees in the valley below; the drivers had hot mint tea ready for us; then we drove on across the uncharted wadis.

The Sinai is a desert, but not of sand. It is rocky, and aromatic herbs and lichens and prickly shrubs thrive in its hard soil and provide scanty but sufficient nourishment for the flocks of camels, goats, and sheep. There are springs in the valleys, where date palms flourish, and tamarisk trees, which in the hot summer months produce a medicinal gum—the manna of the Bible. It is a stark landscape, but not a forbidding one, with constant changes of rock formations and vegetation as we passed from one wadi into the next—certainly nowhere as terrifying as the Bible descriptions of it. Occasionally we saw tent ropes and carpets tied up in the branches of trees, high above the ground, out of reach of wild beasts, and stoutly corded packages that, our guides explained, contained flour, corn, dates, coffee, and sugar. They had been left there by wandering tribes to be collected on their return months later; no one would think of disturbing them.

Camping in the Wadi Mukkatab—the "Written Valley"—was a joy. Our group was alone here, not even a Bedouin in sight, and we lay in our sleeping bags and looked at the stars until we fell asleep. In ancient times this valley was a major thoroughfare for caravans, whose leaders left messages in Semitic, Nabataean, and Greek inscribed on the rock walls. "Look at these old fax numbers!" said our guide.

From there we drove south to the Wadi Feiran, and as we approached the paved road that crosses the Sinai there and I saw electricity and telephone poles in the distance and realized that our three peaceful, spiritually inspiring days and nights in the desert were over, I almost wept; but my tour members burst into spontaneous applause as the Land Rover drove onto the tarmac. True, the ride across the rock-strewn wadis had been far from comfortable, even painful at times, but I would gladly have continued it for much longer. Maybe I am too romantic: not everyone shares my appreciation that part of the pleasure of foreign travel arises from hardship and privation.

The Wadi Feiran, the jewel of the Sinai, lush and green and dense with plantations of date palms, enchanted me less than it did my tour members. There are modern houses, fences, gas stations, metal advertising signs with graceful Arabic letters but also in English and, worse, in German. It was good, I felt, to pass through it quickly and head into the mountains to the Monastery of Saint Catherine at the foot of Mount Sinai.

I had assumed that our confirmed reservations at the guest quarters of the monastery would be within its massive, fortress-like walls. I had expected to be met by welcoming monks bearing trays of coffee and *loukoum* and water as at the monasteries on Mount

Athos, and conducted to comfortable rooms filled with period furniture, opening out onto the wooden balconies pictured in the
watercolors of David Roberts, where monks and visitors are taking
their ease overlooking the courtyard. It was not so. The guest quarters are now outside the monastery, but not in its fine garden or
among the groves of ancient cedars; they are hundreds of feet away,
close to the charnel house, next to the car park and beside the souvenir store. When at last I located the guestmaster, an American
monk with whom I had corresponded, he made a pretense of not
knowing who I was and would not touch the jar of marmalade made
from my orange tree that I had brought him as a gift. "Put it in the
office," he said. A slovenly Jaballiya with rheumy eyes, a dripping
nose, and a sinister cough showed us a depressing dormitory with
double-tiered bunks. (On half a dozen subsequent visits, another
guestmaster, Father George Tzevelekos, who has become a friend,
welcomed me and my groups, allocated superior bedrooms with
clean toilets and washing facilities to us, and took considerable
trouble to ensure that we saw far more of the monastery's treasures
than did other visitors.)

None of us was happy to have arrived at this, the highly lauded
highlight of our Sinai tour. It was dark and we were cold here, at six
thousand feet above sea level, much colder than any of us had anticipated. We were hungry and dirty and thoroughly miserable.

It was one of those moments when even the hardiest of travelers
asks himself, What have I done to deserve this? Why have I left my
snug home, my dear friend, my darling cats, my comfortable bed
with my bedside lamp? Why am I here?

For three days the tour members had looked forward most of all
to the showers I had promised they would find here; and although
there was one rudimentary shower next to the revoltingly dirty
toilets, the water was icy. Dear Evert Dijkema, that immaculately

neat and cleanly Dutchman who had traveled with me so often, set us an example. "Well, let us show that we are pilgrims," he said, and bravely went and stood shivering for a moment under the frigid trickle. None of the others felt the need to prove they were pilgrims. They sulked.

The intense cold and our chilly reception had also broken the normally high spirits of our guides. They came to me and announced that the provisions that should have awaited them at the monastery were not there; they had no food left except some bread; they could cook no supper for us; we would have to go to bed hungry; it was not their fault; it was God's will.

It was one of those moments when the tour leader must exert his authority and stand for no nonsense. "Jesus, the Prophet Muhammad's forerunner, fed a great multitude with only five loaves of bread and two fishes," I said. "Surely you will not let a dozen hungry pilgrims starve? Let us go and see what you have, and trust in God."

We went to the kitchen of the guest quarters. They showed me the bread. "There—that is all we have. You must eat dry bread tonight." I rummaged in our provision boxes and sacks and found a package wrapped in tin foil, two feet long and encouragingly fat—a salami sausage. "You will slice this," I said, "and you will tell the Jaballiya that they must give you tomatoes and peppers and onions—preferably some of each—and you will put it all in your large frying pan and heat it, and pour it over the sliced and toasted bread; and I know that there was a big piece of cheese left over at lunchtime—you will grate that on top of everything. We will have a feast tonight!"

Further search miraculously brought to light four large cans of Israeli peaches in heavy syrup. I started to open them, but Evert, whom curiosity and a desire to assist me in this crisis had brought to the kitchen, snatched the opener out of my hand. "Never open a can until you have thoroughly washed its top with boiling water!" he cried in alarm.

I distributed trail food to the tour members while they lay in their sleeping bags on the metal cots, trying to get warm as they waited for supper. An hour later the guides called us to table. There were festive candles; there were paper napkins twisted into the shape of birds; there was an abundance of the savory and piping-hot salami-and-vegetable stew. The peaches were served in bowls with thick condensed milk and a date on top. There was wine; there was hot tea. It was indeed a feast. We went back to our cots with our bellies full and our spirits much revived.

✧

Since the Israelis built the airport near Mount Sinai and motor roads providing easy access to it, the Monastery of Saint Catherine, which could previously be reached only by camel, horse, or on foot after many days of arduous travel, has become one of the major tourist attractions of Egypt. Its twenty resident Greek Orthodox monks are foreigners there and must conform to the government's order to admit tourists; but they are quite unable to control the increasing numbers who arrive each morning by air from Cairo or who stay at the inns or campsites nearby. "I became a monk to serve God; I never expected to have to serve tourists," said the guestmaster. "It is my penance."

By 9:00 A.M. we watched with a mixture of fascination and distaste as hundreds of tourists assembled outside the narrow gate. It was not a pretty sight. A carnival atmosphere prevailed. Men and women in gaudy and abbreviated beach attire shouted and laughed and sang. Their bare legs, arms, and shoulders were highly offensive to the monks, and acrimonious arguments ensued when the most immodestly clad women were offered the loan of a jacket to cover their nakedness before being admitted into the monastery through the gate. "Forget it! So we won't go in at all!" screamed an obese woman wearing brief shorts and a halter top; and she and her friends indignantly turned their backs on the monastery and instead ostentatiously removed some more garments and sunbathed opposite the gate, angrily threw orange peelings around themselves, and scratched their names on the rocks.

Unable to prevent the tourist invasion, the monks show as little as possible of their ancient precinct. Only a small part of the courtyard is open to tourists; the Burning Bush is almost hidden behind a high stone wall to prevent visitors from taking cuttings; and only a tantalizingly brief glimpse is granted of the interior of the church. The narthex, where some of the monastery's precious icons are on display, is in darkness, and the officious monk on guard forbids the use of flashlights. The American guestmaster had mellowed somewhat—perhaps my jar of homemade marmalade had, after all, pleased him—and he took my group and me past the iconostasis to see the magnificent sixth-century mosaic of the Transfiguration of Christ in the half-dome of the apse, and then, as a further and even greater favor, opened the small chapel of the Burning Bush for us; but the majority of the tourists remained herded together in the narrow courtyard and, there being no guides for them, showed their disappointment, felt cheated. It is a long way to come to see so little. But as I observed them I wondered why most of them had gone to the considerable expense of coming there at all. Almost none of these aimless wanderers seemed to know anything of the creation and the history of the monastery, did not realize how unique is the mosque within its walls. They were intent on buying souvenirs from the Jaballiya.

Later that morning, after the backpackers and the tourists on the day excursion had left, we watched with wonder as several buses brought more tourists from the airport, escorted by the white vans and cars of the United Nations peacekeeping force, a certain sign that these were important visitors. They were expected, and the abbot appeared and personally and deferentially led them through the gate; consumed with curiosity, we slipped in behind this elegant group, several members of which we recognized.

"Quick, where's the Burning Bush? We have a plane waiting," called out the California millionairess who had chartered a jet aircraft to take her and sixty of her friends from Cairo to see the monastery. Among her guests were the ex-king of Bulgaria, the most dangerous woman in the Reagan administration, one pretty young man who seemed incongruously out of place among all these elderly people, and New York's most fashionable sadist, who had thirty years before taken me to his grand flat in London to show me his current slave, a nice chubby American antique dealer, chained to the wall of his bathroom. He did not recognize me with my beard, in my dusty clothes and the black-and-white *keffiyeh* wound round my neck.

The abbot showed the Burning Bush behind its protective wall. One lady in the group looked closely at the venerable shrub through one of the little barred openings. "Oh, it's only a raspberry—and I have a better one in my garden in Santa Barbara!" she called out.

Escorted by the loudly hooting United Nations vans and cars, they all drove back to the airport.

How superior we felt, how smug, that we had not flown in for an hour by jet plane but had crossed the desert and slept under the stars and not washed for three days and suffered bitter cold in order to approach the ancient monastery with reverence and prepare ourselves for the climb of Mount Sinai above it. How proud we were that we were not tourists but *pilgrims*. How glad we were, how fortunate we considered ourselves, that we were not rich Philistines but had with us a knowledgeable Egyptologist from the Metropolitan Museum of Art in New York who read the hieroglyphic inscriptions on the stelae at Serabit el Khadim to us as easily as headlines in *The New York Times;* and a pair of gorgeous young lovers who romantically greeted each wonderful day in the desert by wandering hand in hand away from camp to fornicate in privacy among the rocks at sunrise; and Evert Dijkema, who was deterred by nothing, a travel companion par excellence despite his caustic remarks and scathing condemnation of much that he saw around him and pretended to dislike.

✧

I woke up everyone at 2:30 A.M., and we scrambled into our warmest clothes. It was very cold. Our guides had set up candles in the dining room—there was no electric power at night—and made hot tea for us. At 3:00 A.M. we set off with flashlights to climb Mount Sinai.

To see the sunrise from the summit of the holy mountain had become a universally popular attraction. Backpackers from Australia, South Africa, and New Zealand headed for the Sinai to spend a night on the peak; Europeans of all ages came in droves to make the climb; Jews, Christians, and Muslims came, even Hindus and Buddhists. We were prepared to encounter other hikers on the path, but astonished to see quite so many flashlight beams around us and ahead of us, each denoting a pilgrim. It is not easy to hike in the dark along an unfamiliar and rocky trail, with only the stars to guide one; but the path is an easy one until it ends after about two hours of climbing, and the last five hundred feet or so to the summit are a series of rough, irregular, rock-hewn steps.

It was much colder up there, even, than at the monastery in the valley, and the prospect of scaling those formidable steps was daunting. While my tour members went ahead, I stopped and peeled my orange, more than half-inclined not to follow them; but fortunately two tiny Japanese ladies of advanced age passed me and effortlessly ascended the steps in their high-heeled shoes, blithely chattering to each other. I could not bear to see them do it, and forced myself manfully to stride on and up.

In their eagerness to reach the summit, some of the hikers rudely forced their way past those who walked at a slower pace; and many were unpleasantly noisy. It was all too evident that they were not pilgrims, had no respect for this holy place, had come only because it was "cool," it was "neat," to make the climb.

"Silence, s'il vous plaît: cette montagne est un lieu très sacré pour les juifs, les chrétiens, et les musulmans," I called out to a particularly boisterous group of inebriated French who ran past me and pushed me aside so that I almost fell. They jeered at me and laughed all the more.

On the summit we found dozens of young people lying in bed-rolls among their filth: tin cans, plastic bottles, toilet paper, rotting food. An Australian who was ignoring the famous sunrise and pressed facedown on a girl in their sleeping bag called out "Shut up, mate!" when a priest led his party in prayer. Vendors of tawdry trinkets and cold drinks had set up their stalls outside the small chapel and mosque, both of which were closed. Few of those on the summit except my tour members, the religious group, some photographers behind their tripods, and the athletic old Japanese ladies gave a glance at the sun as it rose and revealed range after range of jagged mountains and turned the biblical wilderness below us from inky purple to pale pink.

When we hiked back to the monastery by daylight, we saw that the whole trail was as profusely littered as the summit. Among the graffiti scratched onto the mountainside were the ominous words FREE CHARLIE MANSON.

Unable to control the tourists or to patrol the holy mountain, the monks remain sequestered within their walls on the five days each week when they must admit visitors. The United Nations like the temporary happenings of the artist Christo, but had been sprayed with paint. The desecration of the Wadi Zaghra is permanent.

We asked who had perpetrated this horror. "A Jew from Belgium came and did it," we were told. "When Israel took the Sinai from us." But Israel, which did so much to develop the Sinai Peninsula during its occupation, and to preserve its historical sites, is quite blameless. When Jean Verame proposed his scheme to the Israeli government in the 1970s, they condemned it as a destruction of nature and opposed it as a violation of the sanctity of ground lying within sight of Mount Sinai. Then the political situation altered; the Sinai reverted to Egypt, and President Sadat, to his shame, permitted the work to begin. "I am not anti-ecology; my work is a marriage between me and nature," announced Monsieur Verame. A *marriage*? Who sanctioned it? It is a ghastly *mésalliance,* and the damage inflicted on the Wadi Zaghra will remain on view for thousands of years if it is left for the desert wind to remove the paint from the rocks and mountains, from the caves and crevices into which it was arrogantly sprayed.

How could President Sadat have agreed to this sacrilege on so vast a scale? Surely he knew that Moses and his followers wandered through this valley; that the daughters of Jethro watered their sheep here; that six hundred years later, the prophet Elijah came there seeking refuge from the rage of Queen Jezebel. Nearby is the tomb of Nabi Saleh, one of the patriarchs in the Koran, where Bedouins from all over the Sinai Peninsula and beyond gather in May to attend the annual ceremonies in this saintly sheikh's honor before ascending Mount Sinai to make offerings at its peak—the place most universally sacred on earth, because on it, side by side, and from reverence for the same event on which both religions are founded, stand a Christian church and a Muslim mosque.

In this serene landscape, made precious by its many religious

peacekeeping force attempts to help by occasionally sending o
its helicopters to the summit and cleaning it; but the refuse
cumulates too fast for them to keep up with it.

We were shocked and saddened. With no tourist police in
dence at the archaeological sites, with no custodians to discou
littering and vandalism, more damage is being done to the histo
and scenic places of the Sinai by tourists in a few years than dur
the previous forty centuries. The Israelis built airports and ro
and created new towns and ports and beach resorts during th
occupation of the peninsula, and left their well-planned infrastru
ture intact when they departed; and now it is the Egyptian gover
ment's responsibility to guard and patrol and preserve the
treasures for posterity. The serious traveler who makes the ascent
the summit of Mount Sinai should not find the cave where G
appeared to Moses filled with garbage, human excreta, and d
carded condoms.

✧

The tourist mess at the summit of Mount Sinai was not the
desecration we saw in the Sinai.

For our picnic luncheon we drove a few miles north of the n
astery to the Wadi Zaghra, to see for ourselves the blue roc
which I had heard strange stories; and we were stunned to find
the rocks, boulders, and mountainsides covering an area of
square miles are indeed a bright, shiny cobalt-blue.

Our first sight of these markings made the tour members
with disbelief: this blue joke on such a monumental scale is nc
done; we were surprised, like Dr. Samuel Johnson on anothe
sion, to see it done at all. But our astonishment turned to
when, as we drove nearer, we realized that the muted colors
granite, ranging from deep purple through every subtle sl
red and rosy pink to pure white, were not hidden under blu

associations, the acres of blue paint in the Wadi Zaghra are singu-
larly and grotesquely inappropriate. Man has imposed his will on
nature in other lands, but the prehistoric representations of men
and horses on English hillsides do not offend us; they were cut into
the turf with humility for tribal or religious purposes. The pre-
Columbian lines and drawings that stretch mysteriously across
Chile's Atacama Desert and the Nazca plain in Peru are an integral
part of the ground; they were created not to shock but to be viewed
by the gods. In the Wadi Zaghra, God and man weep. The Sinai
Peninsula is too precious to be treated like the walls of a deserted
slum tenement where graffiti are tolerated or encouraged. This valley belongs not to Egypt alone but to millions of people who revere
a wilderness where all around, on mountains, sand, and sky, God's
chariot wheels have left a most distinct trace.

We took photographs; in protest, I scratched some flakes of the
acrylic paint off a rock; and we hoped that the government of Egypt
might regret its late president's approval for the scheme, and restore
the natural colors of the rocks regardless of expense, even if it takes
a multitude of laborers forty years to chip off every trace of the
offending blue paint.

We crossed the remaining part of the Sinai and drove down to
the Gulf of Aqaba and camped on a white sand beach and swam and
snorkeled among the fantastically colored fish and coral formations.
There was no one else in sight, but after dinner, as we sat around the
fire, two tall white ghostly figures appeared, lean Bedouin men,
who silently lowered themselves to the ground and lay by us, each
reclining on an elbow, and accepted our offer of coffee. Their presence by the glow of the fire seemed too imbued with romantic
possibilities, too theatrically contrived, almost, to be real. Even I,
old enough to be their father, indeed their grandfather, felt my
bowels grow taut with desire. And then the *amuseur* among us, he
who could always be relied upon in any situation to find the right

word, began softly to sing in a fair imitation of the sultry, throaty, passionate voice of Miss Marlene Dietrich:

> *Give me the man who does things,*
> *Does things to my heart.*
>
> *I love the man who takes things into his hands*
> *And gets what he demands—*
>
> *And when we're alone by moonlight,*
> *Under a big palm tree—*
>
> *Oh, give me the man who does things—*
> *Does things to me.*

Next day we drove to the airport at Ras Nasrani, parted tearfully from our guides and drivers, and caught the plane to Cairo.

16

A

JOURNEY

TO

VILCABAMBA

FOR MANY YEARS I had dreamed of being able one day to explore that almost mythical area in the Peruvian Andes to which the Inca Manco II retreated from Cusco with his followers in 1536 after the Spanish conquest, to seek refuge there in order to preserve the customs, the religion, and the traditions of his people.

Very little has been written about Vilcabamba, which the nineteenth-century historian W. H. Prescott described hauntingly as "the remote fastnesses of the Andes." Even the meticulously detailed and annually revised British *South American Handbook* had almost nothing to tell me about it, and what it did say was inaccurate hearsay. Peruvian guidebooks tantalizingly omit any mention of the area and thus added zest to my eagerness to travel there—but whenever I announced this intention to officials of the Peru Tourist Office and requested travel information, they were horrified at the idea. Vilcabamba was not a place for tourists, they said; the local mestizo population was intensely xenophobic and obstructive; the only road into the area was generally closed by landslides or washed away by torrential mountain streams; there was nowhere to stay, no food could be bought, the rivers were polluted, tropical diseases were rampant, no guides were available—nor was there anything of interest to be seen. Instead they recommended a beach resort near Lima.

I was accustomed to hear such objections when any scheme that is in the least unusual is proposed to government employees; and some years later I consulted my friend Julio Sotomayor, the best guide in Cusco and its surroundings, with whom I had traveled extensively for almost twenty years and who is thoroughly familiar with the Andean region. His grandfather owned a farm in the Urubamba valley below Machu Picchu and had received Dr. Hiram Bingham there in 1911. Julio assured me that there was no danger in traveling in Vilcabamba, that the people in the villages were entirely friendly and, though very poor, welcomed the rare visitors, that the road was good enough to be negotiated by a minibus. He had toured the area twice and visited Vitcos and the famous Yurac Rumi and even penetrated on foot deep into the jungle to Espíritu Pampa; he could arrange for tents, camping gear, food, and staff. Everything I wished to accomplish was quite feasible.

Thus reassured, I was given the final impetus to go ahead with my plans when I came across the *Sixpac Manco* publications of Mr. Vincent R. Lee, a Wyoming architect who made six explorations into the Vilcabamba region between 1982 and 1989 and whose lucid field guides contain fold-out maps, hundreds of detailed and scaled plans and drawings of all the Inca sites thus far discovered, descriptions of two hundred miles of Inca roads along which he had hiked, perspective sketches and architectural-site reconstructions, plus photographs and a satellite image of the entire region. Vilcabamba was no longer a myth—it existed; it was charted; it could be visited; I could follow in the footsteps of Hiram Bingham and Gene Savoy and be guided by Dr. Lee as far as my physical condition and my limited time permitted. I would go not for any scientific reason but merely *because it is there.*

It would be my nineteenth visit to Peru in twenty-five years. I had traveled there from Trujillo and Chan-Chan in the north to Arequipa and Lake Titicaca in the south, from Iquitos and the Amazon River to Paracas on the Pacific coast and the Nazca plain. On each visit I had stayed in Cusco and in the Sacred Valley and climbed steep Huayna Picchu, which rises above the Inca ruins of Machu Picchu. But now I craved for more. I yearned to hike trails that were not trodden daily by hundreds of visitors; I longed to see archaeological sites in remote jungles, too inaccessible for mass tourism, that remained in the heavily overgrown and romantic condition in which Dr. Bingham had seen them eighty years ago and in which Mr. Savoy had still found them in the 1960s. The attraction of Machu Picchu had palled for me. We know nothing of its history, of who lived there and when, whether it was a place of any importance or merely a fortuitously beautiful military outpost. The historically far more important Inca sites in Vilcabamba, only sixty miles beyond Machu Picchu to the north but almost unknown and picturesquely neglected, beckoned to my spirit of adventure—and of them we have the graphic firsthand accounts by sixteenth-century Spanish soldiers and priests, in addition to the recollections of life at the Inca court that the Inca Titu Cusi dictated to his Spanish translators. How stirring were the few photographs I found showing the royal residence at Vitcos, with huge trees thrusting their branches through doorways and windows, and roots relentlessly forcing apart the perfectly fitted Inca building stones. It is only among ruins in a state of such destruction that their great past still lingers, only such relics of the past that appeal to me. "No circumstance so forcibly marks the desolation of a spot once inhabited, as the prevalence of nature over it," said Thomas Whately, writing about the pleasure of ruins in 1770.

The Inca remains of Peru—as well as numerous pre-Inca sites—deservedly act as magnets for many thousands of travelers each year, but they have been tidied up, cleared of vegetation, restored, and reconstructed to such a degree that they are in danger of losing all their mystery and majesty.

Machu Picchu, the most dramatically situated archaeological site on earth, rivaled only, perhaps, by Petra in Jordan, looks each year more like a functional and well-planned modern holiday village whose neat stone cottages (some with cozy sleeping lofts) with running water, sun terraces, and picture windows need only new roofs to make them into highly desirable vacation homes. Towering over them is the spectacular Huayna Picchu, with a trail zigzagging steeply up its west side to the jagged peak fifteen hundred feet above the Inca town. It used to provide a considerable challenge to climbers, but since the early 1980s has been provided with ropes at the more precipitous sections; iron stanchions have been hammered into the rock, so that the ascent has sadly lost most of its terror and become an easy hour's promenade for grandmothers.

My annual visits to what the travel brochures call "the Lost City of the Incas" had become disappointingly prosaic. Julio Sotomayor's encouragement and Dr. Lee's publications convinced me that a visit to Vilcabamba need no longer be a dream. I would go. All I had to do was to find half a dozen people who were as interested to explore the *real* last refuge of the Incas with me—and pay substantially for the privilege of doing so.

✧

Three small advertisements in *Archaeology* magazine announced the first tourist expedition to Vilcabamba in July of 1991 and brought in scores of inquiries and, in due course, six bookings for it. Unfortunately, one couple later canceled their reservations because they became increasingly worried by the barrage of adverse and false press reports about travel conditions in Peru and by the U.S. State Department's politically motivated travel advisory, which, on the pretext of protecting Americans abroad, is used to punish those countries whose governments or heads of state are not currently to the department's liking. By ruining these countries' tourism, it hopes to bring them to heel. Although I assured this couple that during twenty-five years and on eighteen extended tours of Peru I had always found the country safe, they did not reconsider their decision—and deprived themselves of a memorable and completely safe travel experience.

So it was only four intrepid travelers who left Miami with me for Lima; and they proved to be wonderfully congenial. We all shared an interest in wishing to see the country where the last four rulers of the Inca Empire had reigned, with the remains of their palace and places of worship, and our ages were not uncomfortably disparate; but there is always an element of danger when putting together total strangers who must, as on a journey of this nature, live at close proximity day after day, night after night, often in less-than-comfortable circumstances. They may not all jell into a group, one's habits may begin to grate on the nerves of the others, another may feel ignored by the majority and become morose and withdrawn. Fortunately, none of this occurred. We remained from beginning to end a happy little band of fellow travelers, tolerant of one another's individual ways.

Eve Adamson was lively and enthusiastic, and both her soulful, contemplative manner and her flowing, cloaklike garments and exotic sweaters made me think of her as a character in a Russian play. She was indeed active in the theatrical world of New York, had owned a theater there, and had produced Tennessee Williams's last play. She was fascinated by the mysterious, mystic aspect of the

Yurac Rumi, the famous "White Stone" of the Incas, still the most sacred relic of the Andean Indians. Although she was the youngest member of our group, she turned out to be the slowest hiker and liked to stop often to catch her breath; this was extremely agreeable to the rest of us, who longed for a slower pace and a rest and could thus feel that we were doing it for her benefit and not feel guilty.

Constance and Quentin Armstrong, originally from New Jersey and now living in Maine, had been married for more than forty years. He was a retired architect and an avid photographer, and had made a study of urban planning in pre-Columbian America and of Incan methods of construction. They were one of those uniquely American unassuming couples who are an inspiration to us all—devoted to each other, considerate of others, thoughtful of those who serve them, delighting in outdoor pursuits—bird-watching, botanizing, hiking, camping—with never an unkind thought, always a pleasant word for everyone, punctual to a fault—pure gold.

"I thought I'd be the only woman on this rough trip," said Connie when I gave her the expedition membership list at Miami Airport. "I only came along to keep Quentin company—he's the one who is so keen on all those old ruins. And now he is the only man!"

"Don't I count?" I asked.

Ingrid Menon was the widow of a rich Indian industrialist and a remarkably interesting lady. Archaeology had intrigued her since her early childhood, when her father, a Bosnian count, had taken her along on explorations among the Bogomil tombs in the valleys of Montenegro, and she had participated in digs all over the Balkans, throughout the Middle East, in Algeria, the Indus Valley, Tibet, and in the Kamchatka peninsula of eastern Russia—where she had been imprisoned for four extremely disagreeable months due to a regrettable misunderstanding. She had spent several seasons under very rough conditions exploring and mapping pre-Inca sites from

Colombia to Tierra del Fuego; and this was her sixth expedition in Peru.

In her youth she had been a keen sailor and had crossed the Atlantic single-handed in her twelve-foot catamaran. She had taken first place in the grueling Paris-to-Moscow bicycle race in the winter of 1953–54.

She had earned degrees in twentieth-century European literature, South Asian history, and Islamic and pre-Columbian archaeology from the universities of Besançon, Bologna, Istanbul, Madras, and Zagreb. A musician of world renown, she had given piano recitals to high acclaim in her native Vienna and in most of the other capital cities of Europe, in Calcutta and Johannesburg, and had adapted a Monteverdi opera for a jazz-orchestra performance in Tokyo.

She now lived mostly in her Manhattan penthouse and devoted much of her time and all her abilities to numerous charitable organizations of whose boards she was a member and that she also supported financially; but she also maintained homes in the Yucatán, on the Greek island of Samos—"so convenient for taking my fast motorboat across to the Turkish coast to revisit Ephesus, Halicarnassus, and Miletus"—on the Gulf of Kotor, in Darjeeling, as well as a pied-à-terre on the Île Saint-Louis in Paris—"everyone should have a little flat there," she said.

She was equally fluent in eight languages and could, she said, get by in at least a dozen others. She was dedicated to everything she did and extremely hardworking. She allowed herself no leisure. If she had a free morning, she occupied herself with her *broderie anglaise,* of which examples were in the permanent collections of museums in Austria, Canada, Denmark, Upper Volta, and Switzerland; she was a needlewoman of international fame and had embroidered the neckline and cuffs of the dress that her best friend, a former first lady, had worn on the occasion of her husband's inauguration in Washington, D.C.

Ingrid told us about her many diverse accomplishments in a very matter-of-fact way and with admirable modesty; she was a simply and sensibly dressed lady, always appreciative and interested in everything around her, and she cheerfully accepted any unavoidable discomforts—an unusually fascinating travel companion who never failed to astonish us.

✧

In Lima, we dined with my old friend Ricardo Laos, always a pessimist. "Maybe I'll see you when you return," he said. "If you do. The Indians in that terrible Vilcabamba still use poisoned arrows."

Julio Sotomayor met us at the airport in Cusco. Heavy clouds were swirling over the surrounding mountains. "I fear much it will snow," he said cheerfully. "I hope we make it through Abra Málaga." We rested all afternoon to become accustomed to the altitude of eleven thousand feet and then took a walk at a very slow pace through the cobblestoned streets.

In the Sacred Valley—surely the most idyllic valley in Peru, if not in the world—we stayed two nights at the charming Alhambra Inn, a converted sixteenth-century monastery, ideally located for making excursions to the ruins at Pisac and Ollantaytambo. We feasted on Andean river trout, three of the reputed 240 varieties of Peruvian potatoes, and *chica morada,* a sweet puree of red corn, and anxiously watched the snow-laden clouds.

Here in Yucay, our expedition minibus arrived early in the morning for the drive over the Málaga Pass and into the Vilcabamba region. The road over the pass is so taxing that it requires two drivers to take the wheel in turns, each for two or three hours, and I had often traveled with Ascensio and Mario, who were not only capable drivers but resourceful mechanics. The faces of our camp cook and staff were all new to me, and I looked in vain for the ruggedly handsome Braulio Roja, for whom I had on previous tours in the Andes developed a *Schwärmerei* and engaged to be our camp master. He was not there. It was a disappointment; but his substitute, the petite Lourdes Rodríguez, originally from Trujillo in northern Peru, who at first struck me as being incongruously unsuited for the job in a country where women are rarely placed in positions of command over men, ruled over the camp staff with unquestioned authority. She was full of energy, and we camped in considerable style. Half an hour after arriving at a campsite, the tents would all be set up with a bowl of hot water for washing placed outside each of them, and tea and cookies were served in the mess tent—or, if it was close to sunset and becoming cold, hot wine and cheese savories. At first light, the cook's assistant scratched on each tent flap and brought mugs of hot tea and bowls of hot water for the morning ablutions.

When Julio introduced Lourdes to us, she beamed at Ingrid. "Oh, Señora Menon, what an honor to travel with you: I saw you often three years ago when you were excavating at Chan-Chan."

Another member of our team was Edgar Salazar, a policeman from Cusco whom I had hired to provide us with protection, although I doubted very much that there was any need for such precaution. He spoke English well and wore blue jeans and a bulky sweater under which, I assumed, he carried a handgun. I never saw it. He looked upon this trip with us as a paid holiday and was eager to show his appreciation for having been selected by begging us to let him carry our day packs or books or maps and helping us up steep slopes and across rivers; but, as I had expected, his presence was entirely unnecessary. Indeed, if we had ever been in any danger at night—attacked by the nonexistent bandits about which the U.S. State Department gave warnings, or by a roving jaguar—he would have been the last member of our group to know about it. His tent was always pitched next to mine, and whenever I had to get up during the night—at my age, alas, distressingly often—I heard Edgar loudly snoring.

When we left Yucay, Julio explained that our camping staff was not yet complete—we had to stop in the square at Ollantaytambo to collect the cook's assistant. Knowing that the village Indians have practically no sense of time, I expected him either to keep us waiting or not to show up that day at all, but as our bus turned into the square we saw a crowd of villagers standing at a corner, waiting to see off their friend; and a laughing, excited youth with the delicate, soft-brown coloring and endearing, soulful features of the Andean Indians bounded into the bus and embraced our cook. "He is the cook's nephew," said Julio. "His name is Lucho, and never before has he made a journey such as this."

He was a beautiful youth, but as soon as we left Ollantaytambo the bus filled with an overpowering smell. The Indians of the remote Andean villages are averse to the use of water for washing— understandably so, as the streams, fed by snow from the peaks, are painfully cold—and instead they rub their bodies with rancid oil or fat and wear their unwashed garments for many years and sleep in them at night. The rich odor emanating from the angelic Lucho was indescribable, but neither Eve nor Ingrid nor Connie and Quentin remarked on it, and this gave me the final assurance that they were not tourists but true travelers who with resignation accept any unavoidable adversity that fate sends to vex them. I must admit that the prospect of being confined in that bus with Lucho for ten hours or more each day was somewhat daunting, but I tried to console myself with the vain hope that either I would become accustomed to his smell or he might lose some of his pungency.

In any case, there was no alternative. We could not open the windows of the bus because of the dust that rose from the dirt road and, later, when we were above the tree line, because of the intense cold. Julio's fears proved unfounded; by midday the clouds dispersed, the sky was bright blue, and the only snow we encountered was below the Málaga Pass, where we stopped so that Eve, Ingrid, and Quentin could take photographs of the llamas and alpacas who stood huddled together in groups, irresistibly picturesque against the white background, with their little attendant children in bright red cloaks and hats running among them. The tour members were surprised that I had no camera, but when I told them what Le Corbusier had said—"The camera is a tool for idlers, who use a machine to do their seeing for them"—it was not well received and might better not have been quoted. Edgar had never before seen a foreign visitor without a camera. "But you will have no memories of all this when you are back home," he said.

"I will have them here," I told him, and put my hands on my chest.

"Oh, the heart is a very unreliable recorder," stated Ingrid. "Mine has often let me down badly."

The drive from the Sacred Valley over the Málaga Pass and then down into the Huyro Valley must be one of the most spectacular and varied day journeys in the world. The motor road was built in the mid-1960s and follows the Inca road over which Manco II and his people fled to Vilcabamba—first for several hours up seemingly endless and very sharp hairpin bends under colossal glaciers to the pass at almost fifteen thousand feet, with the snow-capped Mount Verónica on the left, then even more giddily down past icy lakes over which the Andean caracara hover in pairs, and through forests filled with orchids and past tea, coffee, and citrus plantations into the lowlands. Three hours after having shivered in the snow at the *ceja de la selva,* the "eyebrow of the jungle," we picnicked in shirt-sleeves by a waterfall in the rain forest.

In the afternoon we called on Señora de Barnuevo. I visit her each time I am in Peru and had brought along a pretty Italian straw hat for her, trimmed with cloth flowers in pastel colors. She is not much over four feet high and has dreadfully neglected teeth. She pulled the hat onto her head and took us to see her fields of coca bushes shaded by fruit trees, where Eve, Ingrid, and the Armstrongs all much enjoyed taking pictures of one another among these greatly maligned plants. The Señora's three annual crops provide her and her family with an extremely modest living; her ancestors have owned this coca plantation for generations; and she had been most distressed by reports that the United States would send troops in helicopters to destroy it, so that she and her children would have no alternative but to make their way to Lima and live in a cardboard or corrugated-iron shack in one of the vast slums and try to sell ballpoint pens outside the luxury hotels and the clubs of the Peruvian grandees. If she planted other crops, like tea or potatoes, her three small fields would not provide her with sufficient income to exist on her property.

Señora de Barnuevo was bewildered. She is a farmer, not a drug trafficker. She cannot understand the gringos' horror of cocaine. To her, coca is merely a plant that has for many centuries been a beneficial staple of the Andean population, that provides energy at high altitudes, and that has the additional boon, for people who rarely have enough to eat, of depressing the appetite. What the rich, the famous, and the powerful in the United States do with a substance manufactured outside Peru from her God-given plants does not concern her. She viewed the possibility of United States military involvement in her affairs with the outrage that a farmer in North Carolina would feel if foreign troops were to descend upon him in helicopters and destroy his tobacco crops.

We tried to reassure her and told her that *yanqui* invaders would not come to destroy her plants; but we failed to convince her and were not ourselves certain that it could not happen. She pressed oranges on us and gave us a mock military salute when we drove away down the valley to the *guardia* checkpoint at Chaullay and on to our first campsite.

It was there that my abhorrence of making use of the claustrophobic and unpleasant toilet tent caused me the only inconvenience of the expedition. Early in the morning, when I had walked away some distance from the camp toward the bank of the Urubamba River with my roll of toilet paper and matches with which to burn it after use, tiny insects swarmed up the inside of my trousers and viciously bit my legs as well as my hands. They were the feared *verracurum* of the Andean foothills, nasty mosquito-like dipterous insects whose bite is painful—but the *verruga peruana* disease they carry is fortunately no longer fatal, as it was in the 1870s, when thousands of workers laying the Andean railroads died of it. I treated myself with steroids and antibiotics and was poignantly reminded that travel conditions on the road to Vilcabamba had not altered in 426 years, for at almost the same place, while camping there before crossing the Choquechaca Bridge into the Vilcabamba region to meet with the Inca Titu Cusi at Vitcos, the Spanish envoy Don Diego de Figueroa had been plagued by these "biting flies" in May 1565. The incident added a touch of drama to my journey. Part of the pleasure of travel, after all, lies in the physical discomfort that increases as we venture to remote and unique places.

The Choquechaca Bridge, built on the site of the ancient Inca rope bridge across the Urubamba River, still provides the only means of entry into the Vilcabamba region.

On the road up the canyon of the Río Vilcabamba, which the officials of the Peru Tourist Office had assured me was impossible for motor traffic, we overtook many empty trucks going to the villages of Yupanca, Lucma, Puquiura, and Huancacalle, and met others returning from there, heavily loaded. It is not an ideal road for anyone suffering from vertigo, but alarming only at several sharp bends that Ascensio and Mario had to negotiate with great caution over loose stones submerged under the running water of mountain streams.

At Puquiura, we were stopped by members of the *guardia* stationed there. Our arrival gave them some rare excitement, so that they engaged our drivers and camping staff in a spirited half hour's conversation. Despite their sinister uniforms—black boots laced halfway to the knees, baggy camouflage pants, and black T-shirts, each man carrying a machine gun in addition to one or two pistols in holsters strapped around his waist and a heavy club and handcuffs dangling from it—they were amiable and delighted to see us. Their T-shirts were handsome, with thickly embossed gold letters— GUARDIA ANTISUBVERSIO—above gold grenades with scarlet flames bursting from them. "I *must* have some of these for my grandson and his buddies," said Ingrid. "He's a member of a gay motorcycle gang in Long Beach, California." And in her fluent Spanish she asked them to sell her half a dozen of them. A price was soon agreed upon, but instead of going to their barracks to bring her new T-shirts, as we had expected, so many of the soldiers began to pull off their own and thrust them at her that it was a problem for her to pick out six bare-chested soldiers whose shirts to accept. I came to her rescue and bought two to give as presents to young friends in Key West who consider military garments the utmost in chic for wearing at the local disco.

Half an hour later we reached Huancacalle, where the motor road ends. A horse trail leads from there through the jungle to the ruins of Espíritu Pampa, probably the last city of the Incas, three days away. The village looked uninviting, its one unpaved street flanked by dismal, dilapidated houses from which sad people in rags looked at us listlessly but with no signs of hostility. The only cheerful aspect was the domestic animals, which appeared to be incredibly fecund: chickens, geese, turkeys, pigs, cats, and dogs promenaded slowly up and down the muddy street with dozens of endearing chicks, goslings, piglets, kittens, and puppies splashing about in the puddles.

On Mr. Lee's recommendation we presented ourselves at the home of the Cobo family, a short distance outside the village, and were made welcome to pitch our tents on their property. Mr. Lee was fondly remembered—"Vicente caught the biggest fish ever taken from our river"—and one of the daughters never stopped telling us how very much ashamed she was of having broken his flashlight.

From our camp on a small rise above the rough bridges over the Río Vilcabamba and the Río Tincochaco, which flows into it here, we could watch the constant activity from early morning to dusk as teams of six, ten, or more horses were led into the village by Indians wearing their traditional scarlet cloaks and flat hats. All the animals were heavily loaded with great sacks and bundles of black plastic, which were stacked in the ruinous village houses until they were loaded on the trucks to take them on to Quillabamba, the nearest town. "Coffee," said Julio. "All coffee." Well, maybe, but I had doubts: the remote valleys of Vilcabamba are rumored to be a very big coca-producing area.

The ruins of Vitcos, for which we set out next morning, are located on the crest of a hill now named Rosaspata. It is a strange hybrid word combining the Spanish for "roses" with the Quechua for "hill," thus, inexplicably, "Hill of Roses" for a place where no roses grow and never did. A gentle hike through shady groves brought us to the great plaza beyond which we saw the crumbling walls with trees pushing their way through any remaining window or doorway. Connie Armstrong appeared somewhat disappointed at not finding a substantial, impressive Inca palace to reward her for her climb, but Quentin strode among the walls and through the rooms and plazas with great enthusiasm, Mr. Lee's site plan in hand, and then sat on the outer wall of the palace and composed a poem about it. Eve wandered off to meditate.

I did not agree with Julio that the abandoned diggings of treasure seekers in many parts of the palace complex disfigured the site—they seemed to add a certain degree of romance to the ruins, had even become part of their history; but I did sense something very sinister here, so high above the fast-flowing Río Vilcabamba and with the jagged peaks of the Vilcabamba range in the distance. No doubt it was thinking about the unhappy events of the last thirty-six years of the Inca Empire that seemed to imbue the ruins with an ominous air as we made our way through the encroaching jungle growth into the halls and across the stone-littered courts. Here, in the large rectangular grassy square facing the royal palace, Manco II had been treacherously killed during a game of horseshoe quoits by the Spanish renegades he had befriended; here his son Sayri Tupac received the Spanish envoys who persuaded him to travel to Lima and into captivity; here his half brother Titu Cusi assumed the royal headband and died. Here Manco's third son, Tupac Amaru, mounted the Inca throne and held it briefly until he fled before Don Martín García de Loyola's expedition in 1572, was pursued deep into the jungle and found in a miserable condition, taken to Cusco with his family, and tortured to death. It was the end of the Inca Empire and its four hundred years of benign rule.

Below Rosaspata, in the valley of the Río de los Árdenes, we followed part of the paved Inca road along which the sixteenth-century Spanish missionary friars had marched with their converts, banners flying, from Puquiura to set fire to the Yurac Rumi and exorcise that site of pagan worship. We found many remains of Inca buildings here, but Julio was not as familiar with the area as he had led me to believe, and without Mr. Lee's site plans and drawings we would have understood and appreciated little of what we saw. It reminded me of forays among ruins in Greece and Asia Minor, where knee-high foundations are all that remain of houses, theaters, and temples, and their former greatness must be imagined. We stopped to rest beside a large stone altar, where Julio pressed his hands against the carved surface and prayed to the god of his ancestors; it gave us a small foretaste of the Yurac Rumi farther on in the valley, which was our chief goal of the expedition, and which, due to the day's heat and the difficult, damp trail and our fatigue, we became impatient to reach.

Soon we saw a huge stone lying among smaller boulders in the distance and made our way with renewed energy across the swampy plain toward it; only as we grew nearer to it could we appreciate its great size. Then we stood silently before it, the shrine to which Hiram Bingham's guides had led him on the afternoon of August 9, 1911, and of which he later wrote, "Here before us was a great white rock. Our guides had not misled us. . . . Densely wooded hills rose on every side. There was not a hut to be seen, scarcely a sound to be heard, an ideal place for practicing the mystic ceremonies of an ancient cult." After almost eighty years, we found the holy place quite unchanged. Although Dr. Bingham described the palace at Vitcos as "a residence fit for a royal king," and the Yurac Rumi as "remarkable," he did not accord them the importance they deserve when he became convinced—wrongly, as it turned out—that Machu Picchu was the last, lost city of the Incas. Indeed, none of the descriptions of the Yurac Rumi—not those of the biased Spanish chroniclers, not that of Dr. Bingham, certainly not that of Mr. Vincent R. Lee, who prosaically refers to it as an "elaborately carved boulder"—had prepared any of us for the sight of this huge granite stone, no longer white as at the time of the Incas but now covered with lichen and dark gray, more than sixty feet long, thirty-five feet wide, and twenty-five feet in height, with its intricately sculpted surfaces—the most sacred site in South America and surely one of the most impressive religious monuments in the world, magnificently situated with the range of permanently snowcapped Andean peaks as its backdrop.

At the time of the Inca Empire, the great stone was partly enclosed by temple buildings, which were destroyed by the zealous Spanish missionaries and of which only some low foundations and walls remain. Bingham saw parts of the temple still standing in 1911 beside the sacred pool of running water, which we found to be a swamp. The absence of buildings serves to display the stone to better advantage, lying now fully exposed in all its majesty and mystery, surrounded only by fallen masonry, upturned lintels, and smaller boulders on whose carved ledges and seats Eve, Ingrid, the Armstrongs, and I contemplated the Yurac Rumi in comfort and at leisure. We sat spellbound and in awed silence for several hours, watching the play of sunlight and shade over the stone's surfaces from different viewpoints, wondering at the meaning of its elegantly carved platforms, the delicately and smoothly rounded edges of the curious steps, the geometric patterns and lines and squared knobs, the intriguing and graceful reliefs, which, we agreed, are so surprisingly modern in style, so appealing to contemporary tastes in plastic art, so "exactly right," as if a Henry Moore or a Brancusi had been at work here.

If historic events had taken a slightly different turn at Cajamarca in 1532, if Atahualpa had killed Pizarro (as, with his vastly greater number of soldiers, he could have done), and if the Inca Empire had continued to thrive without European influence, as did that of Japan, it is not unlikely that this sculpted stone would be today the most revered shrine of all the people of South America from Quito to Tucumán, who would make pilgrimages to it as the Muslims do to their black stone at Mecca.

Quechua is still the language of the Andean people, the rainbow flag of the Incas flies above the city hall in Cusco, the descendants of the Incas continue to pay homage to the Sun before they chew coca leaves, and to the Earth before drinking *chicha;* but their Yurac Rumi is almost forgotten in that field in distant Vilcabamba—no longer a place of worship, but also blessedly uncheapened by mass tourism.

It has a second name—Ñusta Hispanan—which was allegedly bestowed on it by the Spaniards. Dr. John Hemming, in his *Conquest of the Incas,* gives the name as Ñusta España, apparently in the belief that it refers to a princess of Spain, *"ñusta"* being the Quechua word for "princess"; and, when I sat beside Julio Sotomayor as we looked up at the great stone, I asked him what the Quechua word *"hispanan"* meant. He was oddly evasive, and I wondered whether the name was too sacred to be shared with a foreigner, even after twenty years of friendship. No, he said, but it was "a bad name, Mr. Hanns, a bad name." I was naturally much intrigued and urged him to say it. Reluctantly he did so. "It means—it means—it means *urine.*"

Peruvian mestizos are extremely modest, but when I showed no disgust on hearing this word being uttered, Julio explained that the Spaniards, who did everything they could to destroy the Inca traditions, religion, and way of life, had given the holy stone the name "Princess's Urine" in order to discredit the place. It seemed an unlikely name to have invented when something like "the Devil's Throne" would have been more effective—and in Spanish, not in Quechua—and as soon as Julio had spoken the word "urine," the reason for the name was perfectly obvious to me. At the top of the Yurac Rumi is a shallow carved seat, from where the officiating princess or Chosen Virgin of the Sun directed the sacred ceremonies; and directly from this a distinct white stain begins as a thin stream and then fans out across the sloping stone to its edge, from where the fluid fell to disappear into the ground. No one has written about it; no tests have been conducted to ascertain if the stain was made by urine; but the frequent spilling of an acidic liquid over a very long period of time appears to have killed the minute lichen with which the surface of the stone is covered, and its path reveals the original white granite that gave the Yurac Rumi its name.

The prudish Julio was acutely embarrassed when I told him that as far as I was concerned, the name Ñusta Hispanan now made perfect sense and that I believed that it described a rite that had been performed there. He was deeply shocked, both for my discussing an unpleasant bodily function and for suggesting that his Inca ancestors indulged in repulsive practices. "But, Julio," I said, "they did have habits which are by today's standards weird and unpleasant—their warriors ate the flesh of their enemies, Atahualpa spat into the palms of his adoring female attendants, the sun god was honored with libations of animal blood." I told him not to be squeamish about customs of four hundred years ago and that the Bedouin among whom I travel in the Sinai still wash their hair with urine and clean their hands with it before they eat.

He was repelled, and more so when Ingrid came to join in the discussion. "Some of my husband's business associates in Delhi belonged to that large Indian cult whose members drink their own urine because they think that it's good for their health," she told the horrified Julio. "Even the president of India was one of them. Well, *chacun à son goût;* I've always done my best to give my guests what they want, but when I had to entertain those piss drinkers, I served fruit juice and iced tea."

"Never in Peru!" cried Julio. "Even the Spanish chroniclers who said terrible lies about my people never mentioned such a thing." I could not refrain from reminding him that Garcilaso de la Vega, whose mother was an Inca princess, had in his memoirs described that urine was used to wash sick infants and given to them to drink in Cusco when he lived there in the sixteenth century, proof surely that it was not then considered unclean.

Alas, Ingrid and I had deeply shocked and offended my dear Julio. He walked away from us in disgust, and it was several hours before he seemed to forgive us. We never again referred to our interpretation of the sacred stone's second name in his hearing, and when we did so among ourselves, the Armstrongs spoke of it politely as "the Princess's Toilet."

For Eve, who begged Julio and me to allow her more time there, having reached the Yurac Rumi was the fulfillment of a long quest. She sat quite still and with arms folded across her chest, enraptured, as if drinking in the sight of the stone from different sides. I, too, found it inspiring and everything I had hoped for. "How *can* Mr. Lee describe it as an 'elaborately carved boulder'?" I said to Ingrid, who fussily annotated her copy of his *Chanasuyu,* revised his site plans wherever she considered it necessary, and checked his measurements against those that she painstakingly took with her surveyor's tape, of which she made us hold the other end.

She vigorously rose to his defense. "The man is an *architect*!" she cried. "He's a scientist, not a poet, not a *dreamer.* And that's exactly what it is—a carved boulder." And she resumed the labors with her tape, hoping to detect errors in Mr. Lee's measurements.

✧

While we were in camp at the Cobo farm it became obvious to me—and I think that the worldly-wise Eve and Ingrid had their suspicions—that although the beautiful Lucho may truly have been our cook's nephew, he also enjoyed a more intimate relationship with him. They slept together in one sleeping bag, and twice when I went to the kitchen tent to ask for something they were closely entwined as I entered and parted hurriedly and looked at me with fear. I did my best to show that I was not shocked, indeed was happy for their happiness. Lucho was obviously relishing every moment of the expedition. He ran about cheerfully with cups of tea, plates of cookies, and platters of sliced tropical fruits for us, laughed a lot, and played with the children who sat around the kitchen tent and silently watched every camp activity; he merrily pretended to chase away the pigs and cuddled every filthy dog and cat that wandered by looking for scraps. We had all by now become accustomed to his powerful odor.

My favorite meal was always afternoon tea, the thought of which kept me going for the last mile or so on each day's hike. When we arrived back at the camp, the table in the mess tent was elaborately set with hot tea, fruit juices, cookies and chocolate wafers daintily arranged on plates, pound cake with nuts and raisins, crackers, and jars of the delectable jam made of plums, cherries, and berries that is one of Peru's great culinary treats. After this fine repast I felt that at my age I was entitled to take it easy, and retired to my tent until dinner, to enjoy some solitude and Mozart on my Walkman; but Eve and Ingrid and the Armstrongs had stronger legs and stouter hearts and went off to explore the neighborhood, with Edgar always dutifully beside them, to look for birds, or into Huancacalle, whose inhabitants seemed to have nothing to do but follow them around and ask to have their photograph taken.

The villagers had heard that I had brought a first-aid kit with me, and my quiet time was occasionally interrupted when women, usually with a child or two, came to me for a consultation. I dispensed aspirins and throat lozenges and applied iodine and Band-Aids with suitable gravity, but when I was about to treat a little boy's horribly inflamed eyes with an innocuous lotion that could do him no harm, Ingrid happened to be there and was quick to deter me.

"Don't!" she cried. "No medication can help him; he needs an operation, and fast—and remember what these people did to Father Ortiz!"

For a moment I did not understand what she meant. Then I

realized that she referred to the medical missionary who in 1571 had attempted to cure Titu Cusi of pneumonia, had failed, been blamed for the Inca's death, and tortured and killed with terrible cruelty.

I did not treat the boy's eyes.

One afternoon the others urged me to accompany them into Huancacalle; they had met a young man with a guitar who in return for being presented with Instamatic photographs had invited them to his home. We found his family and many neighbors gathered in one small, dark room with its windows tightly shuttered. We sat on broken chairs and wooden crates and listened to some very long, very sad dirges of a religious nature instead of the lively tunes we had expected. It was an excuse for a party, and a large bowl of *chicha* was produced ceremoniously and passed around from mouth to mouth. This favorite and extremely potent drink of the Andean Indians is made from corn that toothless old women ferment by chewing and mixing it with their saliva. Putting the bowl to our lips and taking a sip of the gray, unattractively foaming liquid was the price we had to pay for accepting the hospitality. Even Edgar, city-bred, was clearly repelled; but although the tart *chicha* was not unpleasant to the taste, only Ingrid drank without qualms. "But it's *delicious*! Why don't you drink more? They don't have AIDS here, you know."

We were agreeably astonished each day by the lavish breakfast and dinner in the mess tent, but it was the picnic luncheons we enjoyed most. Wherever we had hiked, soon after noon our cook appeared, having followed us with some member of the camp staff, both of them laden with wooden supply boxes, the large kettle, and firewood they had collected on the way; a cloth was spread in the shade of trees, and we sat around it on fallen tree trunks or rocks. After some speedy and expert preparations a delicious dish was served: a chicken-and-potato salad, a salmon mousse, or our favorite, fresh, cool avocados mashed with olive oil and lemon juice and onions diced very small to give the puree sparkle and added flavor. Accompanied by hunks of buttered bread and followed by pound cake, an orange salad, and hot, strong tea, it was a feast. "But it's *delicious*!" said Ingrid the first time we were served what we named Avocado Vilcabamba. "And so simple, like all the best dishes. I must tell Craig Claiborne about it—most of his recipes are really mine, you know. I taught him everything he knows at my summer cooking school on Lake Annecy."

Toward the end of our stay at the Cobo farm, Huancacalle erupted into unexpected activity. A truckload of heavily armed *guardia* in their black uniforms and menacing dark glasses arrived and took up positions at various vantage points, and patrolled the street; then more trucks drove to the river's edge, and mountains of camping equipment and provisions were unloaded. A dozen villagers were commandeered to carry the gear across the Río Vilcabamba to a field where thirteen tents, including a duplicate of our bright orange toilet tent, were set up with military precision. Fires were then lit on the hillsides to rid the campsite of mosquitoes and other noxious insects. We were informed that the best chef of Cusco, with his assistant, was among the camp staff. The entire population of the village was in a flurry of excitement and anticipation, and its leading men stood about in clean white shirts and dark suits—Dr. Renzo was expected! I had heard about this enigmatic Dr. Renzo Francescutti during previous visits to Peru; he was a man of mystery, with unlimited funds and resources at his command, who often traveled in Vilcabamba, always very much *en prince*. The Peruvian government put army helicopters at his disposal for his explorations of the area, but he had never published reports of his field trips. It was said that he planned to restore the royal residence at Vitcos and turn it into a luxury hotel with a swimming pool and tennis courts and other resort trimmings—a sort of Inca Disneyland—a mind-boggling scheme of ghastliness that fortunately seemed most unlikely to be realized. Others speculated that the Italian doctor was less interested in the archaeology of Vilcabamba than in its potential oil or other resources.

"Oh, anyone can call himself an archaeologist," said Ingrid. "It's the perfect cover for all sorts of other activities. Most of the archaeologists with whom I've worked were really spies or crooks, and all of them were charlatans. What a prima donna that Mortimer Wheeler was at Mohenjo-Daro! We had to get rid of him."

Later in the day a big ugly military helicopter circled overhead and landed on the soccer field, where the great man accepted the homage of the *guardia* and the village elders and then crossed the river to his camp. We did not witness this event or see the famous doctor, but he sent a verbal message by one of his numerous camp staff to assure us that he did not object to our presence. Apparently he considered Huancacalle and the nearby Inca sites as his private domain.

We were disconcerted by all this commotion and none too pleased to have to listen to the helicopter whirring above us all day, sending up great clouds of dust. And we were not happy when all the village children transferred their interest in us to the new arrival and insisted on bringing us hourly reports about the great man's doings: "Come, come quick to see Dr. Renzo's horse" . . . *"El doctor* is very angry and cold; his clothes have not arrived" . . . *"El doctor* is eating his dinner now" . . . and, long after sunset, "Oh, good news—another truck has come with the warm clothes for *el doctor."*

Next morning, as we hiked up Rosaspata, we could look directly down into Dr. Francescutti's camp three hundred feet below; and running about among the Indian staff was a tall man in a bright red shirt. Julio, who can spot a caracara a mile away, said, "It is Braulio. Braulio is there with Dr. Renzo." He cupped his hands and called out, "Bra–uuu–lio! Bra–uuu–lio!"

I screamed, "Bra–uuu–lio! Bra–uuu–lio!"

The man in the red shirt saw us and started running fast up the steep slope of the hill, and a minute or two later the handsome Braulio, with his shock of unruly hair, stood on the trail among us, not even out of breath after his exertion. "Stay with us," I said. "Leave that nasty Italian and stay with us." He laughed, let me give him a hug, and raced back to his camp.

But that afternoon, when we returned to our camp, we were greeted with the astonishing news that Dr. Francescutti had gone. It was very curious. The elaborate and enormously costly operation had been mounted merely in order to permit the doctor and three companions to spend one cosseted night at Huancacalle. His camp staff later told us that he had been most upset when he arrived and saw our tents and learned who we were; possibly his speedy departure was a result of our presence there. Without waiting for his helicopter to pick him up and in his impatience to get away, he had, like Napoléon in Russia, abandoned his troops and hurried off with his companions in the camp staff's trucks, promising to send one of the trucks back for them and the equipment. It did not return, and I had the pleasure of seeing Braulio at our dinner table. No truck came for them the following day, and they sat disconsolate on their packed gear. Our group was leaving next morning, and I consulted with Julio and our drivers whether we could take the Francescutti staff and their gear with us in our bus to Quillabamba. "No problem," they said. It gave me considerable satisfaction to be able to tell everyone in Cusco and Lima that I had rescued the great Dr. Renzo's abandoned staff—and there would be the bonus of traveling with Braulio at least one day.

But when all of Dr. Francescutti's heavy and bulky equipment was strapped to the roof of our minibus, as well as our own, when the two camps' combined bundles of sleeping bags and food boxes and kitchen gear had been packed into the back so that the drivers had no rear vision, and as the members of the absconded doctor's staff filed into the bus and squatted on packages and in the narrow aisle between our seats, I was less sanguine about the arrangement. The bus looked dangerously overloaded and frighteningly top-heavy. Ascensio and Mario inspected it for some time and decided it was safe to proceed. Remembering the condition of the road with its hairpin bends crossing fast-flowing streams, and precipices plunging thousands of feet to the river, I had grave doubts. My responsibility for Eve, Ingrid, and the Armstrongs weighed heavily on me; but Ingrid Menon overruled my fears. "It's perfectly safe," she announced after having made her own inspection of the load and the ropes that secured it, of the wheels, and of the distribution of weight. "I've driven trucks with far heavier loads *sans une panne* across the Caucasus."

We set off, and most of the members of the two camp staffs were soon asleep, unconcerned about any potential dangers. Our cook's head rested on Lucho's shoulder, and the best chef in Cusco dozed arm in arm with his pretty young assistant. Such companions apparently were the perquisites of all Andean camp cooks. Like an attentive stewardess on a plane, Lourdes dispensed fruit, cookies, hard candy, and fruit juices to those of us who remained awake and alert in case of an accident. Braulio sang to us and ate prodigiously. Although I occasionally closed my eyes and held on tight to the seat in front of me, we reached the Urubamba River without the slightest mishap. From there the road down to Quillabamba seemed by comparison like a smooth highway.

We stayed the night at the Hostal Don Carlos, and as soon as he had showered, shaved, oiled his unruly hair, and put on clean clothes, Braulio preened before me in his finery. He was, he proudly explained, setting off on his own journey of adventure, to another hotel in the town. "I am going to see many naked ladies."

Naked ladies?

Lourdes explained that this hotel had an unsavory reputation, and a small swimming pool where shameless women lay around in bikini bathing suits. It was the biggest attraction of the town, but very shocking; there was nothing like that in Cusco. "Braulio should not go there," she told me. "He is a married man, with children grown-up. It is not good."

But Julio joined him, and when they returned in time for dinner, they were both very pleased with the bare female thighs and stomachs they had seen. "There is nothing like that in Cusco," said Braulio.

Edgar was clearly envious and had wanted to go with them but conscientiously remained at the Don Carlos to guard us. Lucho was ill. He had never before been anywhere lower than nine thousand feet and was affected by the low altitude of Quillabamba—a mere thirty-six hundred feet above sea level. I could not be of help to him; I had excellent medications for high-altitude sickness, but nothing to cure the reverse effect. The two camp cooks and their assistants tried to keep cool in the unaccustomed tropical heat by sitting under the sluggishly revolving fans in the dark television lounge. Ascensio and Mario went to sleep in the minibus to ensure that it would not be stolen during the night. "Quillabamba a very bad place," they said.

As the group's only person with an alarm clock, I woke up everyone at 4:00 A.M., and we drove down the cliff to the railroad station. Eve, Ingrid, the Armstrongs, and I bade farewell to our wonderful drivers, to the impressively efficient Lourdes and the camp staff, to our inventive cook and his sadly suffering Lucho, to Edgar, who had been such a pleasant but unnecessary addition to our team, and to Braulio, whom I gave a special hug. They were driving back over the Málaga Pass to Cusco, taking with them Dr. Francescutti's team and equipment. Then, under Julio's direction, we climbed up onto the waiting train and began dislodging the Indian and mestizo passengers from our reserved seats.

At Machu Picchu, the Hotel Turistas had sent a bus to the station to meet us, and half an hour later we breakfasted in its elegantly appointed dining room. The maître d', who knew me well, since I stayed there for two or three nights twice a year, came beaming to our table—but not to greet me. "Oh, my dear Señora Menon, what a pleasure to see you here again," he told her.

Ingrid raised the milk jug. "Please get them to heat this milk," she said. "I don't take cold milk in my coffee. Oh, and, Eduardo, have two bottles of *agua mineral* put in my room—*sin gaz,* of course."

There was no doubt that we were back in civilization.

17

WITH

FATSO

IN

TURKEY

HE WAS NOT, in fact, fat—merely chubby, rotund, and overweight, with a round, smooth, cheerful face—but his name was Joshua Fettsack and it was inevitable that everyone had called him Fatso at school and college. When he joined his family business—it has been said that a third of all Americans are conceived, born, and die on a Fettsack mattress—no one there would have dared to call him anything but Mr. Joshua and, later, Mr. Fettsack. It was always "Yes, Mr. Fettsack; certainly, Mr. Fettsack; at once, Mr. Fettsack."

But when, at the age of fifty-two, he had taken the plunge to acknowledge his homosexuality, had divorced his wife, and had begun to associate with other gay men, he was again called Fatso, at first behind his back, then to his face; and he rather liked it—it made him feel pleasantly young, once more "one of the boys."

He did not come out of the closet—he erupted from it with the thrust of a long-range missile, bought a new convertible, new clothes, and sold the large family home in Newark and moved across the Hudson River into a large condominium in a converted warehouse in the chic gay enclave of Manhattan's West Village, filled by a smart decorator with amusing turn-of-the-century drapes and knickknacks. Outside office hours at the Fettsack Bedding Company, and except for attending Lions and Rotary and chamber of commerce meetings, he no longer wore polyester leisure wear suitable for a respectable middle-aged family man, but instead assumed the brightly colored, crazily patterned, striped, polka-dotted, and abbreviated garments of a teenager: T-shirts with aggressively "gay" slogans, cute tank tops and spandex shorts that had never been designed for a man of his age and girth, and fashionable multitoned sneakers. Unfortunately, he was quite devoid of taste and had no friend to advise him on clothes or anything else. In a futile attempt to hide his bald patch, he wore baseball caps at all times, even refusing to remove them in restaurants, with the bill turned to the back for that boyish, sporty look.

He was a figure of fun, but lovable. He had the mind of an amiable four-year-old child; and more sophisticated gay men wondered how he could be in charge of a corporation that was traded on Wall Street and had six thousand employees. They sniggered about his clothes and his naïveté. He knew they did, and it did not worry him in the least. He was entirely content in the new life he had created for himself, and plunged with relish and abandon into gay sexual activities, making up for so much lost time.

Pretty youths appealed to him, and the elevator boys of the Pera Palas Hotel made him ecstatically happy. He was there with a group of men for whom I had chartered a traditional wooden sailing *gulet* to take us along Turkey's Mediterranean coast, and our tour began with a week's stay in Istanbul.

Turkish men of all ages and with rare exceptions bestow their sexual favors with equal fervor on both females and males; but the elevator attendants of the Pera Palas Hotel are embarrassing in their attention to male guests who are traveling without wives or women companions. So blatant are they in their eagerness to show that they

are available for a moment of pleasure snatched during their working hours or an hour or a night in their free time, so openly do they
fondle their crotch, so grotesquely do they roll their dark eyes, so
adroitly do they contrive with their little white-gloved hands to
brush against the sleeve, the shoulder, and the thigh of the male
guest who is ascending or descending slowly with them in their
ridiculous, narrow, late-nineteenth-century glass cage, that I can
never bear to be confined alone with one of them, and despite the
fact that on this occasion I had an attic room on the fifth floor, I
walked up and down the stairs rather than endure being so embarrassingly propositioned. And after a day or so at the hotel, I noticed
that several of my tour members also preferred to take the stairs, for
the same reason, or waited in the lobby until other hotel guests were
taking the elevator and hoped that the others would go up as far as
their floor and protect them by their presence.

But Fatso adored, worshiped, and desired the thin little elevator
attendants in their threadbare uniforms, and seemed to be oblivious
of their body odor. The boy on the 2:00 P.M. to 10:00 P.M. shift was
his favorite, and could conveniently arrange to join Fatso in his
room when he came off duty and when our group had usually finished dinner. But this undernourished youth boasted to his co-
workers about the emoluments that Fatso lavished upon him, with
the result that the boys on duty from 10:00 P.M. to 6:00 A.M., and
from 6:00 A.M. to 2:00 P.M., became frantic in their efforts also to
charm this generous and undemanding American gentleman and
profit by his generosity.

And soon the handyman who had efficiently mended one of my
suitcases, and the luggage porters, and the waiters and barmen also
winked and postured seductively whenever Fatso crossed the lobby
or entered the dining room or bar, hoping to appeal to him and
combine pleasure with profit; and the houseman on his floor lin-

gered in his room and brought many unnecessary towels and pulled the window drapes open and shut and open again and swept imaginary dirt off the carpet and fluffed up the pillows. Alas, these handsome men were of no interest whatsoever to Fatso, being far too old—many were married men of his own age. But because he was disorganized and untidy to an incredible degree, he was able to occupy these sexually unappealing members of the hotel staff in other ways. With no wife and no one to replace her to look after him, he was in a state of continuous confusion—the contents of his suitcases emptied all over the floor, pairs of shoes separated, spectacles mislaid, his oxblood leather purse containing his passport, credit cards, and money lost, his alarm clock failing to wake him, his electric shaver ruined because he had not remembered to switch it from 110 volts to Turkey's 220 volts before recharging it. Thus the staff members who lingered with erotic expectations were made to separate the dirty clothes from the clean, to search, to wind the alarm clock, to go out and buy a toothbrush and batteries for the camera and the Walkman, to mend the shaver, to bring some sort of order into poor bewitched, bothered, and bewildered Fatso's life.

Because he never remembered to set his alarm clock, he had always to be called for meals and excursions; because he did not read or heed any of the tour literature or the daily itinerary and listened to none of my instructions, he never knew where we were going, what we were to see, how long we would be gone. Traveling with him required infinite patience, was like being in charge of an endearing, utterly mindless child.

"I am confused!" he often cried, plaintively.

"And we are not surprised!" sang out the other tour members.

He never took offense. Having been told half a dozen times on the previous day that we were to see Santa Sophia next morning, and after our guide's introductory talk about it on the motor coach on our way to it across the Golden Horn, he stood outside it and asked, "Why have we stopped here? What is that?" And on being told that it was Santa Sophia, he said, "Are we going to see it?"

"We are seeing it now," I said, "from the outside, and in a minute or two Kemal will take us inside."

"Damn, I left my flash back at the hotel," said Fatso.

"Not permitted, anyway," said Kemal.

"If I can't take pictures, there's no point in going in," said Fatso.

After our visit to Santa Sophia, this being our day devoted to viewing the city's chief monuments of the Imperial Byzantine period, we walked to another, less-known creation of Justinian's: the Basilica Cistern, commonly now referred to as the Underground Palace. It was built to the emperor's order in A.D. 532, utilizing the columns of destroyed pagan temples; and after the Turkish conquest, its waters were directed to irrigate the Topkapi gardens. It is very large—460 feet long and 230 feet wide—and its roof is supported by more than three hundred vast columns in twelve rows. The modern entrance building above it, at street level, is unimposing, so that Fatso, who as usual had not listened to our guide, was overcome by a sudden uncontrolled fit of rage when he saw the guide buy our tickets at the window and the flight of stairs leading down into the earth. "I paid more than five thousand dollars for this tour, and I'll be damned if I'm going to travel in a filthy subway!" he screamed at me.

"Come on, Joshua, it's the Underground Palace," I explained, but he did not take in what I said, hearing only the word "underground."

"I will *not*! You call this a luxury tour—with a subway ride so you can save money?"

Our guide had gone ahead. The other tour members laughed as they walked down past us. I started to follow them.

Furious, but realizing that he could not find his way back to the hotel—the name of which he probably did not remember—Fatso reluctantly, step by painful step, descended after me into the theatrical gloom of the vast chamber, where concealed lights change slowly, almost imperceptibly, now silhouetting a row of columns against a red-tinted wall, now picking out one column, carved to resemble a tree trunk with its branches cut off, now bathing four or six columns in a golden glow. The heads of two gigantic Greco-Roman statues, irreverently used as bases, are dramatically, grotesquely effective, one upside down, one on its side.

We were fortunate in being almost the only visitors, and walked silently, in reverence, along the cleverly placed wooden catwalks that lead the sightseer, to the sound of Beethoven, above the water, among the columns, and through the whole extent of the cistern. The soft music, the mysterious lighting effects, make it one of the great sights of Istanbul.

"*C'est magnifique,*" the awed French-Canadian doctor whispered to his friend. They were the most appreciative and well-informed members of my group—a joy to have them with me.

But Fatso, although his anger had subsided when he discovered that it was an underground antiquity and not a subway for which he had been forced to go into the bowels of the earth, found nothing there to admire. Some drops of clean water fell down occasionally from the high, arched roof of the cistern, less than the welcome sprinkles of warm rain on a summer day; but they disconcerted Fatso intolerably. He tried ineffectively to move out of their way, and whenever a drop touched his T-shirt—THE BALDER I GET, THE MORE HEAD I GET—or his Chicago Bulls cap, he reacted as if he had been sprayed with napalm. While we progressed slowly in order to extend the haunting promenade along the catwalks, he hurried to the exit and waited for us by the souvenir stall at street level.

I was sad that our visits to Santa Sophia and the Underground Palace had failed completely to give Fatso any pleasure; but during

that afternoon's walking tour of some of Istanbul's ancient *hans*—
which I expected him to appreciate even less—I was able uninten-
tionally to save the day and provide him with the opportunity to
enjoy a few moments of rapture.

These *hans*—there are more than thirty of them, still in use—
surround the Covered Bazaar, and many of them are of even greater
interest. They were built between the twelfth and eighteenth centuries to house the merchants who came to Constantinople from
China, India, Persia, all over the Muslim world, bringing the treasures of the East, which they displayed for sale in the *hans*' huge
courtyards. There were stables for horses and camels on the ground
floor, and guest rooms for the merchants above. In varying stages of
neglect, the *hans* are today workshops where one can see men with
primitive tools and in dreadful working conditions, by the light of
a few bare electric bulbs, hammering out silver trays, weaving carpets, repairing automobile engines and television sets, making
gloves and carpetbags, sewing Levi and Wrangler patches onto the
back pockets of locally made blue jeans, adroitly embroidering
Ralph Lauren polo players and Lacoste alligators on cheap sport
shirts.

The grandest and most fascinating of the *hans* is the Valide
Han, reached through a massive gateway and with a Shiite mosque
in the center of its courtyard. Everything is in a state of appalling
squalor. As we walked upstairs, the sound became deafening—it is
the noise of hundreds of looms that were brought here in pieces
from Britain in the late nineteenth century and assembled in the
tiny former lodgings of the merchants, filling them from floor to
ceiling, wall to wall, leaving barely enough space for their operators. In the ill-lit gloom, in the crumbling cells, wide rivers of
scarlet, blue, green, royal-purple, golden, and white cloth pour out
of these old iron machines and are transformed into thick bales of
gorgeous color.

The tour members avidly took photographs, particularly as some of the machine operators, stripped to the waist and moist with sweat, were handsome men with bushy mustaches and superb physiques. "Istanbul!" they cried above the din, and pointed above them: "Istanbul!"

I knew the way to the inconspicuous circular stairway at the corner of the galleries, my tour members followed me up, and we stood on the roof of the *han,* surrounded by the minarets of Stamboul and with the whole of Istanbul below us. It is a magnificent view, taking in the Golden Horn from the mosques of Eyüp all the way to the Galata Bridge, Pera with the Galata Tower, and, beyond it, the modern and less-lovely towers of hotels and banks, the bustle of the waterfront, crowded with ships flying the flags of all the world's nations, the misnamed Leander's Tower on the tiny islet in the Bosphorus, and the misty Asiatic shore.

The earsplitting noise of the looms was lessened up there, reduced to a pleasant, soothing, almost soporific regular beat, and my tour members—as always, with one exception—expressed delight and wonder at this surprise I had contrived for them. "What have we come up here for?" asked Fatso. I pointed out the sights to him as we walked along the roof. Behind one of the lead-covered domes, enjoying a break from their labors, were two of the weavers—or, rather, judging by their age, novice assistants or porters. Barechested, wearing blue jeans, they sprawled on the roof, a pleasant sight, with a bottle of *raki* between them and munching sesame-covered *simit* bread rings. They greeted us with smiles, asked our names and nationality, and with the inborn politeness of Turkish men passed their bottle to us. I thought it friendly to take a sip, but the others declined, no doubt for reasons of hygiene. Conversation being impossible with the youths, as neither knew English, French, or German, we soon waved our good-byes and walked back toward the stairs; but Fatso stopped me. "Give me just five minutes."

"Whatever for?" I asked, astonished; but as soon as I spoke the words, I suspected his intention. "Oh, Joshua, do take care," I warned him.

We waited for him in the courtyard. I was apprehensive, but he kept his promise; after little more than five minutes he rejoined us, elated with his successful, albeit briefly consummated, double seduction.

✧

Men vastly outnumber women in the streets, on the buses and the ferries, and on the bridges of Istanbul. Women stay home, attending to children and household chores. After dark, not a woman is to be seen; the cafés and sidewalk restaurants are crowded with men drinking coffee and *raki,* eating nuts, *simit* rings, the tasty appetizers called *mezes,* and rich cakes; and there is a lot of physical contact among them. They hold hands, they put their arms around one another's shoulders, place hands on one another's thighs. Foreigners who say that this all means nothing are wrong: it means that, certain of their masculinity, the Turkish men can show that they are fond of one another, that they feel easy in one another's company, and, when deprived of a female partner, are perfectly agreeable to enjoy the pleasures of sex with one another and with any male visitor who is likewise inclined.

Kemal, our guide, a married man with a son in college and two daughters, shared Fatso's taste for young boys, and found my and some of my tour members' appreciation of older, rugged Turkish men inexplicable. "Look at those two—aren't they gorgeous?" he would say, pointing out a couple of pretty youths. When I told him that their fathers, maybe even their grandfathers, might appeal to me, he thought I must be joking. One day, when we were having lunch in a simple eating place frequented by men working in that part of the city, a stunning-looking police officer with black hair, a bristling mustache, flashing dark eyes, and a commanding presence was having his meal with friends at a nearby table. "Now there is what *I* call a gorgeous man," I said to Kemal, who immediately put down his knife and fork, and got up.

"I will tell him you like him," he said, "and ask him to come to you at the Pera Palas at ten o'clock tonight." Considerably alarmed, I told Kemal to desist and sit down.

He was perplexed. "But why not? The man would be delighted. At his age he no longer gets many offers like this. He will be honored—and he is a captain, earns a good salary—he wouldn't even want money. Well, a present is always acceptable—a watch is nice," said Kemal, and looked fondly at the gold Swiss watch on his wrist.

At dinner I reminded everyone that the next day's tour would take us to Istanbul's chief mosques, and that we had to be modestly dressed to enter them: long trousers, and shirts with collars and long sleeves. At breakfast, Fatso made his late appearance, well pleased with his nocturnal tryst with elevator boy No. 1, in a pair of monstrously brief shorts and a T-shirt for all Istanbul to know that NOBODY KNOWS I'M GAY. Nothing could have been less appropriate. "I told you last night, Joshua, we're going into mosques today. You can't go in dressed like that." He looked astonished. When he went up to his room after breakfast, I assumed it was to change; but when I called him to say we were all waiting for him in the lobby to leave and he at last joined us, behung with cameras, flash equipment, light meters, and his oxblood purse, he still wore the same shorts and the offensive T-shirt.

"You can't go into mosques like that," I told him.

"Mr. Joshua, you cannot enter mosques dressed like that," Kemal told him.

Fatso looked at us as if we were idiots and stepped into our waiting motor coach.

Our first visit was to the Süleymaniye Mosque. As we took off our shoes in front of the entrance, the attendants pounced on Fatso, pointed at his bare legs and bare arms, and brought him one of the lengths of cloth and long-sleeved cotton jackets that they keep for ignorant, scantily attired foreign barbarians. Fatso did not realize why these rags were being thrust at him, and when we slowly, patiently explained the reason to him, refused absolutely to put them on. "I'm an American, not a Turk," he shouted, greatly affronted. Kemal and I tried to calm him; he attempted to force his way through the green curtains into the mosque; the attendants screamed, laid hands on him, pulled at the straps of his cameras; he struggled and cursed; I feared we were about to have a riot on our hands but managed somehow to detach Fatso from the angrily howling custodians and others who had joined them in their efforts to prevent the half-naked infidel from desecrating their place of worship.

"You have two choices," I told Fatso. "You put the cloth round your waist and wear the jacket and see this lovely, famous mosque—or you stay outside."

"I've taken off my shoes, dammit, isn't that enough for them? Why the hell didn't you warn me about this?" he cried; but he accepted the length of cloth and the jacket, I tipped the custodians for their loan, and he entered the mosque with me. We all sat in a circle on the carpet around Kemal, who explained the basics of Islam.

Then we drove to the Sultan Ahmet Mosque.

"I've been in one mosque. It's enough," said Fatso.

"This one is different. It's the famous Blue Mosque. You can't go home and say you didn't see it," I encouraged him.

The arguments with the zealous attendants, the angry shouts and raised hands, the threats, the rejection and ultimate acceptance of the garments of modesty, were repeated, with variations.

Fatso had heard about the Rüys movie theater, which shows pornographic films to an all-male audience and where Turks of all ages, from teenagers who cannot obtain female sexual partners until they marry, to men who are too poor or too old to find any, are so aroused by the erotic scenes on the screen that they indulge in every known sexual activity. The dilapidated wooden seats are slimy with the spent sperm of randy soldiers, sailors, and bank clerks. Ancient wretches, oblivious of having their pockets picked, gasp their last breath as they achieve their ultimate ejaculation. The air is foul with the stench of noxious cigarettes and hashish, sweet, pungent food, urine, and excreta; the floor has not been swept for decades, and plague-carrying rats scuttle among the refuse; virulent fleas and lice are rampant. The patrons infect one another with every type of sexually transmitted disease and pass on contagious illnesses that have long been eradicated in the West but still linger in the overcrowded tenements of Turkish cities and in remote villages. Scabies, scrofula, and other medieval maladies and Asiatic scourges are brought to the Rüys theater by peasants from the fetid swamps of the Anatolian plains and the fever-stricken valleys of Kurdistan and the Caucasus.

It was definitely not a place into which a pillar of the Newark establishment, the father of a daughter at Harvard and a son at a prestigious military academy in North Carolina, should venture, even disguised in a pair of nylon running pants, a T-shirt proclaiming JUST DO ME, and an L.A. Dodgers mesh cap worn backward; but I failed to deter him. He had to go, and I had to take him there. I felt that my duties as tour leader did not include escapades of this nature; I gave him the address of the Rüys; I drew a map for him and marked his route from the Pera Palas to it—only ten minutes' walk; but he insisted that I take him there.

It was well after 10:00 P.M., and I longed for bed, but I try to oblige my dear tour members. And so I walked with him up the

Istiklal Caddesi, formerly the Grande Rue de Pera, to find the movie theater. During Ottoman times it was said of this main street of Istanbul that it was "as narrow as the comprehension of its inhabitants and as long as the tapeworm of their intrigues," and it is today a narrow, long, winding pedestrian mall where thousands of men, rich and poor, young and old, singly or in couples or in groups, promenade up and down in the evenings. With so many men to look at, so much eye contact to detract us, I realized after a while that we had somehow passed the Rüys. I stopped.

"I think we've passed it. We must go back," I said to Fatso.

His round, normally cheerful face became red and distorted with anger. His anticipation of plunging into the sexual activity of the Rüys had built up into an obsession; to be thwarted even for a moment was intolerable to him. Like a petulant child deprived of its toy, he stamped his feet. "For Christ's sake, find the damn movie house!" he shouted at me.

We retraced our steps and, a few hundred feet on, saw it. No wonder I had missed it—it was merely a small cashier's cubicle in the dark entranceway of a deserted office building. Three or four verminous hustlers hovered around, hoping to be invited into this den of erotic delights.

As quickly as he had lost it, Fatso regained his equanimity, now that he had been delivered to his evening's goal.

"Enjoy yourself," I said as he paid for his ticket, and walked back to the hotel.

✧

It requires at least some little understanding of history, art, architecture, a superficial knowledge of chronology and major events, to appreciate ancient sights. Fatso possessed none. He knew nothing of Greeks, Romans, Byzantines, Justinian and Theodora, the Blues and the Greens, marauding crusaders, pillaging Venetians, the Ottoman dynasty, so that nothing in Istanbul had any meaning for him. Nothing was large or tall enough to impress him, and nothing was *clean*—he complained about the pigeons all over the Yeni Mosque and the entrance to the Spice Bazaar every time we drove past them. Nothing pleased him—not the frescoes and mosaics in the Church of Saint Saviour in Chora, not the Chinese porcelain in the Topkapi Palace Museum or its Seljuk armor or the masses of Ottoman jewels or the gorgeous ceremonial robes or the gem-encrusted thrones or the Prophet Muhammad's mantle and bow, or the pretty Baghdad Pavilion, with its inviting divans. Our drive along the vast Theodosian city walls bored him, and he did not bother to get out of the motor coach when we stopped at the section where, as Kemal told us, the last Byzantine emperor died defending his city and where the young sultan Mehmed II entered to loot Constantinople.

Only once did he seem to enjoy a sight-seeing tour. As a sort of joke, I took the group to visit the Şale Palas in Yildiz Park, to which the mad sultan Abdülhamid II had retired, closely guarded, in constant fear of being assassinated. It is a monstrously oversized Swiss chalet from the outside, and its interior is a huge late-nineteenth-century French bordello in stupenduously bad taste. Fatso happily photographed every hideous room of it.

When we left Istanbul to spend the day at the Princes Islands before flying south to join our yacht at Marmaris, Fatso's infantile lack of self-control annoyed me to such an extent that, just once, it caused me to lose my temper with him.

We checked out of the Pera Palas after breakfast, embarked in our chartered boat at the Galata Bridge, and sailed into the Sea of Marmara. The sea was smooth; the day was warm but not unpleasantly hot. The tour members took off their shirts and sunbathed on deck; a slim deckhand in seductively tight white pants brought up coffee, tea, and pieces of Turkish delight. Kemal identified the buildings on the Asiatic shore—the gargantuan rectangular military barracks in which Florence Nightingale tended the British soldiers during the Crimean War, and the ornately turreted Haydarpaşa railroad station, from which Agatha Christie often took the *Orient Express* to Mesopotamia and from which trains still go all the way to Baghdad.

Büyükada, the largest of the Princes Islands, is to Istanbul what Capri is to Naples, what Fire Island is to New York: a peaceful summer resort with horse-drawn carriages and bicycles instead of cars, charming old villas in well-kept gardens, and a few good small hotels among the pine groves.

Because there would be no dinner on the plane to Dalaman, I provided a more lavish luncheon than usual at a waterfront restaurant, with plenty of the local wine from the Monastery of Saint George; later we sat in a café in the main square over coffee and watched the crowd, and I bought two dozen assorted pastries for which Turkey is renowned—not only the famous baklava, but flat, round almond biscuits, apricot Baghdad cakes, substantial pastries filled with honey and walnuts, with sliced apples, with sweet white cheese and raisins, with delicious poppy seeds, each piece individually wrapped.

We returned to Istanbul in the late afternoon and had tea in the waterfront park at Seraglio Point, with toasted cheese sandwiches. Fatso refused to eat them. I reminded him again that there would be no dinner on the flight south and that we would not reach our yacht until almost midnight. "I can't do without my dinner," he said. I suggested he have a sandwich at the airport. "No way. I have to have a proper dinner." The flight was delayed; we had ample time at the airport.

"Let me buy you a sandwich or a bowl of soup, Joshua," I said.

"No way," he said. "I paid for breakfast, lunch, and dinner each day on this damn tour, and I'm going to get it."

During the flight, when coffee and cold drinks were being served, I handed round my carton of pastries to my fellow travelers. Fatso refused to take one and pointedly turned his face away from me. The members of a German tour group were seated near us, assumed by my dark suit and black tie that I was a flight attendant, and loudly demanded that I serve them also. I did not disabuse them of their mistake. *"Nur für Amerikaner,"* I told them. They gasped with disbelief.

On the long drive from Dalaman Airport to Marmaris the last of the pastries were eagerly accepted by my tour members but, again, not by the sulking Fatso. "Oh, Joshua, don't be so stubborn; do take the last one," I said.

"Goddammit!" he burst out. "You've starved me all day long, and now you offer me a rotten piece of cake that no one else wants!"

It was too much. I had heard enough of his whining for one day. "I saw you eat an enormous breakfast. You went back to the buffet at least three times. You had a four-course lunch. I offered you toasted cheese sandwiches at teatime and pastries on the plane. Missing dinner just once will do you no harm: you could do with a few less pounds."

It was cruel, it was hitting below the belt, and I bitterly regretted my words as soon as I spoke them; but he had goaded me beyond endurance. I was ashamed of myself and sat in silence for the rest of the drive.

In Marmaris, finding where our yacht was berthed, waking the crew, seeing to the transfer of the luggage, allocating cabins, distributing towels, looking for light switches, learning how to flush the toilets, and settling us all in our quarters fortunately kept me too busy to dwell on my regrettable outburst. Next morning, when we sailed from Marmaris after a substantial breakfast on the covered part of the deck, the previous day's unpleasant words happily seemed of no consequence to either Fatso or me. The yacht, the attentive crew, the meals, the calm sea, and the deep blue water all far exceeded everyone's high expectations.

"*C'est magnifique,*" said the French Canadians. "It's paradise," said the Minneapolis executive with the ravishing smile that quite melted my heart. "We love it," the Californian lovers told me. It was Sunday, and after luncheon the pastor from New Hampshire moved most of us to tears with his brief, poignant reminder of how fortunate we were to be there, together, and in good health.

But Fatso could not be at ease, even on this wonderfully relaxing cruise. Those of his belongings that were not mislaid or lost were prone to accidents. His T-shirts ripped, the zippers of his shorts snagged, the laces of his sneakers broke at the most inopportune moments during shore excursions, his toilet water leaked all over the clothes in one of his suitcases, his suntan lotion had exploded during a flight and made a shocking mess. His new Walkman, bought especially for this trip, froze into inaction on the second morning of the cruise. He had seen that I listened to music when I sat apart from the others on deck to watch the sunset, and asked to borrow my Walkman. I told him he could use it, with pleasure, but that I needed it every morning at six and every afternoon at five, for half an hour or so, when I enjoyed listening to a flute or harp concerto; my dawn and dusk sessions with Mozart were the most cherished moments of each day. But five o'clock came, and Fatso continued to listen to disco rhythms; I waited in vain for him to hand me back my Walkman but was too embarrassed to claim it—nor did he return it after dinner. I was furious with him for depriving me of my moments of pleasure, although I realized that he was less thoughtless than merely forgetful. Small joys become of major importance when one is almost seventy. I fumed with anger, and on the following days could barely be polite to him when I saw him with my Walkman clapped over his ears, happily snapping his fingers to the ghastly noises that could be heard coming through the earphones. On the third evening, as I sat feeling miserable and deprived on deck, waiting for the sun to set, the French-Canadian doctor handed me his Walkman. "You must hear this, it is so beautiful," he said. The music was indeed beautiful—some romantic French *chansons* I could not identify, enchantingly combined with the recorded sounds of birds chirping and trilling—but it was the kindness of the young doctor that made the tears run down my face as I lay there on deck and watched the sky turn from rosy pink to deep red to pale blue and dark, dark violet as the stars began to appear high over the Mediterranean. He had noticed; he had a soul; he knew what the loss of my half hour of music meant to me. His thoughtful, gracious gesture was a rich reward for three days of gnawing disappointment.

Perhaps someone spoke to Fatso, or maybe he remembered my request at last. When I went to my cabin after dinner, my Walkman lay on my bed.

It was Fatso's washcloth—or, rather, the lack of it—that occupied most of his thoughts during the cruise. He had either forgotten to pack it in Istanbul or mislaid it, but no matter how often he searched for it in his closet, in his chest of drawers, under his bunk, in his bathroom, in his half-unpacked suitcases, and among the growing piles of discarded clothing all over the floor of his cabin, his washcloth was not to be found. None of us had a washcloth to give him. My suggestion, that he use the end of his towel or a T-shirt or tank top, was indignantly rejected. "I want my *washcloth,* not a towel or a T-shirt," he said tearfully. "Don't they sell washcloths on this ship?"

There were no washcloths. It was a major problem. It was ruining the cruise for him. "Tomorrow we will be at anchor in Ekinlik Bay," I said. "We will go ashore to visit ancient Caunos and the Lycian rock tombs. There is a village; maybe they will have washcloths." But the shops had none. The basic yachtsmen's stores at

Tersane Creek and at Cleopatra's Bay (where she is reputed to have bathed with Antony) had never heard of such a thing. Their offer of a dishcloth was curtly dismissed.

"Goddammit, I want a *washcloth,* not a rag," cried the frustrated Fatso.

I was hopeful that Goçek would not fail us. This little port had lately flourished and become an elegant small haven for luxurious yachts, with smart restaurants and shops catering to a rich and discerning clientele. "We will find a washcloth in Goçek," I said.

"I damn well hope so," said Fatso. He was quite desperate.

Happily, Goçek did not fail us. In the first store we entered, opposite the jetty, I found a stack of washcloths at the back. I selected one at random and triumphantly brought it to Fatso. "I have the honor to present you with a washcloth!"

"Dammit, not plain white!" cried Fatso.

Life aboard our yacht was peaceful and pleasant, and swimming in the clear, warm, and truly turquoise waters in the sheltered coves of this Turquoise Coast was perfection. Our cook prepared excellent meals and was wise in not attempting to ape Western dishes but in giving us the traditional Turkish fare at which he was an expert: great lamb stews with vegetables, meatballs with lemon sauce, kebabs and rice pilafs, plenty of seafood bought daily from fishermen at the small ports or at anchorages. Our favorite was a luncheon dish—*menemen,* previously unknown to me, because it is apparently too simple to be featured on the menus of city restaurants. It is scrambled eggs with melted white cheese, tomatoes, and green peppers, highly seasoned, and amazingly good. We demanded "many men" as often as possible. Fatso was worried about hygiene. "Are you quite sure the cook washes his hands before he cuts up the tomatoes and peppers for our salads?" he asked me.

"Dear Joshua, I'm sure everything in the galley is much cleaner than the Rüys movie house," I could not resist answering.

Whenever we dropped anchor for swimming at a bay that had a provisions shop, and at the small ports, one of the deckhands went ashore to buy fresh fruit, vegetables, eggs, yogurt, milk, cheese, and meat; and instead of swimming with the other tour members, Fatso went ashore with him. He loved to shop, and returned in the Zodiac with some purchases of his own: often candy bars, packets of cookies, nuts, sometimes postcards, once a pair of hideous plastic sandals. "What do you find to do ashore for so long?" I asked him. He smirked mysteriously, preened, but after some days could keep his naughty secret no longer. He had come to an arrangement with the pretty deckhand who shopped for fresh produce, who looked so innocent but was astonishingly experienced in giving happiness to yacht passengers and, at the same time, deriving profit for himself. He knew the shopkeepers whose stores always had a dark storage space at the back, and the owners of little rooming houses in the alleys of the ports where a room could be rented for ten or twenty minutes.

Now I understood why Fatso so often sat on deck as we cruised along the coast, looking unhappy, and whined over and over again, even after he had replaced his washcloth at Göçek, "When are we stopping *somewhere*? When are we getting to a *town*?" It was only the brief trysts with our deckhand, snatched during the shopping expeditions, that made the cruise along the glorious Turquoise Coast bearable for him.

We went ashore at Gemiler Island, the home of Saint Nicholas, the original Father Christmas, to explore the Byzantine remains; but when we assembled on the shore to return to the yacht in the Zodiac, Fatso was missing. Gemiler is uninhabited; there is no shop, no café, but boys from the mainland occasionally row across to it to tend the goats. I climbed a hill and soon saw goats, but no goatherd. I called out, "Joshua! Joshua! We're leaving!" And, as expected, his sheepishly smiling round face appeared from behind a thick bush.

"Did Father Christmas give you a nice present?" quipped the others when he joined us.

✧

Our cruise ended at Fethiye, where Lycian tombs in the cliffs dominate the town. We drove up into the mountains to a wondrous place of which I had read. Baedeker, in his monumental *Konstantinopel und das Westliche Kleinasien* (1905), devotes a whole page to the Sultan Han and designates it with two asterisks, his highest approbation—"an unsurpassed example of the finest Seljuk nonsecular architecture. . . . The custodian expects a gratuity." Robert Byron visited it in the 1930s and was greatly impressed with its walls and fluted towers—"the bricks are long and thin, as sharp as when they left the kiln, thus dividing the shadow from the sunshine of each tower with knife-like precision"—and wrote of it years later, "Rereading my diary now I still hold the opinion that the Sultan Han is possessed of a character outside anything else in architecture and ranks with the great buildings of the world." My friend Jan Morris reached it—"that delectable caravanserai"—by jeep in 1965. I had to go there. I had to see it.

No one went there; it was barely accessible; the drive would take no less than three—some said four, even five—hours over a terrible road. But I always enjoy a challenge. It would be something special to offer my tour members, something other tourists do not know about or attempt. We would have a picnic luncheon on the way and avoid the hordes of German and Scandinavian sunworshipers at Fethiye and its nearby beaches.

The road, though not exactly terrible, was certainly rough, and I began to have misgivings about my rash decision to undertake this expedition into the unknown. The landscape was not appealing. Luncheon under the shade of trees somewhat revived our spirits, but when we continued into the bleak, barren mountains, I waited for my travel companions to begin to demur, to grumble, to object. But suddenly, and much sooner than I had expected, the crenellated walls and towers of the Sultan Han were before us. We walked between two of its guard towers through the gate and darkness into the courtyard; an old man in ragged clothes and slippers—the custodian—waddled toward us, extremely surprised but obviously happy to see and greet us.

The Sultan Han is a brick-built citadel with nine fluted towers crowning a hill that commands a pass through the Lycian Mountains, of immense importance in past centuries. Royal *han*s were located throughout Turkey along the ancient trade routes and provided travelers and their animals with accommodations and safety; but the Sultan Han is of exceptional interest. Its unusually massive walls and towers, built by the Byzantines and rebuilt by the conquering Seljuks, enclose a gorgeously tiled early church—it was turned into a mosque by the addition of one slender, steeply roofed minaret, a thin pencil pointed to Allah—and the palace of a minor thirteenth-century Seljuk sultan, which combines grandeur with dignity and good taste. A series of hexagonal pointed domes of increasing size, arranged in pairs, admit light to the windowless rooms, kitchens, and audience chamber.

The courtyard has open porches on three of its sides, each with a fountain for the ablutions of the travelers; on its fourth side, three tall arches reveal the walled garden at a slightly lower level, planted with fruit trees, trellised vines, and rosebushes, all sadly neglected and in need of ruthless pruning. Here, as in the courtyard, is a central and elaborate marble fountain, and more fountains are placed along the walls above narrow, shallow troughs, in some of which exotic fish used to be kept, in others trout for the sultan's table. Beyond this, built against the outer wall, is the multidomed palace.

With my 1905 Baedeker to guide us, we began to explore,

but the custodian would not let us proceed. He smiled, gestured to us to stop, looked mightily mysterious and secretive, put a finger to his pursed lips to command us to be quiet, and walked to a corner of the courtyard. There was a tap, and laboriously he began to turn it.

There was a choking, rasping sound, then a soft gurgling began, and a moment later we heard the rush of water, and then, amazingly, the fountains erupted. Water spurted from the marble mouths of dolphins and mythological beasts and the beaks of double-headed eagles and cascaded over basins, began quickly to fill the shallow troughs, spurted high into the air, so that as we watched with astonishment, the drab, dusty courtyard and parched garden were transformed: everything glistened and shone; the air was filled with delicious sounds of splashing; birds appeared from nowhere, came to rest, drank their fill, and frolicked in the clear running water. It was magical, a fairy tale come to life by the turn of an ancient, rusty tap.

The decrepit old custodian rarely had visitors and was enchanted to see the pleasure he had given these Americans by contriving this aquatic display for them. He hobbled along with us, pointing here and there, making explanations we could not understand, laughing merrily at us, at the running and spurting water, at the birds. I was thrilled now that I had arranged the expedition to this remote, decaying, neglected, but wonderful place, a vision of a more gentle, more gracious age, and the perfect last experience of our Turkish tour.

Fatso, alas, saw nothing of all this. He was totally absorbed in bemoaning the loss of his camera's lens cap, and annoyed with the custodian. "He's after a tip! That's all the guy wants—*a tip*! I'll be damned if I'll pay him anything just for making the water come on. No way!" he cried, angrily stamping his feet.

I calmed him. "Dear Joshua, no one expects you to give him

anything. This book says that the custodian expects a gratuity; and he deserves one; and I will give it to him."

The driver of our bus became impatient and sounded his horn. We had to leave. I pressed a bundle of pound notes into the custodian's hand. He smiled at me. *"Güle, güle*—give more money? *Bisschen mehr Gelt?"* he asked, without counting the money. I gave him more, gladly, seduced by those cleverly learned, useful English and German phrases.

From the dark doorway I looked back into the courtyard where he was turning the tap to shut off the flow of precious water. I saw the jets subside, the mouths of dolphins and lions and eagles run dry; the lovely plashing sound ceased.

"C'était très formidable," said the French Canadians when we boarded our bus.

"There was really nothing there, was there?" said Fatso as we drove away.

18

THE

NILE

BY

FELUCCA

"I CAN CONCEIVE nothing more delightful than a voyage up the Nile with agreeable companions in the winter, when the climate is perfection," wrote the Honorable Robert Curzon of his cruise in the winter of 1833–34.

He traveled in a dahabiya, a well-appointed and competently staffed houseboat with sails and oars, as did all the travelers of discernment who came to Egypt in the nineteenth century and often spent many months there. Dahabiyas, flat-bottomed, drawing little water, light, and easily poled off when stuck, were considered to be the only civilized way of traveling on the Nile. Florence Nightingale, who sailed with friends in one she named *Parthenope,* in the winter of 1849–50, expressed disgust at the sight of the Nile steamers that were beginning to ply there. "A journey on the Nile is a donkey ride and a boating trip interspersed with ruins," wrote Ampère. Amelia B. Edwards, author of *A Thousand Miles up the Nile,* remained moored in her dahabiya at Abu Simbel (where modern travelers barely have an hour during their air excursion) for eighteen days in February of 1874 and, finding the northernmost statue of

Ramses II to be disfigured by the plaster left on it when a cast of it had been taken some fifty years previously for the British Museum, made her sailors tint the white patches with coffee, using sponges tied to the ends of poles. "Ramses' appetite for coffee was prodigious. He consumed I know not how many gallons a day," she wrote.

Gustave Flaubert, who later achieved fame with his novel *Madame Bovary,* and his friend Maxime du Camp sailed and whored along the Nile in the winter of 1849–50 and must have passed the prim and pious Miss Nightingale, but neither party appears to have been aware of the other. "We were of inquiring minds and were not idle tourists. . . . What we wanted was to learn," wrote Du Camp, and he and Flaubert patronized prostitutes, sodomized boys in bathhouses, and became infected with venereal disease. It was all part of the great travel experience.

By the end of the nineteenth century, the tourist invasion of Egypt had increased to such an extent that when the writer Pierre Loti sailed the Nile in a dahabiya, he bewailed the exploitation of the river: "Soon there will scarcely be a river more dishonored than this, by iron chimneys and thick, black smoke."

The graceful dahabiyas have vanished, and ever-larger and uglier (but cost-efficient) passenger ships have replaced the Nile steamers in which I was fortunate to have cruised with my parents in 1929, when the Aga Khan was a fellow passenger and made me sit on his lap, and again as late as 1964, shortly before the last surviving of these gracious, spacious, romantic ships were abandoned to rot on the riverbanks or sold for scrap metal. They had become uneconomic to operate; they had been built for a small number of leisured travelers who no longer existed, with vast, ornately decorated staterooms, and canopied beds of state, and space for dozens of wardrobe trunks, and modest cabins below for valets and maids. On today's huge, hideous floating hotels, hundreds of sunburned tourists crowd the decks, frolic in the swimming pool, are subjected to blaring disco music all day and night, and are rushed from one temple to the next to suit the convenience of the large competing cruise operators.

There is, now, only one way to see the Nile as it should be seen and deserves to be seen, in the manner in which the nineteenth-century travelers experienced it—by felucca.

✧

Since childhood, the Arab world has held an overwhelming appeal to me—the male-oriented world of Haroun-al-Raschid and Sinbad the Sailor, of the Arabian desert with its proud, hawk-eyed Bedouin, so poignantly evoked in the travel books of the eccentric Charles M. Doughty and the equally odd, homosexual Lawrence of Arabia; of Rudolph Valentino in *The Sheik* and the Red Shadow in *The Desert Song;* the Egypt of Robert Hichens's novel *Bella Donna,* in which an English adventuress throws herself at a rich, powerful Egyptian who rejects her in favor of what at the time of the book's publication had to be described as a lovely local girl but that was surely meant to be a lovely local youth.

Arabia is closed to me because I am not a Muslim and neither a soldier nor an oilman. I must die without having seen Mecca; but Egypt, where I can roam as I wish, has an irresistible and continuing attraction for me. As in the phrases of the 1920s song, the sand seems to kiss the moonlit sky, the desert breeze whispers an enthralling lullaby to me; it is the most sensuously satisfying place I know—and added to its Islamic attractions are the stupendous ancient monuments and those of the Hellenistic and early Christian periods, covering a span of civilization five thousand years long. In the words of my old friend Lord Kinross: "No other country in the world can show a history so varied yet so continuous and so consistently rich in artistic achievements."

Nothing one has read, or seen in pictures or films, prepares one for the enormous scale and the extent and the awesome majesty of the monuments of Egypt's past, many of which, incredibly well preserved by the climate, were thousands of years old when Joseph and Mary of Nazareth brought their son, Jesus, there—and the legendary tree under which they rested, and the temple in which they are said to have worshiped, can be seen in the suburbs of Cairo.

The name of the game, for today's traveler in Egypt, is to avoid the crowds. In the Egyptian Museum in Cairo, at the pyramids of Gizeh and Sakkara and at Abu Simbel, in the temples of Luxor and Karnak and the tombs at Western Thebes, the press of mass tourism must be tolerated—except at such times as immediately after President Sadat's assassination and during the Gulf War, when we found the temples, tombs, and sites blissfully empty of tourists—but the usual tourist route is a very restricted one, and wonderful places exist where almost no one goes.

Every visitor to Cairo is led to the mosque of Sultan Hassan, but few seek out that of Ibn Tulun, built in the twelfth century in the Persian style, with its great open court and curious tower; and of those who do go there, very few step next door into the Gayer-Anderson House, which is actually two houses of the sixteenth and seventeenth centuries joined by a bridge across an alley. They were painstakingly restored by a British physician who served in the Egyptian army, Major Gayer-Anderson, who willed them to the Egyptian government on his death in 1942. To wander through the rooms of these houses is to get an idea of how the leisured, privileged, rich classes of Egypt lived in the past, in the harem with the elaborately carved window screens from which the ladies could view the activities in the streets below, in the men's *salamlik* with its grand, gorgeously tiled rooms where central fountains provide cooling. The major lived here with his lover, a beautiful Nubian youth, whose portrait in a white turban and robe dominates one of the rooms. "Oh, that Major Gayer-Anderson, he very naughty man!" smirks the custodian.

The areas around the pyramids at Gizeh and the approaches to the pyramids and tombs at Sakkara are filled with row upon row of tourist buses and cars and sellers of postcards and cheap trinkets and soft drinks; here the captive tourists are beset by rogues offering the spurious promise of a sexual adventure and photo opportunities atop a camel. But halfway between these major sites, only a few minutes' drive off the main road, are the pyramids of Abusir, happily unrestored, where we can see how the pyramids of Gizeh and Sakkara were viewed by late-eighteenth- and early-nineteenth-century visitors before the tourist rush to Egypt began, before antiquities were "cleaned up," still rising in ruined dignity from the surrounding desert sands, with no motor coach or seller of fake scarabs or soft drinks in sight, but charming youths who come running from the houses in the nearby oasis of palm trees and take us by the hand and lead us among the fallen stones.

Egyptian tour companies discourage visits to such places off the accepted tourist route and by making many excuses try to prevent anyone from going there. The road is closed—it is a military zone and forbidden to go there—it is dangerous—there is nothing to see. The government authorities, too, strive to prevent visitors from seeing anything except the well-known, overcrowded sights, and fail to appreciate that many travelers return to Egypt again and again and expect to view sites they have not previously visited, of which there are thousands. At Sakkara, only half a dozen of hundreds of tombs are shown; but it is the double tomb of Ni-ankh-Khnum and Khnum-Hoteb, court manicurists of the Fifth Dynasty, of which many members of my tours for men have heard, which is never open to the public, and in which they wish to inspect the paintings of these so-called brothers embracing each other and rubbing noses—the ancient Egyptian equivalent of kissing. When, after twelve years of unsuccessful effort, writing letters and making formal applications and pleading with the authorities, permission for us to view this tomb was still not granted, I simply went with my group to that tomb and found a guard who knew another guard who was said to have its key; I made it abundantly clear that money would be forthcoming; and half an hour later the tomb was opened for us. I felt sorry for Evert Dijkema, who had been to Egypt with me three times and always wanted so much to to enter this tomb. "Evert will be *livid* when I tell him we got in," said Freeman Gunter, our accompanying Egyptologist.

A week later, at Western Thebes, we managed to achieve another triumphant "first" and inspected a profane site of ancient Egypt that dear Evert would also have relished seeing. For years, none of our guides admitted knowing of its existence, and no custodian at the Temple of Queen Hatshepsut could ever be persuaded to direct us to it. I had read of this cavern in John Anthony West's *The Traveller's Key to Ancient Egypt,* and guided by the directions in it, we clambered up the steep, rocky cliff while custodians and guards below called to us to desist. As the book says, the cavern remained invisible until we were almost upon it; then we pulled ourselves into it and trained our flashlights on its walls. It was cut out of the rock, and apparently used by workmen who built the valley temple to escape from the fierce midday heat when they ate their lunch; and they amused themselves—and us, thirty-five hundred years later— by scratching graffiti onto the walls, drawings that are still quite clear and explicit, and several of which depict, in Mr. West's words, "a character graphically portrayed engaging another in a position normally found today only in a Times Square rest room." Our climb to the cave rewarded us with a glimpse of ancient Egypt at its earthiest.

✧

Nowhere in the world has the greed for the tourist's money caused greater havoc than along the Nile.

In Aswan, the grotesquely ugly Oberoi Hotel on Elephantine Island, like a tall airport control tower, dominates the landscape for many miles. Huge resorts for tourists, like monstrous concentration camps, have been hurriedly erected on the shore of Lake Nasser and on the Nile south of Luxor, utilizing the cheapest, nastiest materials. They contain swimming pools and gymnasiums and tennis courts and miniature railroads and nightclubs and beauty parlors and Bavarian and Tyrolean restaurants where the factory workers of Europe are kept, far removed from Egypt's antiquities, in sanitized isolation during a week's or a two weeks' package tour, to become painfully sunburned—for it is not Egypt that calls the inmates there, but the *Drang zur Sonne.* Few of them ever leave the confines of these tourist prisons, which have well-stocked shopping arcades—so there is no need to go to the expense of signing up for the tour to the native bazaar.

There, when the monstrous regiments of 350 uncouth sun-seekers arrive from their charter plane in a fleet of motor coaches bearing the ominous words MIT HETZEL ZUR SONNE, 350 glasses of a sick-making purple concoction are waiting for them on long tables in the hot sun; they greedily gulp them—"Welcome Drink Included," states the tour brochure—and head for the swimming pool.

The Japanese have no time for such rest and relaxation in the sun. In swarms of a hundred or more, with their noses and mouths covered by hideous gauze masks, they docilely follow their leader's banner. They stay one day in Cairo to photograph the pyramids and the golden mask of King Tutankhamen in the museum, spend an hour at Abu Simbel fiddling with the light meters of their cameras, and thirty-five minutes in the Valley of the Kings at Thebes. Then, having done Egypt, they fly on elsewhere. A few youngsters are more adventurous: when two of my tour members climbed the Pyramid of Cheops to see the sunrise from its top, they were disconcerted to find six young Japanese in sleeping bags who had spent the night up there.

But it is on the Nile itself—and the Nile *is* Egypt—that the commercialization has been most uncontrolled. The band of arable land on its banks is often less than a mile wide, and within this narrow strip almost all Egyptians eke out their living and grow the country's crops. This fertile ribbon of land is so precious, so great is the need to preserve it, that villages are often set back from it in the desert. Here the crocodile still occasionally shows its fearful head; here herons and storks rise from the reeds; here, in the cool of the evening, and exactly as in the ancient tomb paintings, a fisherman loudly slaps the surface of the water with his oar to attract the fish, while his companion in the punt spreads the net in hopes of a good catch.

And here, now, hundreds of floating hotels—three-, four-, and five-storied barracks for tourists—race up and down the river between Luxor and Aswan, causing small boats to capsize in their wake, discharging refuse, belching black smoke and diesel fumes, the terrible noise of their dynamos announcing their approach from miles away.

It is impossible to avoid these monsters, but fortunately the river is wide and the felucca crews are expert at tacking to keep out of their way; and they rarely appear singly but advance in packs, having passed through the lock at Esna together and been moored there at night, so that there are many hours each day without a floating barracks to disturb the peace and tranquillity of the river. Cruising quietly and slowly on the Nile in a felucca sailboat provides an unforgettable experience, with views of village life along the palm-fringed shores; and the days and nights removed from the press of mass tourism are, as a much-traveled member of one of my

groups told me, "as near to paradise as you can get on earth." These
open, thirty-foot, one-masted, lateen-rigged boats have been used
on the Nile for thousands of years and have no engines; a canvas
canopy provides shade during the day and retains the warmth at
night, when sleeping bags are unrolled on the padded deck. There
is space for eight passengers in each felucca, plus the *raïs,* or captain,
and the crew, who expertly sail the boat and prepare typically Egyptian meals and, after dinner, entertain with songs and music.

The nineteenth-century dahabiyas must have been more comfortable with their cozy cabins and washing facilities; but travelers
then made them their homes for many months. For four days of
cruising, today's feluccas are surprisingly enjoyable, and the most
hesitant members of my groups adapt themselves to them immediately on stepping aboard, take off their shoes, and recline luxuriously among the colored cushions on deck in the shade of the
canopy, relax, and call for sweet mint tea to be brought to them.
Then, when the offensive floating hotels pass us, we feel tremendously superior as the passengers crowd along the railings and look
down and take photographs of us in our little boats and of our
black-and-white flag with the Sagittarius symbol; and we wave
back graciously and suspect that they are envious and realize that
we are cruising the Nile in more style than they.

For many years I have sailed with *raïs* Aïd Fahwy and watched
him mature and become more than fond of him. He is almost six
feet tall, very dark, and superbly muscled; and Gustave Flaubert
and Maxime du Camp's description of their *raïs,* Ibrahim, fits him
exactly: "Meticulously, almost elegantly clean and neat, and despite the simplicity of his costume, which consisted of a blue gown
and a white turban, he had a somehow lordly air, which gave even
greater distinction to his dark, animated features, his soft and contemplative eyes." Like *raïs* Ibrahim, Aïd is very devout and regu-
larly says his five prayers a day. Each time I come to Egypt, we hug

and kiss each other on the cheeks when he greets me at the dock and when we part at the end of the cruise; for the rest of the time I content myself with adoring him as he reclines gracefully at the stern of his felucca, expertly controlling the tiller with one of his beautiful brown feet, a glass of mint tea on the seat beside him.

His crew varies from year to year. For some years he sailed with Moursi Madani, the most experienced felucca man on the river, a legend who was affectionately hailed by every passing boat and from all the villages, a tiny, busy little eighty-year-old gnome who was never idle, constantly washing the deck and the hull, mending ropes, peeling potatoes, sewing up a tear in a canopy, and who sang in a high falsetto voice. Perhaps he has retired at last; lately, Aïd's sailors are younger and more vigorous, capable of swiftly climbing to the top of the twenty-five-foot mast to unfurl the great lateen sail, and there is always one who is quite young, a boy who dances provocatively and raises his galabiya seductively when Aïd plays the drum, and sings after dinner, and with whom Aïd sleeps at night on the bow, tantalizingly wrapped in a blanket. Gustave Flaubert and Maxime du Camp had a young sailor like this with them on their boat in 1850, and wrote of him that "he served as wife to quite a few of the crew."

✧

When we sat on the terrace of the Old Cataract Hotel in Aswan, having drinks at sunset on the evening before we were to embark in our feluccas next day, I explained once more how we would live during our cruise down the Nile to Luxor, so that everyone would be sure to wear suitable clothes and pack all the necessities for the next four days and fill their canteens with bottled water; and when I described the food we would eat, our sleeping arrangements, the absence of conventional toilet facilities and of running water other than that of the river, I saw surprise, then dismay, and finally horror in the face of a real-estate entrepreneur from Los Angeles, a charming and good-looking man with the body of a teenage swimmer who was ashamed to enter any hotel pool in case his sparse strands of hair might be disarranged, although his bald head was in fact his greatest attraction. He was greatly concerned, he said, about the hygienic conditions of the galley and the preparation of the food.

I told him that there is no galley in a felucca; that the food is cooked on a minute paraffin stove in the small, narrow well between the rope locker under the boat's bow and the passenger platform; that there are two or three pots, a kettle, and a frying pan. The crew prepares breakfast, luncheon, afternoon tea, and dinner between sailing the boat; they handle ropes and blow their noses with their fingers and pick at their sores and cut up tomatoes and cucumbers for delicious salads; to clean the utensils they dip them into the Nile, which is not only the lifeline but also the sewer of Egypt; hygiene as we understand it is unknown—but I stressed that on more than a dozen cruises I have never had anyone with me who became ill.

Dick had perhaps been too busy before the tour to read the brochure in which all this was unequivocally stated; he heard me with astonishment, and after dinner asked me to direct him to the bazaar. "I have purchases to make," he said.

Next morning we boarded our two feluccas—Brian Kenny in Awad Yousef's *Rose* with five tour members, and I in Aïd Fahwy's *Sapreen* with five others, including Dick—and as soon as we were settled on deck with our belongings arranged around us, Dick unpacked a number of packages and took them to Aïd in the stern. "This disinfectant is very strong," he told him, "so you need only put five or six drops of it in the bowl when you wash up the plates and glasses. These pads are for scrubbing all the pots and pans; anything that comes into contact with Nile water must be thoroughly wiped with these impregnated cloths. Here are rubber gloves: be sure to put them on before you prepare any food or cut up any vegetables or fruit."

Aïd looked at me; I looked at Aïd; we understood each other perfectly. I knew that none of Dick's purchases would be used during our cruise, or any cruise, that they would be stored under the deck and sold in Luxor. I crawled across to sit beside Dick and told him that he had embarrassed me and humiliated Aïd. "He is so proud of his clean boat; it is only on the big ships that all the two hundred or more passengers invariably get sick. You must put your trust in our crew—and in God."

"Very well," said Dick. "I will, if you say so. But I'm a Californian, and for us hygiene is the greatest priority at all times. If I get sick, I'll have my lawyer sue you."

Two days later, in the afternoon, I suddenly realized that Dick was missing. I called across to Brian in the *Rose*—had Dick changed to the other felucca after our luncheon stop? No, he was not there. "Oh my God! We've left Dick behind!" I cried. The tour members in my felucca giggled at my consternation and pointed to the rope locker under the bow.

I made my way to it and peered into the dark and saw Dick with a very strange, flushed look on his face.

"Dick, are you ill?" I cried in alarm. But then I saw that he was not alone in that dark, filthy hole; he was with one of the crew and engaged in a carnal act in which hygiene played no part whatsoever.

"If you get sick now," I told him later, "I shall deny any responsibility."

✦

Sailing by felucca between Aswan and Luxor, where sight-seeing is dutiful and obligatory for the serious traveler, and exhausting, provides the relief of wonderfully restful, contemplative days and nights. Sailing down the river, with its sluggish current, against the steady and often strong wind from the north, means that the boats must tack constantly; rarely, when the wind drops, the crew must row and sometimes pole the boat along through the reeds at the riverbank.

There is no timetable. One wakes at dawn, and tea is brought to each passenger in his sleeping bag; then one walks the precarious plank and steps ashore to attend to one's ablutions in private. Breakfast follows, later a stop for luncheon, then a nap under the canopy until teatime. At sunset the boats are tied up against the bank while dinner is being prepared; later there is a little music, a little gossip, and so to sleep. One is free to go ashore when and where one pleases, on any whim.

After more than twenty visits to Egypt, over a period of more than sixty years, I had never succeeded in seeing the Step Pyramid of El-Kula. "Stop there!" I commanded Aïd. "There, on the west bank! The Pyramid of El-Kula must be quite near; we will walk to explore it."

Aïd, who knows every inch of the Nile but nothing of anything that is more than a few feet from its banks, shrugged dramatically. "You crazy man. No pyramid here. Pyramids all near Cairo— Gizeh, yes; Sakkara, yes; Maidun, yes. No pyramid here."

Poor ignorant Aïd did not understand that the Step Pyramid of El-Kula was clearly marked on my map and is listed in Baedeker. We went ashore and walked through the green fields toward a village, where we aroused considerable interest and were invited into the schoolhouse so that the children could show off their few words of English. We asked for directions to the pyramid, but no one had heard of it; it was quite unknown to everyone although only a mile or less distant on my map. "No pyramid here—pyramids all near Cairo!"

The thoughtful Aïd had tea and cookies ready for us when we returned. "Good pyramid?" he asked mischievously, knowing quite well that we had not found it. But we much enjoyed our walk. A pungent smell arose from the big cook pot simmering on the little stove in the well of the felucca, promise of another succulent stew for dinner. We sailed on. Aïd, delighted that our expedition to the pyramid had been futile, lounged by the tiller and laughed. "Mr. Hanns—you crazy man!"

The days are so leisurely that between watching life along the riverbanks, picking up a book with the intention of reading, and dozing, there is a great deal of time for chat. We heard from one of the doctors who attended ex-President Nixon that, much to everyone's surprise, he was courteous and always considerate of his staff; we heard from Professor Alfred Borrello, who looked absolutely splendid in his stately black galabiya and turban and was always bent over his embroidery, that Evelyn Waugh, in whose house in Wiltshire he had spent a weekend, was indeed as unpleasant and rude as my shipmates on the SS *Hermes* cruise in 1958 had said. "I had no idea how exquisitely relaxing this cruise would be," said the learned Alfred. "All this fresh air has sharpened my appetite."

Almost all felucca passengers prefer, after a day or two aboard, to wear Arab garments. Nothing is more sensible, and galabiyas suited both the middle-aged, stout dentist from Chicago and his slim, lively young Puerto Rican lover. Many hours each day are spent in learning to tie turbans, and then tying them most artistically, most authentically. Aïd and his crew, and Awad and his sailors in the felucca that sailed along close to us and tacked in and out of ours, all laughed uproariously at these prolonged and rarely successful efforts. They, of course, simply took their long pieces of cloth, folded them, swirled them fast and expertly around their heads, tucked in a corner here, another there, and looked superb.

Brian Kenny, who can (and frequently does) quote poetry and obscure sayings, and who disdains wearing a turban—"I am not going to a costume ball"—disparaged the others' attempts to tie them and declaimed a rhyme about Beau Brummell, the early-nineteenth-century English dandy:

> *My neckcloth, of course, forms my principal care,*
> *For by that we criterions of elegance swear,*
> *And costs me, each morning, some hours of flurry,*
> *To make it appear to be tied in a hurry.*

Yes, there really is nothing more delightful than a voyage on the Nile with agreeable companions, when one feels free to be so frivolous.

There is time, too, and plenty of opportunity, for me to show off my knowledge as a paramedic, acquired when I was a volunteer with the Saint John Ambulance Association in the early part of World War II. During more than forty years of conducting tours and expeditions, often to places where no medical assistance is available, I have perfected the contents of my traveling first-aid box so that I can deal adequately with anything short of a major medical calamity. Along the Nile my reputation as a hakim precedes me; and the plastic box with its red cross and red crescent is always beside me on deck.

My tour members place little trust in me and generally prefer to rely on their own and one another's medications; but when all else has failed they come to me, somewhat contrite, to be dosed with my magic mixture, Dr. J. Collis Browne's Chlorodyne, which I obtain in large quantities from England, where it is sold over the counter, and which never fails, after judicious administrations, to cure diarrhea, nausea, colic spasms, chills, and travel fatigue—but whether it also prevents or cures cholera, asthma, neuralgia, sickness in pregnancy, renal calculus, and uterine affections, as it claims, I have never found out.

The felucca crew always come to me to be treated. They suffer from almost continuous coughs (but cigarettes are never out of their mouths); they have splinters deeply embedded in the tough skin of their feet and hands; there are nasty sores; they vaguely describe pains in the head, the shoulders, the back, and the legs that are probably imaginary. I look grave and dispense lozenges and aspirin and rub on embrocations and provide sympathy. Even Aïd does not disdain applying to me for something to ease his cough, or begs for a pill to cure some fictitious affliction, or, since he surely knows my feelings for him, gives me the pleasure of holding his foot in my hands and removing a splinter from it.

But it is the people in the villages who are my most devoted patients, who bring me their children and sit cross-legged with wonder when I unlock the box and lift its lid and pull out its cantilevered trays with all their compartments, in which are bottles and tubes and capsules in gaudy colors, scissors and tweezers and needles, mysterious jars, snakebite kits and Band-Aids and fluffy cotton balls and bandages and adhesive tapes and packets of Fisherman's Friend with pictures of a trawler on them. It is touching to see the faith with which these people deliver their little boys and girls into my hands; but as I am never confronted with a serious case of illness or injury, I suspect that it is all a game of make-believe, that they wisely take anyone who is in need of proper medical attention to the nearest doctor or hospital, that this consultation with the funny old hakim with the golden ring in his ear is only an entertainment, an excuse to obtain some nicely colored, sweet-tasting pill, preferably one that is half-pink and half-white. I play the game and demonstrate great concern as I study the trivial cuts that are presented to me, and I slowly and with grave deliberation select a soothing ointment to apply to a wound, or let a drop or two of some innocuous lotion fall into an eye or an ear. Applications of the pretty iodine, Merthiolate, or Mercurochrome are always well received, and the children run off proudly showing off a clean bandage or a Band-Aid on their brown skin.

Then, well pleased with his handiwork, the great hakim closes his box of tricks.

✧

For no reason whatsoever—I do not know how this nonsense started, but I suspect that Freeman Gunter was the instigator of it—we began and continued to use French expressions and intoned them in the most pompous manner, as if we were reciting choice phrases of Racine and Molière on the stage of the Comédie Fran-çaise. We rolled every *r* with rich, reverberating Gallic fervor; we stressed every accented letter as far and as long as it was humanly possible to do so, and further; we thought we were tremendously funny and laughed so much at our silliness that we were often in danger of wetting ourselves. The Nile was not the Nile but *le Nil*! Cairo was *le Caire*! Every delectably spiced stew that Aïd produced from the stove and set down before us was greeted with cries of *"Oh, un repas très formidable! Oh, les oranges douces de l'Orient! Oh, les dattes du désert!"* The crew of both feluccas—for our boats were tied to-gether while we all dined under the lamp aboard the *Sapreen*—thought that we had gone totally out of our minds—as perhaps we had. "All crazy mens," said Aïd.

"Oh, le raïs—un homme très formidable! Un homme très magnifique! Oh, le Nil—le plus grand fleuve d'Égypte!"

But Freeman Gunter's far-greater contribution to our cruise, and a remarkable four-day coup de theatre, was his presentation, at sunset each evening, of one act of *Aida,* Verdi's opera that the khe-dive of Egypt had commissioned for the opening of the Suez Canal but that was first performed in Cairo in December of 1871.

It is one of my rules that no recorded music is played aboard the feluccas during the day, so that we can listen to the sounds of the boats as they move through the water and to the wind lashing the sail and, near the shores, to birds singing and children laughing as they splash about in the river, and in the villages to the muezzins' call to prayer.

Freeman has a passion for all things Egyptian and for opera, diverse interests in which he is exceedingly knowledgeable and that converge with great felicity in his love for *Aida*. He had brought with him a powerful portable cassette player capable of reproducing the opera with great clarity out of doors, and had used his nineteen complete recordings of *Aida*—some being very rare and dating back as far as 1919—to put together one ultimate, unsurpassable performance of the opera in its entirety, preserving its continuity in the proper order, created by selecting for each moment of it the most choice rendering that he believed best captured the essence and atmosphere of the drama. Thus we heard Radames sung by Kurt Baum and Jussi Björling and Enrico Caruso and Placido Domingo and Carlo Bergonzi; Amneris by Rita Gorr and Giulietta Simionato and Agnes Baltsa; Aida by Maria Callas and Renata Tebaldi and Montserrat Caballé and Zinka Milanov and Leontyne Price; and Amonasro by Piero Cappuccilli and Tito Gobbi. It was a feast. Sometimes, for added effect, a duet was repeated, even three times, so that in the final scene we listened first to the noble voice of Jussi Björling with Zinka Milanov, then to Carlo Bergonzi with Renata Tebaldi, and, most thrilling of all, to Kurt Baum with Maria Callas in a recording made of their second night's performance in Mexico City in 1950.

How nostalgic it was for me to hear again after so many years the sensuous, plummy voice of Leontyne Price, radiantly shimmering in her high notes—and now on the Nile! For many years she had been Brian's and my neighbor on Vandam Street in New York, and when we gave a party in the garden of our little apartment, she walked among our forty-six rosebushes and, unaccompanied, sang "Summertime." A guest who did not know that she was our neighbor ran up to me. "My God—that's Leontyne Price!" he cried, amazed and enormously impressed.

"Yes, I always have some kind of entertainer at my parties," I said.

We listened, quite still, in the fading light as the feluccas tacked to gain the exact place for the night stop. It became too dark for Professor Borrello to do his embroidery. On the western shore, the palm trees were silhouetted against a sky as vivid orange as in the paintings on black velvet, but in reality the scene was not hideous at all but sublimely lovely, biblically serene. Oh, Aïd! Oh, *Aïda*! Soon, very fast, the garish orange sky turned pale violet and the stars began to pierce it. The day was done and we were tied up against the riverbank, we agreeable companions with the magnificent Aïd and Awad and the wonderful crew, alone in the still, dark night. Aïd lit the oil lamp. Beyond the palm trees, sand was kissing the moonlit sky, the desert breeze was whispering a lullaby. The flowered oilcloth was laid for dinner; our eating bowls and spoons were passed up.

"*Oh, le Nil!*"

"*Le Nil—le plus grand fleuve d'Égypte! Les dattiers sur un fond au soleil couchant! Oh, regardez la lune, beau visage du ciel!*"

"Dinnertime, you crazy mens!"

"*Oh, un repas très formidable!*"

"*Oh, c'est très magnifique!*"

Oh, how wonderful to be so silly.

19

FELLOW

TRAVELERS

ALL HAPPY TRAVELERS resemble one another, but (as Tolstoy wrote of families) all unhappy travelers are unhappy in their own way.

Happy travelers possess resilience, stamina, patience, and indifference to personal discomforts in varying degrees, and, above all, the ability to make the most of adverse situations. When traveling as a member of a group, they are considerate of others. Seneca said, "He that would make his travels delightful, must first make himself delightful."

Unhappy travelers are interested chiefly in the shortcomings of their hotel accommodations, worried always that they are being cheated and imposed upon, ignorant and thus not impressed with anything they see, discontented, impatient, and unable to adapt to unfamiliar conditions. Nothing pleases them, and a shower of rain, a short flight delay, or the absence of hot croissants at breakfast is a disaster. Some are merely nasty; others are chronically ill-mannered, crude, rude, obnoxious, and evil.

It is gratifying to be able to enhance the pleasure of travel for happy travelers; unhappy travelers can rarely be comforted and roused from their misery.

I have spent many happy weeks among charming, interesting, considerate, and appreciative people camping in the Andes and the Sinai or on the open deck of a felucca on the Nile, where living at such close proximity puts a considerable strain on both newly made acquaintances and old friends. A common interest must be found. When married couples talk to me at length of their children, I talk to them of my cats, and thus we bridge the gap between us. It is strange, though, that after having shared so many adventures, the best of times and the worst moments that occasionally occur, it is often some totally insignificant or trivial incident by which I best remember a fellow traveler. Thus, when I think of Mr. and Mrs. Brian Stephenson of Bermuda, it is less because of our happy weeks together in the Chilean Lake District and on Easter Island than because before they joined one of my tours to India, Patricia Stephenson telephoned me from Bermuda and asked me to make a hotel reservation for them in New York for the night before the tour departure: "Please get us a room at the lowest rate."

I told her that a room at the lowest rate in New York would not be at all to their liking but that I would make a reservation at a reasonably priced, respectable midtown hotel.

When the Stephensons arrived at the hotel, they expressed astonishment at my choice. Surely I knew, said Brian, that they preferred something better than that? "Yes, I do know," I said, "and I was quite surprised when Pat asked me to get you a room at the lowest rate."

"No," he said. "She asked you to get us a room at the Loew's Drake."

The Loew's Drake was, at that time, one of New York's finest hotels; and we have laughed about this ridiculous telephonic misunderstanding ever since.

✧

Ineradicably stamped on my memory are recollections of the most parsimonious, the oldest, the nastiest, and the gentlest persons with whom I have traveled.

To be thrifty is, in many respects, a quality to be commended; but I find it less easy to understand and approve of travelers who are rich and self-indulgent but so amazingly parsimonious that it strikes me sometimes almost as an indication of insanity. I see travelers who have cheerfully paid ten thousand dollars for a ten-day tour and who, bored on a rainy afternoon, buy a gold chain or a wristwatch for fifteen thousand dollars, but then bargain with a pathetic little peasant girl who has spent three months making a rag doll to reduce its price from the equivalent of a dollar to fifty cents.

Even after forty years of conducting tours I have not become reconciled to seeing so many travelers' aversion to tipping for services rendered. Tipping is an unpleasant, often awkward part of travel, but whether we like it or not, it has become the almost universal way for the traveler to express his or her thanks. In those few places where tipping is not the custom, as in French Polynesia, I am embarrassed to leave the dining table, the chaise by the pool, and my hotel bedroom without offering a tip. A tip may not always be obligatory, but if it is not forthcoming—or falls short of expectations—there is disappointment, chagrin, sometimes anger. A delightful lady member of one of my tours in the Chilean Lake District found a pretty little local coin on a path and asked me its value—it was one tenth of a United States cent—and at the end of our stay she handed it to the guide who had for four days helped her on and off the motor coach and the steamer on Lake Todos los Santos, assisted her up and down stairs and across the catwalks above the Petrohue waterfalls, carried her tote bag and her camera, and ran back to fetch her sweater and her rain poncho.

He came to me in bewilderment. "Is she insulting me?"

I told him to keep the coin as a souvenir.

When I reminded the lady that the coin she had given as her tip was worth one tenth of a cent, she said, "Oh, but it's the thought that counts!"

Inexplicably, it is often the nicest people who are the most parsimonious, like the rich, retired English gentleman, so generous with his hospitality and so gracious a host in his home, who invited an impecunious young guide in Ecuador to share a bottle of wine with him at luncheon and then, after the meal, asked him to pay half the cost of it.

"How much shall we give Julio?" my tour members ask me at the end of ten glorious days in the Andes, during which the superb Julio has not only guided them from dawn to dusk but has arranged special treats for them, has sat with us at breakfast and luncheon and dinner, always ready to answer questions, eager to instruct us and stimulate our interest in the places he loves and where he is at home. I stress that he is a university graduate with a degree in anthropology; I remind them how devoted he was to us all and how concerned about our well-being. I point out how deserving he is of a substantial token of our appreciation. "At least ten dollars from each of you," I say.

"Ten *dollars*! That seems most excessive!" they cry.

Fortunately there are also, often, many travelers who do reward good service; indeed, some are so generous that by contrast they make the others' lesser gratuities seem even more paltry in the guides' estimation.

The most parsimonious person I have encountered was a nephew of Professor John Garstang, during a Mediterranean cruise.

Professor Garstang, born in 1876, had begun his career as an archaeologist in Egypt in 1899, had excavated at Abydos with Flinders Petrie in 1907, worked for several seasons at Meroë in the

Sudan, and in 1931 discovered the ancient city of Jericho in Palestine. He then turned his attention to Hittite sites in Asia Minor, where his discoveries near Mersin, in Cilicia, constituted one of his greatest triumphs.

He had joined a Society for Hellenic Travel cruise in September of 1956 because one of its ports of call along the southern coast of Turkey was Mersin, and he wanted after more than thirty years to revisit his site—or what remained of it. He traveled with a lady secretary, a nurse, his sister, and a nephew, and was so frail that when I first saw him being led along the platform at Victoria Station in London, I thought he would not survive the train journey to Venice, where we embarked on the SS *Proleterka*. This Yugoslav ship, chartered for the cruise, was run for the benefit of its crew, not the passengers. Loud jazz music, highly offensive to the scholarly travelers, blared on decks and throughout the public rooms, and the deck chairs were always occupied by burly crew members. When I remonstrated with the purser, he swept my complaints aside. "The men in the engine room work very hard; it is very hot down there. They deserve to have some fresh air and sun. And they like the music."

"But the passengers—"

"Say me nothing about the passengers. They are of no importance to us; we will never see them again. Our crew stay with us for many years and must be made happy."

Professor Garstang remained in bed in his cabin for ten days in order to conserve his little strength for the excursion at Mersin, where the SS *Proleterka* anchored out in the bay. While the other passengers were ashore, one of the ship's stewards and I carried him down the ship's ladder and into a small boat for the ride to the dock, lifted him into an old taxi, and drove with him and the nurse to the site of his excavations some miles west of the town.

The entire cruise group awaited us there, with cameras at the ready, as well as twenty or thirty men who had been the professor's laborers at the site thirty years before and who had come to pay their respects to the grand old man, bringing their sons to be present at this historic occasion. The place was barely recognizable as having once been an archaeological site—it was nothing, in fact, except a low hill of rubble. The steward and I raised up the professor, who hung like a puppet between us in his shabby old gray suit, now far too large for his emaciated body. His feeble eyes were shielded from the sun's glare by a green celluloid visor. He rallied for this, his big moment.

"Ladies and gentlemen," he whispered hoarsely, "you see before you the ruins of a site, and the wreck of a man." He slumped in our arms; we carried him down the slope to the taxi; the nurse gave him a spoonful of brandy; we carried him from the dock into the boat and up the ship's ladder and back to his cabin. We sailed that evening, and early next morning, when we were in Beirut Harbor, he died.

The nurse was quite useless, and it was the wife of one of the cruise lecturers who closed his eyes and laid him out. There was a great deal to be attended to—telegrams to be sent to England, decisions to be made about the removal of the body, harbor police and health officials to be dealt with, the British embassy to be informed and their assistance requested—but when the professor's nephew strode into my cruise office, his prime concern was with another matter.

He was a Gurney, a scion of an old, highly respected, and exceedingly rich banking family from Norfolk; "as rich as a Gurney" is an English expression that is more readily understood there than a reference to Croesus, of whom not everyone has heard.

"Now look here, Ebensten," he said, "I take it you will not be able to resell the professor's cabin for the remaining seven days of the cruise, more's the pity, but I will retain its key to make quite sure that you don't give it to anyone else or make any use of it; but of course, the family expect and demand that a refund is forthcoming for the three daily meals which the professor will not eat, as well as for the electric power he will not utilize, and for laundry service, since no fresh bed linen and towels will be required from now on. And then there is the matter of water—fresh water aboard is a major item of expense, as you should know even if you don't, and I have calculated that the professor would have used no less than fourteen pints of fresh water per diem, so the cost of ninety-eight pints of water is to be refunded. I expect to have to incur considerable expenses here in Beirut—it is all most tiresome—so let me have the total refund by six o'clock, in cash sterling, no fancy foreign currency, together with your itemized statement of the refunds."

He did not wait for my response, and I was too stunned to have been capable of making any, and he marched briskly out of the cruise office.

✧

The oldest tour member I have had with me—and also one of the nicest—was John Laurence Seymour, the composer, who was ninety-two when he went to Egypt with me in November of 1985.

His opera *In the Pasha's Garden* had been performed at the Metropolitan Opera House in New York in 1935, and he thought it was high time that he compose another, which was to be based on the emperor Hadrian's love affair with Antinoüs, the Bithynian youth who drowned in the Nile. Unlike my prudish old admirer and biographer of Hadrian, Stewart Perowne, John Seymour believed that Hadrian and Antinoüs's love had been passionate and carnal.

Despite his age—perhaps because of it, because people who reach old age understand their physical limitations and know how to take good care of themselves—John Seymour was cheerfully ready at 4:00 A.M. for a dawn flight to Aswan, ate sparingly and wisely, and proved to be the most delightful of travel companions, an entertaining raconteur at meals, an inspiration to all the tour members, who never suspected his real age. When we talked about Halley's Comet, which was to appear in the sky the next year, he said he had seen it last time and thought it was vastly overrated. "Don't even bother to go out on the porch to see it," he advised us. The others argued that he must have been very young when he saw it in 1910, and that children never appreciate things properly. "Young! Not at all! I was a man of voting age," he said. (This was not, I believe, strictly true, unless men of seventeen years were eligible to vote at that time.)

When he spoke amusingly of his meetings with President Roosevelt, it was Theodore to whom he referred. He looked elegant at all times and was always suitably dressed—blue jeans and a red flannel miner's shirt for explorations, and a fine old-fashioned tuxedo and an elaborately frilled dress shirt for dinner. He omitted no part of our taxing program of sight-seeing, and being unable to bend and crouch low in order to enter some of the tombs and pyramids, he scrambled in and out of them on his stomach, to everyone's admiration.

There are no remains at Antinoüpolis, the city Hadrian built at the place where his lover drowned in the Nile; but we sailed past it very slowly and scattered rose petals. John Seymour was highly appreciative of this little ceremony arranged in his honor. "As long as I linger on this planet I'm going to plan on sampling some of your other tours—in which I won't have to crawl on my belly," he told me. Alas, he lingered only another month and did not see Halley's Comet again.

✧

Twice in my life I have been physically abused by women. The first attack on me was by a member of the Archives of American Art, a group of people interested in art and artists who made a fund-raising tour each year. The organizers of these tours are generally hardworking and amiable ladies, but those who travel with them often have little interest in foreign travel and pay the tour price, and make the tax-deductible contribution that is a requirement for participating in it, because it furthers their social ambitions.

I was at Kennedy Airport in New York one evening in September of 1968, when the group's flight was delayed. I had been involved in an automobile accident some months before, and had a broken leg and was on crutches. Mrs. Bernard Gimbel and the tour's organizer, Mrs. Eloise Spaeth, arranged their topcoats over themselves, and with quiet resignation each lay down across three chairs to sleep. Others did crosswords. But a rich Chicago meat packer's wife, a woman as grossly fat as a Japanese wrestler, took full advantage of the free drinks and became belligerent. When I had to announce yet a further flight delay of two hours, she advanced upon me, punched me hard in the chest, and pulled the crutches from under my arms so that I fell to the ground. No one came to assist me. I crawled across the lounge to a chair and raised myself onto it. Inside the plaster cast, my broken leg throbbed with pain. Presently, another lady member of the group sat beside me, and I thought she had come to comfort me and apologize for her friend's attack, but no—"We all feel so sorry for Mollie," she said. "She'll be quite upset tomorrow morning when she realizes what she did."

Mrs. Bernard Gimbel, who accepted the flight delay with such admirable calm, was the eighty-year-old widow of the New York department-store owner, an enthusiastic traveler, a grande dame of the old style, and a shopper of considerable discernment. When she went to Turkey, she bought two carpets. She did not, of course, buy them in one of those carpet emporiums in Istanbul where suave salesmen capture tourists within their marble halls and sit them down with a drink or a cup of coffee and sell them machine-made horrors at stupendous prices. She did not buy them in the Grand Bazaar, said to abound with bargains if the traveler knows how to play the game and devotes many days to it. She did not even buy them in one of the old *han*s, which are almost unknown to tourists and where knowledgeable collectors, dealers, and museum directors find lovely old things of value at sensible prices.

She did not buy her carpets anywhere in Istanbul, but waited until she was in a small provincial town in Eastern Anatolia, far off the normal tourist route. There, in a dirty alley, after hours of good-natured but hard bargaining, she secured two choice silk-on-silk carpets. She did not claim to be an expert, not quite, but she recognized the real thing when she saw it, and knew its true value. She was delighted with her purchases and had them wrapped in sacking and made into a big package, for which she paid the excess-baggage charge and took it back to New York on the plane with her.

On the parquet floor of her apartment, the carpets looked even more stunning than in the humble shop in Anatolia. She was thrilled with them, and invited her son, then running the Gimbel's store on Thirty-fourth Street, to see them. "Aren't they wonderful?" she asked him.

"Yes, Mother, very fine."

"And you won't believe what I paid for them—you just won't believe it! This one was twelve hundred dollars, and this one, fifteen-fifty. So what do you say to that?"

"Oh, Mother," said her son, "we have the same carpets in the store, at less than half that."

◇

The second assault on me was made by a nineteen-year-old liberated female member of another fund-raising group, that of the Peabody Museum Associates of Yale University. I had felt honored when its organizer asked me to arrange their fourth tour, to Peru, until I heard later that no one else would handle them; they were well known to be, with few exceptions, the nastiest people imaginable, arrogant, imperious, aggressive, and opinionated ladies who, en masse, became a hellish band of vulgarly competing viragoes. Some of them brought along their docile husbands, men at the top of their professions who wanted only to have a peaceful vacation; but for this monstrous regiment of women, the tour provided a challenge to exert their power, to fight for what they claimed to be their rights, to vie with one another for the best seats on planes and buses, and for the best rooms in hotels. "My husband is a very, very important man, I'll have you know," they would cry. "We must have a room facing the front."

The most horrible of these women was so puffed up with self-importance as to be almost a caricature of a shrew. Her husband said never a word while she ranted and raved, and I found it hard to understand how he had tolerated her demands and tantrums for fifteen years. No doubt she had the money; but he should have poisoned her long ago.

The teenage female had been sent on the tour by her parents to further her education, but she was less interested in the archaeology and anthropology of Peru than in trying to seduce the bus drivers and guides. She was so uncouth, so lacking in manners, so rude, and so devoid of any feminine grace that it was impossible to feel sorry for her lack of success.

When we boarded a very large motor coach for the drive to Paracas, from where we were to visit the Guano Islands, I stood by its door to help the tour members up its steep steps; and the liberated young female indignantly knocked down the arm I held out to assist her and hit me, hard, twice across my face. Very little surprises me, but I was considerably shaken. When we arrived at the hotel in the afternoon, she left her diary on the motor coach, and I took it to my room. It was a graphic record of her sexual escapades in Connecticut, her disgust with the tour and her fellow travelers, and her condemnation of me. With a red felt-tipped pen I corrected her orthographic errors, the misspelled place-names, the wrong figures for altitudes and distances; and where she referred to me as an "officious pig" and a "sick-making fag" I struck out these offending descriptions and wrote "attentive tour leader" and "agreeable bachelor." At dinner, I returned the diary to her. We did not speak to each other for the remainder of the tour.

The misery of conducting this group of nasty people was redeemed by the presence of the two oldest members of it, whom the organizer of the tour had not wanted to accept because of their age but who, when I was introduced to them at Yale some months before the tour departure, appeared to me to be physically fit and mentally alert, so that I urged the organizer to relent and include them. They proved to be stalwart travelers indeed; nothing deterred or worried them; and they were a constant joy to me. They ate sparingly, as I urged all the tour members to do—the others ignored my good advice and, consequently, frequently became ill—and after luncheon they dozed off in the motor coach to wake refreshed an hour or so later, ready to tramp around extensive archaeological sites in the hot sun, descend into dimly lit catacombs, and hike up steep mountains to clamber around Inca ruins.

In Puno, on Lake Titicaca, which we reached after an exhausting sixteen-hour drive from Arequipa over 15,500-foot passes, bitterly cold and delayed by a fearful thunderstorm, the shrew led a revolt: the group would no longer be imposed upon and make another horrible overland journey across the miserable Andean landscape. Instead of taking a filthy old train next day to Cusco, as planned, they would fly and I must bear the extra cost.

The two indomitable old ladies, stoutly shod and warmly dressed, had looked forward to the adventure of this railroad journey across the altiplano, with its promise of vendors of handicrafts boarding at its many stops en route; and they showed their disappointment at the shrew's decision. I told them that no matter what some tour members decided to do, I would proceed with the program as set out in the printed tour brochure and would travel by train next day. They enthusiastically announced that they would join me—and so, to my astonishment, did the shrew's husband, who was no doubt delighted to take an opportunity to escape from her domination for the twelve hours during which we were a party of four happy travelers.

At Nazca, I had arranged for Miss María Reiche to talk to us and show us the strange lines and drawings that stretch for miles across the desert, some of the representations of spiders, monkeys, and lizards being more than six hundred feet long. They were quite unknown until the 1930s, when air travel began in Peru and they were first seen. Miss Reiche had come to Peru to tutor the children of a rich family and became enthralled and totally absorbed by the mystery of the lines on the pampa and made their study and interpretation her life's work. Our guide brought her a letter from friends in Germany; she read it and then tore it neatly into tiny pieces, which she gave back to him. She did not wish to be encumbered with anything that was not absolutely necessary. She wore sandals and a very simple dress, like a shift, and slept on a cot in the desert and owned no hat and no watch. She could not begin her talk, she said, until she was provided with a piece of chocolate to lubricate her mouth, and a piece of string with which to demonstrate her theory about the desert lines. I was able to supply her with these items.

After her talk, I put numbered pieces of paper in a bowl and asked the tour members to draw lots for their places on the flights over the pampa next morning. There was one small plane with three passenger seats that was to make ten twenty-minute flights over the lines and drawings; due to the heat rising over the desert, the earliest flights were the least bumpy. The shrew indignantly refused to take a paper from the bowl. "My husband and I will not play your stupid game," she announced. "We are important people and will take the first flight, when the air is calm."

After the flights, Miss Reiche had arranged an opportunity for us to see details of the huge drawings from twenty or thirty feet above the ground. "The *bomberos* are my friends," she explained, and the helpful firemen of Nazca brought their ladders out to the desert and invited us to climb them for a close-up view of a spider's foot or a monkey's paw, each more than fifty feet long.

Few of the tour members ventured up these flimsy, perpendicular ladders that swayed in the wind, but the two eighty-year-old ladies followed my example and clung high above the desert. "What was it like?" they were asked when they were safely back on the ground.

"More thrilling than an orgasm," said one of these wonderful travelers.

In Cusco, the organizer of the tour, urged on by the shrew, expressed dissatisfaction with our capable guide. "We are not run-of-the-mill tourists," she told me. "We are the Peabody Museum Associates of Yale University. For Machu Picchu, whose finds we have in our museum, you must get us a scholar, not just a guide." I managed to persuade the authorities at the Museum of Archaeology to send one of their staff members along with us—but this young man was not in the least intimidated by the tour members.

"I understand you are from the Peabody Museum in Yale," he told them. "Well, I suggest that you return to us everything that Dr. Hiram Bingham took away from Machu Picchu in 1912 and that has been lying in your cellars ever since. You will not let anyone see it. If we write to you for information, you do not reply. If we request photographs of items that are of special interest to us, you do not send them. You have 164 mummies, 555 pieces of pottery, plus 350 trays and jugs, more than 200 pieces of bronze, including that unique knife with the fishing boy on its handle of which I wish to make a detailed study, and hundreds of stone objects. For more than sixty years you have not even bothered to catalog all these treasures of ours; so please, ladies and gentlemen, give them back to us."

This was not at all what the tour members wanted to hear. "Who does this guy think he is? Get rid of him!" the organizer told me.

When we arrived back at Kennedy Airport in New York, the shrew managed to upset me once more. We were waiting to pass through U.S. immigration control, and she left her husband in the line and ran up to me, her face distorted with fury. "How *dare* you insult us by making us stand here!" she screamed. "We are important people. Couldn't you even handle *this* properly?"

Fifteen years later, and again at Kennedy Airport, I knew that I was going to have other unhappy fellow travelers with me as soon as I saw two members of my group to Egypt: those mean, narrow lips, pursed with disdain, those shifty eyes darting about with suspicion of being cheated, that pompous way of addressing the airline staff, were all unmistakable signs of trouble ahead. They had made reservations in economy class on the plane but demanded to be seated in first class. "What sort of travel agent are you, if you can't even fix *that* for us?"

Neither I nor the other tour members ever understood why these two men had come to Egypt with us. They showed no interest whatsoever in the country, its history, its antiquities, or its people. After the first few days they did not join the sight-seeing tours or excursions. "You'll find us by the pool," they said. In Luxor, although by then I was thoroughly disgusted with them, I persuaded one of them to cross to the west bank with us, but the tombs in the Valley of the Kings did not please him. I begged him to stay and come to see the tombs of the nobles—"They are the gorgeously colored ones—the walls all painted—grapevines on the ceiling—really a must!"—but when we arrived there and he realized that he would have to walk a hundred feet or so from the car park to the tombs, he hailed a taxi to take him back to the ferry and returned to the Luxor Sheraton. "You'll find me by the pool."

They could not attend the sound-and-light performances at Gizeh, Philae, and Karnak. The hours were inconvenient. "That's when we nap before dinner." At Abu Simbel, they did not bother to enter the rock temples and took off their shirts and sat with their backs turned. "We're working on our tans."

Their hotel accommodations were of paramount importance to them, and they created a noisy scene on arrival in every hotel lobby. Their room was never acceptable, always the worst room they had ever seen in their life. They raced along the corridor to compare theirs with those of the other tour members, and ran back to confront me at the reception desk. "Our tub is six inches shorter than that in Jeff and Craig's bathroom—we measured them! So what are you going to do about *that?*"

"Nothing," I said.

They ran to our eminent accompanying Egyptologist, who had nothing to do with room allocations and travel arrangements. "If *you* don't get us a better room, we'll make your life hell!" they cried.

Sometimes, after having moved into a room they considered to be better, they then after an hour or so insisted on being moved back into their original room. It was like some evil game.

Maids showed me how these men left their room. They did not flush the toilet bowl, and wiped their bottoms with towels and threw them onto the floor. They blew their noses copiously on their bed sheets. The hotel staff despised them so that they rang in vain

for room service; their curtains were not drawn at night nor chocolates placed on their pillows; theirs was the only luggage not picked
up from outside doors. "For Christ's sake, use some of that money
we paid you and get us a bit of service around here," they told me.

They were too grand to sit with the other tour members for
meals and summoned the maître d' to be given a table for two in
what they believed to be the best part of the dining room. They
would not eat in the delightful, typically Egyptian, and well-tried
restaurants in Cairo, Aswan, and Luxor where I took the group to
enjoy local food among local people.

They were even more obnoxious than a similar pair of New
York men who had been with me in Egypt some years before and of
whom a fellow tour member wrote in *Mandate* magazine that "their
jaded sourness was typical of overprivileged homosexuals at their
worst" and described how, in the tomb of Thutmose III, one of
them had said, "I can't believe I'm wearing my Cartier watch in this
filthy tomb."

The other tour members referred to them as the Jewish Faggot
Princesses, and I had to appear to be shocked when I overheard
this, but it perfectly described this venomous pair. I wanted to
send them home, because it is only by ridding itself of such creatures that a travel company can continue to conduct pleasant, so-
ciable tours; but as the tour progressed we saw less and less of
them, were only troubled by them on the drives to and from airports (when they insisted on occupying the first row of seats) and
when checking into hotels, and I tolerated their presence to the
end. To the relief of everyone, they did not attend our farewell
dinner. As soon as I was back in my office, I removed their names
from our mailing list.

Why, oh why, do the wrong people travel?

✧

One of the participants in my group of "discerning gentlemen" in China in May of 1982 was Mr. Calvin Culver, known in homosexual circles as Casey Donovan, star of the epoch-making *Boys in the Sand* and many subsequent porno films in which, so I was told, he performed—or permitted to be performed upon him—a variety of amazingly erotic sexual acts.

This, the most famous—or notorious—gay sex symbol of the time, was, surprisingly, a highly educated, enormously well read, and considerate man with impeccable manners who dressed in a most conservative style. Good-looking but in no way either pretty or aggressively handsome, with a teenager's slim and graceful figure that he had maintained for more than twenty years, he was the sort of man with whom one could be seen anywhere and whom one could unhesitatingly introduce to one's mother.

He had done his homework on China, was well informed about its history, archaeology, art, religion, peoples, and politics, and was one of the most organized travelers I have known. Although he carried only one small duffel bag, he was appropriately and neatly dressed at all times during our two-week tour, be it for an arduous two-day mountain climb, for a formal dinner with the governor of Anhui Province and high officials at the Government Guesthouse in Wuhu, or for a cruise aboard the presidential yacht on the Whang-poo River in Shanghai. Amazingly, he rarely seemed to wear the same clothes twice.

He was extremely diplomatic. When a young Chinese woman guide, having heard that we had a movie star with us, asked him to describe a film in which he had appeared and the other tour members held their breath, he said that it was about a group of people from New York who went to an island resort for the summer and dealt with the complications of their relationships there. When one member of the group, a retired and formerly brilliant university professor who had become negligent of his appearance, slovenly in his habits, and incapable of looking after himself properly since he had last traveled with me, was shunned by many of the others so that he sat alone and rejected during a six-hour journey, Calvin left the lively men at the back of the bus and moved to sit beside him and later shared a table with him at dinner and assisted him to his bedroom.

The Chinese authorities, always eager to make everything as unpleasant for us as possible, had given the bus driver and guide orders to stop nowhere en route under any circumstances. We raced through villages as if the people there would be contaminated merely by the sight of us foreign devils waving at them from behind the sealed windows; and we begged in vain for a comfort stop, completely out of sight of any habitation and with no human beings within many miles of us. The guide gloated at our discomfort. "Is for security," he said, smiling.

China is the only country I know that I thoroughly disliked. It may be unfair to condemn a vast country, and one with a recorded history going back more than five thousand years, after only one two-week visit; but I will not listen to a good word said about a country where there is no reverence for the past; whose capital city was callously desecrated by destroying the walls that enclosed and contained it and gave it its unique character; where plastic sandals and shoddily made souvenirs are sold in the Temple of Heaven and the halls of the Summer Palace in Beijing; where one is taken to and expected to express enthusiasm for a Russian-built bridge and made to wait by it for an hour for the thrill of seeing a train come crashing over it; where all the artistic achievements of past centuries are forgotten and the highest form of art today was demonstrated in a factory to which we were taken to see hundreds of little girls sitting in rows and embroidering pictures of nauseatingly realistic kittens onto thin cloth, the fronts of the kittens on one side, their backs on the reverse; where one is surrounded and hemmed in and pushed and shoved by millions of spitting, coughing people; and where everyone is always smiling, smiling, but I felt that as they smiled at me they wanted to drive a long sharp knife into my stomach, turn it, and then giggle as they watched me expire slowly at their feet.

It is a country totally lacking in charm. When we were one room short at Angler's Rest, the excessively expensive tourist complex outside Beijing, and I had to sleep on the floor in the corridor and asked for a mattress, or at least a blanket and a pillow, they smiled and smiled and said, "We give you *nothing*!"

And the *food*! The ingredients of the witches' brew in *Macbeth* would have been preferable to the evil, slimy fungi and rodents and slugs and unidentifiable bits of pallid nastiness floating in those bowls of tepid soup that were set before us. How well I remember with revulsion those balls of rancid tallow artfully died pink and baby blue; the hard-boiled eggs whose yolks were livid scarlet, with white spores like poisonous toadstools, and whose whites resembled Gorgonzola cheese but stank far worse; the congealed lumps of rice; and everything else that had been sapped of its original color and reduced to the same unappetizing shade of gray—hunks of coarse meat entwined with gristle, entrails, potatoes, and weird roots— and cooked so long that any taste these delicacies may ever have had was entirely obliterated. We saw no fresh vegetables or fruit for two weeks, and when, toward the end of the tour, I admitted to Calvin that I was actually hallucinating about an orange, a piece of Camembert cheese, and a glass of cold milk, he laughed. "So what else is new? We've all been fantasizing about salads and juices for the last ten days!"

Everything in China repelled me. I found nothing appealing. I admit I was prejudiced and have never lost the fear of the "Yellow Peril" about which I had been warned so often as a child. The Great Wall was a great disappointment, meandering as it does so aim- lessly across the land, useless for keeping the Manchu out and the

Chinese in; and it did not help to endear it to me when we were made to line up beside a stinking communal toilet before being permitted to climb it. I thought the oversized stone animals lining the road to the Ming tombs grotesque and hideous; but Calvin, who was enchanted by everything in China, thought they were funny, and vaulted onto their backs to be photographed.

There was one incident only during our China tour that I enjoyed—and it was contrived by me and enlivened by my tour members. We were being led through the masses of tourists that surged all over the Summer Palace near Beijing, and in one of the halls stood a throne where female visitors could pose and be photographed, for a fee, wearing a court robe dating from the reign of the last empress of China.

Dozens of these gorgeous robes hung in rows in a long glass-fronted closet, and Calvin gave one look and begged to be allowed time to dress up and have his picture taken. In a moment of inspiration I told all the tour members to select gowns and headdresses—I would pay for the group photographs—and my "discerning gentlemen" accepted the offer with alacrity and began to pull the heavily embroidered, flowered, bejeweled gowns from their hangers, snatched them out of one another's hands, put them on, discarded them for other, even more elaborate and gaudy robes, selected the most magnificent and largest diadems, enormous hats with feathers and bells and pom-poms, headdresses with glittering stones of paste and cut-glass ornaments like chandeliers, with silk fringes hanging seductively over their faces.

The women attendants were frantic. "Is dresses for *ladies*!" they cried. "We *know*! We *know*!" cried my excited tour members. It took a long time before everyone was satisfied with his costume and could be marshaled into position for the group photographs; and by then the throng of Chinese tourists, who refused to be moved on through the hall but stayed on, watching with fascination, became so dense that the doors had to be closed, and hundreds of people climbed onto benches outside and fought for a vantage point from which to be able to see the spectacle through the barred windows.

Our guide was disgusted with us.

In the Huang Shan Mountains, we were the first group of Americans to make the two-day climb of the holy mountain, staying at the large dormitory-type lodge at the peak in order to rise at dawn and see the spectacular sunrise while thousands of Chinese hikers stood stone-faced around us and spat on our shoes. One of the rock formations we passed, and for which the region is celebrated, was pointed out to us as being named "Eight Fairies Crossing the Sea"; the guides did not understand why this made us laugh.

When we returned to the village at the base of the mountain, we had been promised the luxury of a hot thermal bath and anticipated a large pool filled with hot, therapeutic water in which we would relax and swim. Not so. Our guides led us into a run-down bathhouse, far from clean and distinctly smelly, where we had to wait on wood benches while individual cubicles, each furnished with a tub, were made ready for us. Remarkably small, suspiciously gray towels and minute cakes of soap were handed out. I waited for my tour members to be taken to their cubicles, and Calvin, in his usual considerate way, also let the others take their turn, so that finally only he and I were still waiting; and both of us were then led to a cubicle that had two bathtubs. Here we politely turned our backs on each other, undressed, stepped into our respective tubs of very dubious-looking tepid water, and soaped ourselves. It was not the gloriously soothing experience we had hoped for as a reward for our long and challenging climb; and we did not linger in our tubs, but picked up our towels before stepping out of the water, rose decorously, and again turned our backs on each other, dried ourselves as best we could, and put on our clothes.

As we were the last tour members to return to the waiting room where the group was assembled, there was a certain amount of innuendo when it became known that while all the others had each been allocated a single bath, Mr. Culver and I had shared a cubicle.

"So that's what you get for being the tour leader!" someone called out; and on our walk back to the inn in the village, several tour members came up to me and whispered: "Is he really so well hung?" "Is he cut?" Alas, I could not tell them; I had not looked. Indeed, profane thoughts had not occurred to me, so intent was I on ridding myself of at least some of the grime and sweat after our two-day climb and getting dressed again without delay in order not to keep the others waiting.

Throughout this tour of China, and during later travels I made with Calvin, I realized that he possessed to a high degree the qualities that are essential for a tour leader: meticulous attention to detail; the patience of an angel; the ability to charm not only his fellow travelers but also airline, railroad, ship, and hotel staff and overzealous officials, and to turn a potentially troublesome situation into an unexpected, interesting travel experience. After some years he became a leader of many of my tours—not only for men but also for the general public, readers of *Archaeology* magazine and *The New Yorker,* where I advertised—to Egypt, India, and Nepal, to Peru and the Galápagos Islands, down the Grand Canyon of the Colorado River, and across the Canadian Rockies; and he endeared himself to all who traveled with him. Because he knew many members of the international *bon ton,* he was able to enhance the pleasure of those who toured with him by chance encounters: during a tour to the Carnival in Venice, when he led the group into Harry's Bar, a distinguished Italian prince arose from his banquette and called out, "Calvino, *mio caro*! What a surprise!"—and promptly invited him and his tour members to afternoon tea next day in his palazzo.

Occasionally a potential tour participant would express reservations on being told who would be the leader of the group. "Isn't that Casey Donovan, the actor with the big dick?" I retorted that it was not Mr. Donovan who was leading the tour, but the extremely proper and professional Mr. Calvin Culver, a former schoolteacher, and that his genitalia would be at all times hidden under his Brooks Brothers trousers.

He was a mystic and very spiritual, so that he contrived to be alone in the Inca city at Machu Picchu at night in order to meditate and chew coca leaves for many hours under the stars; and when he climbed with our group down the thousands of rock-hewn steps from Mount Sinai after sunrise one Thanksgiving Day, which happened also to be my birthday, and a strange white bow appeared suddenly in the clear sky and dipped down directly onto the Monastery of Saint Catherine in the valley below, he took this for a heavenly sign and stood in awe, then quickly captured the phenomenon with his camera and later named his photograph "The Miracle of the Sinai."

His death was as happy as his life had been. He looked trim and fit but complained for a week or two of a pain in his chest. "I think," he told me, "that I caught something on my last trip across the Sinai desert. It was awfully dusty, and I coughed a lot." His parents persuaded him to have some tests done, and he admitted himself to a hospital in Inverness, Florida, on Thursday, August 6, 1987. I telephoned him there on Saturday afternoon. He said he was feeling well but that the doctors had found "a lot of white spots, like a snowstorm," on the X rays of his lungs. We talked for some time, then he said he was very tired: " 'Bye, love you." He fell asleep and did not awake.

It was a merciful death for him, but a far greater shock for me than when other dear friends had died after months and years of dreadful suffering and increasing disability. Sadly, very few people who heard of the death of the mythical Casey Donovan, the porno star of the 1960s and 1970s, ever suspected what a quiet, responsible, dedicated, loving, and truly gentle gentleman the real Calvin Culver was.

20

CLOTHES

MAKE

THE MAN

Je ne blâme ni approuve: je raconte.
—Talleyrand

WHY DO SO MANY homosexual men in this country dress like schoolboys? Men nowhere else in the world do so. It is a phenomenon unique to gay men of the United States.

Young, slim, attractive men put on little boys' clothes because they wish to show off their physiques; but far more frequently it is paunchy, balding, physically unfavored men who cause adverse comment and embarrassment by appearing in this childish garb—middle-aged and elderly doctors, lawyers, judges, and corporation executives who seem to be unaware how grotesque they look and that they are, at best, figures of fun. Why do they do it? Is it an attempt to shock, to attract unpleasant attention, to be conspicuous, to arouse indignation?

Close-fitting tank tops and the briefest, thinnest of shorts are fine on beaches and around the pool when worn by lean young men who look good in them, but are unsuitable attire for men of any age anywhere else. In all countries except ours, men of all races and colors and classes and statuses and ages realize that there is a time and place for wearing abbreviated, provocative clothing; and foreign homosexual men are particularly concerned not to expose themselves to ridicule and adverse comments by flaunting sexually revealing infantile clothes where it is inappropriate. Only our homosexual men seem to be unaware that the clothes in which they hope to be admired on Castro Street and at Fire Island are out of place in a famous restaurant in New Orleans, in an historic hotel on the Grand Canal in Venice, on the *Orient Express,* and while touring ancient sacred places.

Two men wrote about their vacation in New Orleans in the *New York Native* in September 1991, and photographs of them on sightseeing tours showed them wearing the tank tops and shorts in which they spent the week in that city. How much better these middle-aged, balding, stout men would have looked in shirts and long trousers; and no doubt they would not have been so badly treated as they described at the K. Paul Restaurant if they had worn appropriate clothes there. Why provoke unpleasantness in order to wear clothes that any sensible man is glad to have cast off when he reached his teens?

I send the members of my foreign tours detailed instructions regarding appropriate clothing, and warn them what not to wear abroad in order to avoid being made to feel uncomfortable; but despite this, and my and our local guides' requests to wear acceptable clothes, tour members often cannot resist a mania for going forth dressed ludicrously in T-shirts or tank tops and tiny shorts that last suited them thirty, forty, or fifty years before in kindergarten.

What impulse drives an amiable fifty-year-old Texan executive to enter the splendidly ornate lobby of the Hotel Europa and Regina on the Grand Canal in Venice in a tank top at least one size too small for him and in shorts that are not walking shorts or serviceable army-style khaki shorts to just above the knee, but that are as thin and brief as underwear, with his stomach protruding through the gap between these scanty garments? He was not a pretty sight and I did not hide my dismay at his appearance, but he was quite unaware of the highly unpleasant impression he made. When I had given him his key and sent him up to his room, while I was still at the reception desk an assistant manager of the hotel came to me and asked me to ensure that this member of my group would not again be seen anywhere in the hotel in that state of undress. "It is not Carnival time, now," he said. I hoped that the Texan might on reflection have realized how unsuitably he was dressed and would come down to luncheon in long trousers, a shirt, maybe even a jacket—but there he was again, in the elegant dining room, among the well-dressed guests and to the consternation of the formally uniformed staff, in open sandals, a green tank top, and scanty shorts. Did he think that the people who were staring at him were admiring his biceps and bare thighs? That they were avidly hoping to see the tip of his penis appear from the edge of his shorts? I explained to him why he should go and change, and asked him to look around at the dress of everyone else eating there—but he adamantly refused. "To hell with it; I dress as I like on vacation."

When our guide—a historian of Venice eminent in his field—came to pick us up for our first sight-seeing tour, he said to me, "Why is that old gentleman dressed like a child? I cannot take him into churches in those clothes; in fact, I must say to you that I do not wish to be seen anywhere in my city with a man like that."

What lack of decorum makes a retired, widowed university professor from Ohio, on a hiking tour of the monasteries of Mount Athos in northern Greece, where the ecclesiastical authorities require visitors to be in every respect modestly dressed, becoming to the holiness of the area, flaunt a gaudy Hawaiian shirt and a hat of bright red, giving him the appearance of an aged garden gnome?

(The hat was, fortunately, lined with white cloth, and I persuaded him to wear it inside out.)

What urge to be different makes a surgeon from Chicago and his attractive young lover who are participating in one of the most luxurious travel experiences available—the journey from Central Europe through the Balkans to Istanbul for three cosseted days and nights aboard the *Orient Express*—enter the gorgeous Art Deco dining car of that train for breakfast and luncheon wearing tops and briefs that the other, appalled passengers consider to be underwear? And for dinner their desire to stand out in the crowd continued—their matching tuxedos were of shiny black cloth, with red lapels and piping, worn with huge red-striped bow ties and cummerbunds. They looked like the members of some tacky Latin American band of the 1930s; and a lady in the dining car turned to me and facetiously asked, "Oh, are we having the Gay Caballeros to entertain us after dinner tonight?"

What absence of tact induces two well-educated professional men from San Diego to ignore my tour instructions regarding clothing for traveling in Muslim countries, to reject my and our guide's earnest, polite requests not to wear sleeveless shirts and shorts, and makes them persist in entering the churches and mosques of Istanbul with bare legs and arms, knowing that they are giving great offense to the custodians and the other visitors to these sacred places? They were the only men wearing shorts in Istanbul—a city of eight million inhabitants, plus thousands of visitors from all over the world—during our five-day stay. Even the many teenage European backpackers we encountered on our sightseeing tours knew better than to be scantily dressed.

What lack of respect made these tour members in their half-naked state enter a small mosque in a village on the Bosphorus during a prayer service, to the shocked outrage of the worshipers?

"Dear Mr. Hanns," our guide asked me on this occasion, "why

do these men force us to consider them to be barbarians? No other tourists do this; only your American gays dress like that. It is not amusing."

How can I prevent it? My only remedy would be not to accept such men on future tours; but apart from their curious preference for wearing revealing, childish, offensive clothes, they are charming, delightful, entertaining, and appreciative travel companions. When I can persuade my tour members to wear suits and ties for dinner at a fine restaurant, they look superb; and if one or two refuse to conform sartorially and appear in blue jeans and work shirts, people assume that we are an extremely democratic group and have invited our bus driver or luggage porter to dine with us. Occasionally, when I tell tour members to dress properly for dinner or the theater or for a visit to a private home, I am denounced as being old-fashioned, old-maidish, fussy, a snob. Apart from showing my displeasure—which is generally obvious to all the members of the group *except* to the culprits—I hope that the others will bring peer pressure to bear on the offenders and make them dress more acceptably. It does not always succeed.

Occasionally, it is comments by total strangers that resolve the issue.

At Machu Picchu visitors to the Inca site appreciate that these ruins are not only uniquely interesting and awesome but that the place is sacred to the Andean people; they approach it with reverence and decorum.

One year, three of my tour members—including a judge—appeared there wearing tank tops and very brief, very tight-fitting, dazzlingly colored gym shorts of extremely thin cloth through which their genitalia were clearly outlined. They were well-endowed men and proud of it—but the ruins of Machu Picchu, filled with hundreds of travelers bent on archaeological pursuits, are not the place for men to provocatively display the size of their manhood.

All the hundreds of other male visitors that day wore long trousers, but my tour members seemed oblivious of the unpleasant sensation their revealing shorts created. When I saw them walk between the tables along the hotel terrace toward where I was sitting, I felt acutely embarrassed and hoped fervently that they would not greet me. Conversation all around me stopped as the trio approached; everyone was staring at those tight, gaudy shorts and the bulges under them. As they came near, I turned my head away as if to look at the view.

And then a girl of about ten, sitting at a nearby table with her family, said in that loud, piercing voice that many children affect, "Mummy, why are those men wearing such funny clothes?"

And even louder, in the arrogant and strident voice of the English upper classes, stressing every syllable of each word, the mother replied, "Be-cause they are ho-mo-sex-ual po-seurs, darling."

Everyone who understood English on the terrace laughed or giggled.

My three tour members walked on, rather faster than before.

They were dressed like adults that evening.

✧

Outside the United States, "casual" wear is not understood and not appreciated except on beaches. Men who wear blue jeans or shorts, and tank tops or T-shirts, are considered to be impecunious and are treated accordingly. Men who wear neat clothes when traveling on planes, ships, trains, and buses, in hotels or inns, and while sightseeing in cities, will receive prompt and courteous attention.

Being over the age of forty, dressed conservatively, and having gray hair is of distinct advantage when dealing with airline and hotel staff and customs and immigration officials in foreign countries. Ostentatious jewelry offends underpaid clerks and officials who wield considerable power behind their desks as we stand humbly before them, and they can vent their anger by creating annoying delays and difficulties. Such signs of wealth are also an irresistible invitation to thieves. Wristwatches should be simple and tell the local time, not the phases of the moon, and need not be capable of functioning at five hundred meters below the surface of the ocean. To wear eyeglasses adds to one's appearance of trustworthiness, and it is best to be clean-shaven, though a neatly trimmed beard enhances an old man's dignity. Hair should be as short as possible. (Long hair is recommended only for women traveling abroad, who thereby appear suitably feminine.) I find long hair most enticing when worn by young men, especially if it is straight and blond; and one of the great pleasures of living in Key West is to see so many attractive young men, stripped to the waist, with long hair and sexy ponytails, at work and riding around the town on their bicycles. Alas, if they should think of traveling abroad, they are well advised to trim their hair.

The model male traveler wears a dark suit, a white shirt, a plain dark tie. His luggage consists of hard suitcases, the more the better. An attaché case, an umbrella, or binoculars are additional symbols of respectability. Cameras are vulgar. Dark glasses denote the terrorist, drug trafficker, or other criminal. It is preferable for white men to be pale-skinned when first entering a foreign country; a suntan conveys the impression to the underpaid officials and clerks that the traveler is an idler, and arouses their envy and jealousy. The pale traveler is welcomed because he looks as if he has worked hard and deserves a vacation.

Above all, the traveler should dress modestly and sensitively so as not to anger or upset the local people, or offend their culture and customs.

In the Muslim world, from Morocco to Indonesia, men in shorts and shirts without collars and sleeves are assumed to be whores (as are scantily dressed women) and are propositioned accordingly—and rarely by the sort of men whose advances they might enjoy. Two friends of mine who traveled from Europe through Turkey to Afghanistan on their motorbike and were oblivious of Muslim sensitivities were disconcerted when stones were often thrown at them as they passed through villages and small towns. When they told me about this later and I discovered that they had worn shorts and no shirts, I explained to them the reason for the animosity that had been demonstrated toward them.

A man who toured Africa alone recently in search of an AIDS cure told me of the bad treatment he had often received at frontier crossings, at the counters of airline and steamer and bus offices, and at hotels. I asked what he had worn on his travels. "Khaki shorts and a T-shirt, of course," he said. That explained everything: in Africa, as in most undeveloped areas, snobbery is rife, and travelers who are not prosperously dressed are suspected of being on the run from the police, involved in the drug trade, or so poor as to become a burden on the country they attempt to enter. Long trousers, a clean shirt, and a jacket easily dispel this impression; and it amazes me again and again that men do not adopt such simple measures to avoid being misunderstood and mistreated on their travels.

It is also an advantage for the traveler to be thin. Fat foreigners, big eaters, are not popular in poor countries. I well remember how one of my tour members in China, a grossly overweight elderly man, was stopped in the Forbidden City by a group of Chinese miners on vacation. They surrounded him, lifted his shirt, and poked their fingers hard into his fat stomach. "What are they doing?" he cried out in alarm. How could I explain to him that these simple men had never seen such a living fat Buddha?

Awkward or potentially inconvenient situations when traveling can be avoided merely by wearing a suit and tie. During one of my tours to Greece, Olympic Airways—the only air carrier in that country—suddenly announced a strike. We had reservations on the 9:30 A.M. flight from Athens to Mykonos for the next day, and the airline advised me that it would try to get at least one forty-seater plane off the ground to the island before the 8:00 A.M. strike deadline. When I arrived with my tour members at the airport at 6:30 A.M. next morning, we found hundreds of passengers who had been there for many hours, crowding around the Mykonos check-in desk, where the harassed clerks were stacking up the tickets of all passengers on flights for that day and saying they would decide later who would be accepted for the one flight before 8:00 A.M. There was a rumor that all ferry services to Mykonos and other islands were going on strike in sympathy, and the frustrated passengers were angry and noisy. They consisted mostly of the travelers for whom Mykonos is a haven: European unisex freaks with safety pins through their noses, with orange-and-blue hair, dressed largely in beads and patches, and others loaded with bulky backpacks and bedrolls. I did not have to attempt to bribe or charm the airline clerks, but at the sight of me in my neat dark suit and tie, when I opened my attaché case and presented my group's air tickets, they believed (erroneously) that I must be a person of importance and power, and without a moment's hesitation they accepted our tickets and handed me the boarding passes for the flight. The scantily dressed vacationers were highly indignant and made loud remarks in German and other languages about me and my tour members that were not complimentary. But my conservative clothes had saved the day for us.

My friend Brian Kenny and I learned in the early 1960s how the prejudice against "casual" clothes can limit the traveler's activities. When we toured Europe on Brian's motorbike, of which the carrier had space for spare shirts and socks and sweaters but none for city clothes, we encountered unexpected inconveniences because the ubiquitous blue jeans and leather jackets in which we traveled, and which were so suitable for our mode of transport, were quite unacceptable outside the biker fraternity.

At Harwich, having seen the bike loaded into the hold of the night ferry to Hook of Holland, when we attempted to walk up the first-class gangway, the seaman on duty brusquely ordered us to third class—"You go up there, mates!"—and when we showed him our first-class tickets, he grudgingly allowed us to walk up but did not disguise his scorn for us. In Amsterdam, a friend who had often been our guest in London apologized profusely for not being able to invite us to his grand house on the Singel. "What would my servants think?" he explained. He wanted at least to repay our hospitality by inviting us to luncheon, but dared not be seen with us at a restaurant where he might be recognized in such raffish company; so he took us to the railroad buffet—"No one I know is likely to see me there with you."

He made us feel so uneasy in our blue jeans and leather jackets that we were afraid to go to the theater to see the musical *Going Madly Dutch,* for which we had tickets. We went to the box office in the afternoon and explained to the lady that we had no other clothes and asked whether we would be permitted to attend that evening. "Where are your seats?" she asked us suspiciously, but when she saw that they were toward the back of the theater, she told us there would be no problem.

Our tour of Europe was not the carefree jaunt we had planned. We were embarrassed to check into decent hotels, we did not dare to enter fine restaurants, we felt that sight-seers in castles and churches and museums were eyeing us with disfavor. Blue jeans and leather jackets have become less objectionable in thirty years, but our tour was a salutary lesson to us, and ever since then we pack a dark suit, a white shirt, a somber tie, wherever we go; and I recommend every man on his travels to do so, even if he is on a strict budget or backpacking. One never knows when one may be invited to afternoon tea by the bishop, to dinner at an embassy, or to the opera. It is best to be prepared.

✦

Very early in the morning on January 1, 1986, I was woken up by a telephone call from Santiago, Chile, and informed that the plane I had chartered to take my group of gentlemen to the Antarctic for a black-tie New Year's Eve celebration as guests of the Chilean air force had crashed on landing. There were no survivors. The tour members included several men who had traveled with me three or four times and had become good friends; the leader was a bright, handsome young man of whom I had grown to be as fond as of a son.

I have dressed conservatively all my life, but since that dreadful day I wear clothes that are white, gray, or black, and the same black knit tie every day. The only exceptions to this rule that I make are for garments that are traditionally colored: serviceable Levi's, which are unsurpassed on expeditions, where they can be worn day after day, become worn and dirty and even torn, but never look scruffy; khaki trousers and shirts, which do not scare off every animal and bird in sight on field trips; and yellow rain jackets or ponchos.

For sixty years I had never thrown away a tie and possessed hundreds of them: the thin little knit tie of Yeoville Boys School, and the hideous red-yellow-green-striped tie of Athlone High School in Johannesburg, South Africa; the no-less-ugly tie of the Corps of Signallers dating from World War II; "slim-jims" and grotesquely wide "flounders," British status symbols for a fashionable young man at different periods of his career; pretty, frivolous, "ever so gay" ties of brightly flowered Liberty silk; ties that my well-meaning stepmother had sent me for birthdays and at Christmas and that I had never worn; ties made for me from strips of old Andean cloth by Mary-Ellen Taylor when she went to live in Ecuador; batik ties from Bali; a tie made of very thin black leather, which, when worn with a business suit, was intended to convey a message to those who understood it; the elegant ribbed tie of the yacht *Golden Cachalot,* in which I had arranged cruises to the Galápagos Islands and, later, along the coast of Belize; and the tie by which people who know such things could recognize me immediately as a fellow of the prestigious Royal Geographical Society.

For many years I kept them all in cardboard boxes as mementos of a long life of vanity and ambition, until without regrets I gave them to an old Conch lady in Key West, who used them to make patchwork quilts.

21

TEA

ON THE

TERRACE

FRIDAY, JUNE 17, 1960, was a fine, warm summer evening in London, and I put on my black leather jacket and blue jeans and went to Speakers' Corner at Marble Arch. There, on a large gravel section within Hyde Park, sparsely lit by ornate nineteenth-century lamps, speakers were traditionally permitted to expound their opinions, no matter how outrageous, provided only that they did not criticize the institution of the British royal family and its individual members. Antireligious, antigovernment, antiestablishment views were all tolerated, and weirdly garbed fanatics could proselytize to their hearts' content. It was a free show that attracted good-natured hecklers and anyone who wanted to be entertained but could not afford the cost of a theater or cinema ticket or even the price of a beer in a pub. It also attracted lonely homosexual men who came in search of a quick thrill in the dark among the dense crowd of idlers, or in the hope of finding romance.

At that time there were no bars or restaurants or gymnasiums where homosexual men could meet. A few private clubs, pretending to cater to men interested in the arts or the history of uniforms, were tolerated by the police in obscure locations. Six or eight homosexual men who sat down to a genteel dinner in the home of one of them could (and occasionally did) hear the front door being broken open by the police, who burst in and arrested them and took them to jail, accusing them of having "gathered for an immoral purpose."

The Homosexual Reform Society was courageously founded to bring pressure to bear on the government to alter the archaic law, and the Albany Trust was created so that contributions by check would not have to bear the dirty ten-letter word. Volunteer helpers who addressed, stuffed, sealed, and stamped envelopes by hand for mailings to members of Parliament and members of the House of Lords, educators, jurists, and religious leaders presented themselves at staggered hours in the evenings at a house in Islington; and the society's officers were greatly worried whether, if they provided us with tea and cookies while we worked, our activity could be construed as being social gatherings and thus illegal. Their lawyers advised them that providing we all sat at our separate tables or desks and that the cups of tea and cookies were brought to us at our work stations, the danger of our being taken to prison was minimal and a risk worth taking.

In this atmosphere of fear, furtiveness, and guilt, Speakers' Corner at Marble Arch was the only safe public place for homosexual men to meet with impunity; and no matter how inclement the weather, and despite surveillance by policemen who patrolled the area in pairs, many men, well wrapped up against the rain or cold, sauntered from one group surrounding a speaker on his soapbox or platform to the next, and provided them with their most loyal and regular, albeit totally uninterested, audience.

While speakers extolled the advantages and joys of polygamy or the benefits of veganism; demanded the restoration of public hangings, slavery, or the Romanovs; advocated the abolition of income tax, the Church of England, the pope, or National Service; elo-

quently informed their listeners that communism, fascism, or Zen
Buddhism would save mankind and that the world was flat—and
that a capitalist plot was attempting to persuade us otherwise—
men stood closely pressed together, pretending to be engrossed in
these fiery speeches, while their eyes darted about constantly to spot
other men whom they unerringly recognized by their clothes or
gestures as sharing their own inclinations. And having selected a
likely candidate, they adroitly disengaged themselves from the
closely packed crowd around the speaker and hurried off to follow
or entice the object of their choice into the darker sections of the
park.

Motorcycle jackets and workmen's donkey jackets of serge with
leather elbow patches were the homosexual's favored uniform; and
when I set off in pursuit of an attractive man in motorcycle gear, a
nice effeminate youngster in an imitation-leather jacket who had
been sidling up to me said, "Don't waste your time: he's a real
biker." I would not be deterred. I had many more years of experience than the youth in distinguishing between a real biker and a
man attired like one, and although the gorgeous man I followed
strode to his big black Triumph 550cc motorcycle, the artfully
studied way in which he leaned provocatively against it indicated
quite clearly, as it was meant to do, that his aim in coming to
Speakers' Corner was the same as mine. "I'm sorry, but I can't take
you back to my place," he said. "My landlady is very strict."

I told him that not only could I take him back to my place, but
that I also had a room to let and was not a strict landlord.

His name was Brian, he was an Australian, and I mounted his
bike behind him and we drove to my flat in Long Acre. It was a very
small two-room flat, but being so very centrally located in Covent
Garden, the rent was high and I had to let one of the rooms; and the
artist friend who had stayed in it for six months had recently returned to South Africa. Brian was a well-paid construction worker

with a university education who read the London *Times* du̶
lunch break at the building site and who could afford to pay t̶
for the room; but by the time he moved in two weeks later, we̶
mutually and enthusiastically agreed that the room would be fit̶
up as a sitting room and that we needed only one bedroom; and w̶
have lived together ever since.

When two people know instinctively that they are meant for
each other, and decide to become a couple, they do so "to have and
to hold, for better, for worse, for richer, for poorer, in sickness and
in health, to love and to cherish, until we are parted by death"; and
so we have lived, content and in harmony, cheerfully honoring our
commitment to each other.

Until I met Brian Kenny, and unless I was invited to luncheon
or dinner, I existed on a diet of beans on toast and chocolate fingers.
He made me eat healthy food, swim daily, jog, ski, and brush my
teeth after every meal. He failed to teach me how to drive his motorbike and maintain it or to appreciate poetry, but as we began to
travel together, he did teach me how one can make one's stay at a
hotel bearable.

Gone were the days when I allowed the arrogant, supercilious
staff of hotels to intimidate me and when haughty receptionists
handed me the key of, and I accepted without demur, the most
miserable bedroom in the hotel—one of those garrets that the
world's grand hotels keep to accommodate the valets and maids of
the rich and the bodyguards of the fashionable international crooks
on whom the staff fawns, nasty little rooms that are rarely cleaned
and where the inmate is obliged to make his own bed.

Brian knew how to travel with style. He required *Lebensraum* to
be happy and felt constricted within the four walls of a mere bedroom. A suite suited him better, or at least a room with a door
opening out onto a balcony or a terrace. As soon as we are shown into
it, and if he considers it acceptable, and even before his four, six, or

are brought up—one especially heavy case
—he proceeds to rearrange the furniture
the pamphlets, brochures, directories, and
with which hotel managements litter the tops of
, and cabinets, and hides them in a drawer together
the ashtrays. Then he unpacks all his cases, even if he stays
only a day or two, calls maid service for more hangers, extra
pillows, another blanket, stronger light bulbs for the bedside
lamps, calls room service and orders a beer and a cheese sandwich,
or lemon tea and English pound cake, summons housekeeping and
hands over the suit, tie, shirt, underwear, and socks in which he has
traveled, to be instantly dry-cleaned and laundered, and discovers
some tap or fixture in the bathroom that needs immediate repair or
adjustment.

Maids, waiters, and maintenance men appear within minutes of
Brian's call, and as he never knows the local currency and treats it
like play money, all are magnificently overtipped. Within half an
hour of his arrival in any hotel, he is well known to the staff and
treated like a prince or film star. Vases with flowers appear magi-
cally, and cellophane-wrapped baskets of fruit; and then he arranges
his books, some between bookends on desks and shelves, others
artistically displayed on tables and beside his bed, and sets up the
photographs in their leather frames with which he always travels
and that almost fill one of the many cases: Mother in furs, Mother
as a soubrette on the stage, Father's pearling lugger, in which Dr.
Kenny sailed round Australia with chorus girls as his crew, Mother
and Father with the aviator Charles Kingsford-Smith in the first
airplane in Western Australia, sister and self in 1925 and 1985
posed identically and wearing the same type of neck-to-thigh black
bathing suits. There are, too, smaller framed photographs of his
favorite cats, and placed near these and thus linking the distant
pets, our children, to the present, is the jar of dry cat food without

which he never leaves home and with which, as he opens its lid, he attracts the half-starved cats at airports in Africa, Asia, and South America.

He is the only man I know who travels with *two* tuxedos. No man has more bow ties, and no man has more sets of cuff links, the color of whose stones must match or compliment that of the tie selected to be worn on each day. Naturally, he always changes for dinner—even when camping in the desert. Beau Brummell lives.

By the time that his books and photographs are displayed to his satisfaction, his suits hung up in the closet above his carefully lined-up shoes, his shirts and sweaters, each in a plastic cover, and ties and handkerchiefs and underwear all placed in their proper order in the chest of drawers, his splendid and costly toilet articles neatly set out on the bathroom shelves (leaving almost no room for my few basic necessities), room service arrives and is asked to take the tray out to the terrace, where, before he takes a bite from his sandwich or of the cake, he spreads crumbs on the balustrade to attract birds.

Brian relishes the luxury of these terraces—at the Mena House Hotel facing the Pyramids of Gizeh near Cairo and at the Old Cataract Hotel overlooking the Nile at Aswan, at the delectable Auberge du Père Bise at Talloires on Lake Annecy, at the disreputable but enchanting Hotel Stuart on the waterfront in Papeete, and that of Room 28 at the Hotel Turistas at Machu Picchu—and his favorite time of the day for enjoying the privacy they provide and the view they command is teatime, in the late afternoon, after the day's sight-seeing is done. He believes, as Henry James wrote in 1880 and Brian likes to quote, that "under certain circumstances there are few hours in life more agreeable than the hour dedicated to the ceremony known as afternoon tea."

How proud of our achievement we were that day in Zermatt, when we had set out very early in the morning over the Theodul glacier to ski to Cervinia in Italy for an alfresco luncheon and then taken the cable car back to the Theodul Pass and, before skiing down to return to Zermatt, stopped for our well-deserved afternoon tea on the sun terrace at Schwarzsee below the ominous rock cone of the Matterhorn.

How pleased with ourselves we were for having skied so well and for looking so youthful and vigorous with our alpine tans and commando-like crew cuts.

I ordered tea and pastries from the waitress in German, and a British family that sat behind us assumed that we could not understand English. Long hair had recently become almost ubiquitous in Europe for men of all ages, and to our horror we heard one of the children ask, "Why do those two old men have their hair so short?"

"In olden times, all men had their hair so short," explained the mother.

Our egos were utterly deflated.

✧

Room 28 at the Hotel Turistas at Machu Picchu is the only room with a sitting room, and I reserve it more than a year in advance for the two nights I stay there each year with my groups, not only in order to provide Brian Kenny with ample space to arrange the photographs of his family and our cats and his traveling library, but because it also has a large terrace overlooking the narrow gorge of the Urubamba River toward the snowcapped Vilcanota range of the Andes and the dramatic peak of Huayna Picchu, which towers above the Inca ruins.

Here, at the big circular table under the sunshade, we invite the tour members to afternoon tea, for which the hotel chef bakes us a plain pound cake. Surrounded by the dense mass of hydrangeas, the huge leaves of elephant-ear plants, bamboo, bromeliads, and begonias that cling to the sparse soil between the rocks of the almost perpendicular mountainside that forms the back of the terrace, we

sit high above the day-trippers whose often inane remarks we over-
hear with amusement and who look up at us on our privileged
vantage point with disgust or envy.

"Are these ruins Aztec or Mayan?" we hear some ask their long-
suffering guides. "What a fuss about nothing," announced a German to his party as they came through the gate after having
inspected the Inca city. "When these miserable little thatched huts
were built, my ancestors were worshiping in Cologne Cathedral!"
The backpackers complain loudly and at great length about the
prices of cold drinks and candy bars. "What a rip-off this place is!"

These afternoon-tea ceremonies on terraces in foreign places are
indeed as agreeable as Henry James said, but it is more pleasant and
more deeply satisfying to have afternoon tea snug at home. In our
little wooden house in Key West, we carry the tray with the blue-
and-white onion-pattern china, modern replicas of the Meissen my
parents had, and with the thinly cut cucumber sandwiches and the
fruitcake, which Brian's niece bakes and sends us from Western
Australia, out onto the front porch. There we sit on weekends, side
by side, watching our neighbors' activities on the lane from behind
a screen of umbrella trees and *Thunbergia grandiflora* vines, as does
Miss Jane Marple from behind the lace curtains of her village house
in the Agatha Christie murder mysteries.

Hilary, the airline hostess, crosses the lane to bring us yesterday's edition of *The Times of India, Le Figaro,* or the *Frankfurter
Zeitung,* depending on where her last flight took her; we look across
to Lola, who knits on her porch and who has lived in her house since
she was brought to it as a young bride seventy years ago, who gives
us all her key limes and whose late husband was born in our house;
we watch Louis, the handsome ex-cop with the ponytail, going
barefooted to the corner store; and we wait for the House and Garden Bike Tour, whose members stop to admire the very ordinary
bougainvillea, frangipani, and hibiscus along the lane but give no

glance at the neatly labeled flora that Brian has assembled in the smallest botanical garden in the world, all grown from seeds and cuttings that he has brought back, in defiance of the regulations that forbid it, hidden among his socks, from his travels to India and Persia and Egypt and Kenya and Peru, from Easter Island and the Galápagos Islands and the San Blas Islands off Panama.

Not every plant in our garden is an illegal migrant, of course. We also have, all identified by their small wooden signs, tall, fast-growing poinciana trees, which were planted from inch-high seedlings and whose pods are so grotesque—like carpet slippers, Noël Coward said; cream-and-yellow Plumerias; *Dieffenbachia seguine*, with their beautiful green-and-white veined leaves, which used to be fed to recalcitrant slaves in the South, where it was known as dumb cane because it punished them by swelling their tongues so that speech was impossible; *Euphorbia caput-medusae*, a fast-growing succulent whose long, slender branches have given it the name medusa's head; and the wonderful *Aloe barbadensis*, whose sap miraculously and with amazing speed cures cuts, burns, and all kinds of skin rashes, so that it is like having one's own pharmacy.

Candide-like, Brian cultivates dozens of *Hippeastrum amaryllis* bulbs, which he dug up from the edge of the airstrip at Aligandi in the San Blas Islands, where we often waited in fear and trepidation for the small charter planes to come and take our groups back to Panama City. They are commonly known as beach lilies or fire lilies, are salmon-colored, and still, after twenty years, burst into spectacular bloom when the rains come in June.

From Persia came the rare jujube tree, planted from a minuscule seedling picked in the foothills of the Demavend Mountains in those distant days when it was possible to operate tours in that fascinating country; and from Egypt came the *Cyperus papyrus*, which looks so pretty in our green-and-white screened Florida room at the back of the house but whose slim leaves our cats cannot resist chewing. The African milk tree—*Euphorbia trigona*—and the candelabra euphorbia, with its strong, curving branches decorated with pale green banding, both flourish on the front porch and remind Brian of the camel safaris he made in the Northern Frontier District of Kenya with the naturalist Denis Zaphiro, who was originally a hunter.

From Peru came the seeds of our daturas, misnamed flower of evil and more aptly called angel's-trumpet, with their lovely trumpet-shaped white blooms; and in the garden of the Larco Herrero Museum in Lima, and from under the eyes of the suspicious curator of the erotic collection, Brian took the small cuttings of the jade plant—*Crassula portulacea*—a succulent that, with its tightly massed small circular leaves, resembles a bonsai.

Our calla lilies are souvenirs from Easter Island—but that was not their original home, for like almost all the flora of that windswept island in the South Pacific, they were introduced there from Tahiti, having earlier still been brought to Tahiti from the Orient. Our *Opuntia inebriata,* however, are indigenous to the Galápagos Islands, from where Brian took their pads and planted them in pots on our porch—one from the jaws of a tortoise that was beginning to feast on it, the other from the small white sand beach at Tower Island. They require no watering and derive their nourishment from the humid air; and wasps have made their nests between the spines of these cacti, whose pads are apt to collapse as drunkenly as their name implies.

Key West is an ideal place for a gardener of advanced years whose time is somewhat limited and who wants to see his seedlings grown into tall trees. The two banyan trees that shade our house were planted from suckers in 1977. They are held sacred in India, where it is believed that if a child is desired, a saucer of milk must be placed beneath them. We have made no attempt to achieve this result. From India, too, Brian returned with several *muttkas,* large spherical clay pots with very narrow necks, which are porous and used there to keep drinking water cool, and which it required all his considerable charm to persuade the airline staff to let him bring on the planes with him. He has planted dracaenas in them, and their weird brown blooms perfume our rooms for many days.

While we were swimming in the lagoon at Tetiaroa, Marlon Brando's private island near Tahiti, a coconut floated by close to us, showing a tiny spout of palest green. It was irresistible to Brian; he hid it among his snorkel gear and, terrified of arrest if the U.S. Customs inspector at Los Angeles Airport were to find it, brought it safely home. For its first months in the United States this *Cocos nucifera* sat on a windowsill in our sunny office on West Forty-second Street in New York; then, demanding a warmer climate and an island home, no matter how far removed from its native Pacific, it was taken to Key West and planted in our back garden. For many years it barely grew, then its roots found water, it adapted itself to the alien soil, and it now stands forty feet tall, Brian's most daring and audacious global transplantation.

More spectacular even than this palm tree is the night-blooming cereus cactus—*Cereus peruvianus*—which made a considerably shorter journey to Key West from Fort Jefferson in the Dry Tortugas, in the Gulf of Mexico. With his ever-ready Swiss Army knife, Brian took a six-inch cutting; fifteen years later it has grown into the most exotic and conspicuous plant on our lane, soaring high above the roof of the porch, which, with the weight of some of its great limbs leaning on it, it threatens to pull down. Its white and lemon-colored flowers are a foot in diameter and incredibly beautiful, and as the sun rises they become filled with bees. Next day, collapsed, they fall to the ground like rotten bananas.

And as Brian and I sit, surrounded by all these botanical wonders that, like us, have come to our lane from afar and put out their roots here, and enjoy our afternoon tea on our porch—not a terrace, because it has a roof, and lacking a view of the pyramids or the Nile or Lake Annecy, of neither the harbor of Papeete nor the bay of Hangaroa, not of the Matterhorn or Huayna Picchu but *home*—as we sit there we hear, every half hour, the voice of the guide of the Conch Train sight-seeing tour as it passes the end of our lane: "Ladies and gentlemen, if you feel some slight discomfort in your ears as we approach the next corner, it's only because we are coming to the highest point of the island—Solares Hill—sixteen feet above sea level."

Like tour guides all over the world, he is not entirely truthful. It is only fifteen feet.

FOR THE BEST IN PAPERBACKS, LOOK FOR THE

In every corner of the world, on every subject under the sun, Penguin represents quality and variety—the very best in publishing today.

For complete information about books available from Penguin—including Pelicans, Puffins, Peregrines, and Penguin Classics—and how to order them, write to us at the appropriate address below. Please note that for copyright reasons the selection of books varies from country to country.

In the United Kingdom: For a complete list of books available from Penguin in the U.K., please write to *Dept E.P., Penguin Books Ltd, Harmondsworth, Middlesex, UB7 0DA.*

In the United States: For a complete list of books available from Penguin in the U.S., please write to *Consumer Sales, Penguin USA, P.O. Box 999—Dept. 17109, Bergenfield, New Jersey 07621-0120.* VISA and MasterCard holders call 1-800-253-6476 to order all Penguin titles.

In Canada: For a complete list of books available from Penguin in Canada, please write to *Penguin Books Canada Ltd, 10 Alcorn Avenue, Suite 300, Toronto, Ontario, Canada M4V 3B2.*

In Australia: For a complete list of books available from Penguin in Australia, please write to the *Marketing Department, Penguin Books Ltd, P.O. Box 257, Ringwood, Victoria 3134.*

In New Zealand: For a complete list of books available from Penguin in New Zealand, please write to the *Marketing Department, Penguin Books (NZ) Ltd, Private Bag, Takapuna, Auckland 9.*

In India: For a complete list of books available from Penguin, please write to *Penguin Overseas Ltd, 706 Eros Apartments, 56 Nehru Place, New Delhi, 110019.*

In Holland: For a complete list of books available from Penguin in Holland, please write to *Penguin Books Nederland B.V., Postbus 195, NL-1380AD Weesp, Netherlands.*

In Germany: For a complete list of books available from Penguin, please write to *Penguin Books Ltd, Friedrichstrasse 10-12, D-6000 Frankfurt Main 1, Federal Republic of Germany.*

In Spain: For a complete list of books available from Penguin in Spain, please write to *Longman, Penguin España, Calle San Nicolas 15, E-28013 Madrid, Spain.*

In Japan: For a complete list of books available from Penguin in Japan, please write to *Longman Penguin Japan Co Ltd, Yamaguchi Building, 2-12-9 Kanda Jimbocho, Chiyoda-Ku, Tokyo 101, Japan.*